A LIFE

Alun Lewis

A LIFE

John Pikoulis

SEREN BOOKS

Seren Books is the imprint of
Poetry Wales Press Ltd
Andmar House, Tondu Road, Bridgend, Mid Glamorgan

A Cataloguing in Publication record for this title is available from
the British Library CIP Office

*The publisher acknowledges the financial support of the Welsh Arts
Council*

Typeset in 10½ pt Plantin by Megaron, Cardiff
Printed and bound in Great Britain by
Dotesios Ltd, Trowbridge, Wiltshire.

Contents

List of Illustrations		vi
Preface		7
I	Cwmaman	9
II	Early Schooldays	16
III	Scholarship Boy	21
IV	Aberystwyth (1)	29
V	Manchester: Love and Work	41
VI	Aberystwyth (2)	49
VII	The Mountain over Aberdare	55
VIII	The Gathering Storm	68
IX	Longmoor (1): Death and Beauty	77
X	Longmoor (2): Taking the Plunge	92
XI	Marriage and OCTU	105
XII	Second Lieutenant Lewis	115
XIII	Passage to India	140
XIV	Death and the Maiden	172
XV	Waiting for the Pistol	198
XVI	What Survives?	234
Appendix A: The Caseg Broadsheets		244
Appendix B: 3 Kent Terrace		247
Notes		260
Index		284

List of Illustrations

Frontispiece Engraving by John Petts
1. Cwmaman, looking down valley to the north east
2. Cwmaman, looking up valley to the south west
3. The Lewis family, 1924
4. On holiday at Penbryn, 1932
5. Cowbridge Grammar School Hockey First XI
6. Aberystwyth Students' Representative Council
7. Alun Lewis, 1938
8. Alun Lewis, 1942
9. The Lewis Family, 1941
10. 158th Regiment, R.A.C., The South Wales Borderers
11. With Jack Gush, Poona Hospital, February 1943
12. With Jack Gush, Poona rifle ranges, April 1943
13. Freda Aykroyd
14. Caseg Broadsheet No. 1: Two poems by Alun Lewis
15. Caseg Broadsheet No. 5: 'In Memory of Ann Jones' by Dylan Thomas

List of Maps

1. Wales, showing locations named in the text   23
2. India, showing locations named in the text   141
3. The North Burma Coast, showing locations named
   in the text   231

Preface

For this second edition of my life of Alun Lewis, I have revised the original to produce a predominantly narrative account for paperback readers while still preserving its character as a critical biography. At the same time, I have taken the opportunity to correct some errors and reintroduce passages dropped through pressure of space in the hardback edition as well as making use of information that has become available since 1984, most notably the mass of material published in *Alun Lewis: Letters to My Wife.* In order to preserve the unity of the text, I have rewritten the original entirely. The portrait of the poet that emerges is, I believe, unchanged.

I have already thanked the many who helped me to write my biography, including the poet's wife, Gweno Lewis, who made available to me much unpublished material, his mother and brothers, Gwladys, Glyn and Huw (alas, all now dead), his sister Mair Fenn and Freda Aykroyd, who also made available unpublished material and helped deepen my understanding of the poet and his work. I must now also thank Rhiannon Davies, daughter of Edward Lewis, uncle of the poet, who talked to me on a recent visit from Australia. David Leslie Davies arranged the meeting and I must thank him also; he drew my attention to various errors in my account of the Lewis family and life in Cwmaman generally, so I am doubly indebted to him. I have benefited from the work of Ulrich Schäfer, of Frankfurt, who has been collecting materials for a Lewis bibliography and has generously made the results of his research available to me. Further thanks go to Chatto and Windus and Michael Bott, Keeper of Archives and

Manuscripts at the University of Reading Library, and Christopher Sheppard, of the Leeds University Library, for making copies of lately-discovered Lewis correspondence held by them available to me.

Some reviewers of the first edition were disconcerted by my high estimation of Lewis's worth but they may have misunderstood the nature of my praise. Evidently, his career was cut short before its promise could be realised but in a handful of works (mainly the ones I concentrate on here) the abundant nature of that promise – and more than promise – is, I believe, amply demonstrated. But that was not the only grounds for my praise, for it has become apparent that Lewis played a significant historical role in effecting the transition from the 30s to the new styles of English poetry after the war and particularly in the 1950s and it is as much for this reason that I claimed his centrality as in any more absolute terms.

However that may be, I hope critical debate will help enhance the reader's appreciation of Lewis's life. He was a remarkable man and the more we know about him, the better we will be able to understand his work and the age in which it was produced.

John Pikoulis
1991

I should also thank Unwin Hyman for permission to quote from published Lewis material as cited, and Granada Publishing for the quotation from *The Funny Bone* by Julian Maclaren-Ross.

Photographic material was contributed by Gweno Lewis (ills. 7, 10, 11, 12), Huw Lewis (ills. 3, 4, 5, 9), Freda Aykroyd (ill. 13), Evan J. Hopkins (ill. 6), Cynon Valley Borough Libraries (ills. 1 and 2) and John Petts (ills. frontispiece, 14).

The maps were drawn by the Centre for Educational Technology, University College, Cardiff.

I

Cwmaman

Alun Lewis was born on 1 July, 1915, in Cwmaman, a small coal-mining village in Mid Glamorgan, South Wales. His father, T. J. Lewis (Tom), was an English master at the Glynhafod Council School in Cwmaman, a certificated graduate of Bangor Technical College. His mother, Gwladys Elizabeth, was also an English teacher. They had married the previous July, when they were both just short of their thirtieth birthdays, and set up home at 16 Llanwynno Road in one of the two Glanrhyd Villas. There was an open prospect of Cwmaman mountain across the way; just down the road lived the colliery manager and under-manager, their houses separated from the detached house of the colliery policeman by the track of the railway which carried the coal down to Aberaman at the mouth of the valley.

Cwmaman (pronounced Coomáman, the valley of the Aman river) lies in a blind, narrow valley some three miles long. At its head are the original pastures and woodland of farming country, the river Aman descending from Craig Bedwlwyn (Ferndale or Mardy mountain), which separates the valley from the Rhondda valleys to the west; it runs down to the Cynon valley, disappearing every now and then beneath the surface. Craig Tirllaethdy lies to the south, Craig Fforchaman (or Brynhyfryd mountain) to the north. The earliest iron furnaces in the area were worked in Cwmaman in the sixteenth century, but the establishment of the modern village followed the opening of Sheppherd's Pit in 1848, the first of five that were to be sunk in rapid succession in the valley. (None exists today.) Before the coming of the railway, the coal was carried in sledges to Cwmbach canal and then by barge to Cardiff docks. This was steam coal for domestic use. Along with the pits came stone quarries for building purposes so that, even today, the hills have a bleak, forbidding appearance, despite the forest of firs that has grown to cover them and the levelling and grassing-over of tips.

The first colliers' train appeared in 1892, the first passenger train in 1906. Otherwise, it was by horse and cab or Shank's mare to Aberdare, the main town of the area five miles away. The path over the Graig (mountain) from Cwmaman to Aberdare was commonly used, as were the countless walks and paths threading the hills, offering relief from the restraints of a confined environment. As in the other valleys of South Wales, the most blasted pit-head sprawl and crowded mining terrace lay within a few yards of open country so that escape was always near at hand (one reason, perhaps, for the absence of rural sentiment in even the most built-up areas). This contrast between valley and upland plays a crucial role in the imagination of South Wales writers, one part of them devoted to their communities, another to the mountains, the former associated with an intensity of communal experience such as only close physical proximity and the tribulations of a shared occupation within a common culture can provide, the latter with a countervailing isolation, imaginative reverie, physical exercise, beauty.

By the time of Lewis's birth, Cwmaman was a village of under 2,000 houses, small two-storey structures, for the most part without bathrooms or indoor sanitation. The streets were crammed into the valley floor and north slopes no more than five deep. These were named after the English poets, Spenser, Milton and so on. As it happens, over a hundred and fifty poets flourished in and around the Cynon Valley in the past hundred years, more than in any other valley in Wales. There was a Miners' Institute, built on a levy of $\frac{1}{2}$d (and later 1d) in every pound on the colliers' wages. The original structure was destroyed by fire in 1896 and rebuilt ten years later. In 1907, a Lesser Hall was opened for concerts, meetings, lectures and the like, the Main Hall being reserved for films. In 1912, the library moved into a building of its own, including a billiards room (three tables, one for boys), two bathrooms, a shower bath for sports teams, a gymnasium and various club rooms.

The first schools were built in the 1860s and '70s, also on a levy on wages. These, like the many chapels, clustered round the centre of the village. By the time Alun went to school, the family had moved to 61

Brynhyfryd, at the head of the valley, in an area know as Glynhafod, between Fforchwen and Sheppherd's pits and Brown's pit at the centre of the town itself. 61 Brynhyfryd was bought for them by Tom's elder brother, Edward. It lay next door to the Nant Aman Fach (the small Aman river), a tributary of the Aman, which separated the house from the Glynhafod Infant and Junior Schools on the other bank. These, built only a few years before in 1911, were reached by a little iron bridge which lay about twenty yards away. Behind were some allotments and then the steep incline of Brynhyfryd mountain, covered with bracken and stony outcrops, a few blasted trees leaning into the hillside. In comparison with Cwmaman it was almost rural.

Behind Glynhafod lay another, secret spur of the valley, a mile or so long, almost completely untouched. Within the main valley, the mechanical screens grading the coal into trucks sent up a tremendous rattling and a cloud of coal dust. Small coal, being uneconomical, was screened at the pit head and the men paid only for what was left in the grader — hence the arduous nature of piece work and the rich pickings to be had on the tips during emergencies. At night, these burned with slag, adding to the spontaneous combustion of the smoke in the air. The smell was powerful. Up in the mountains, with the wind whistling and the skylark and curlew crying to the sheep below, one could look down on the timber yards, workshops and screens, the small stone cottages and chapels and, with the peculiar melancholy of upland regions, contemplate the presence of things.

The Lewis family could not be said to have been typical of Cwmaman. Tom Lewis was born there in 1885 and, though he went down the pits briefly as a boy ("enough," he recalled, "to have a definite distaste"), he managed to escape the occupation that had drawn his father, Job, from the slate quarries of Pembrokeshire in the 1880s by becoming a schoolteacher — the classic escape route from the pit. Accordingly, life for him did not revolve round the pit or the Institute or the South Wales Miners' Federation. Nor did his wife and children speak Welsh or attend chapel or sing in the choirs at Cymanfaoedd Canu (religious singing festivals), for all that Tom himself was bilingual (as was most of Cwmaman). Gwladys was the daughter of a preacher, Melchizedec Evans. He had been born in Cwmavon (Port Talbot), where his father worked in the furnaces of the copper works, but had been raised by relatives in the Rhondda after his mother's death and rescued from the mines by a schoolmaster who recognised his singing ability. Eventually, he went to Carmarthen Theological College but did not attend university, as he could have done, because his health had been impaired by the mine and long hours of study. He was ordained at Saundersfoot as a Congregationalist in 1879. Later, he was attracted to Unitarianism, both for its practical character and for doctrinal reasons, and, after nearly twenty years preaching in Hope Chapel (Cardigan), Brecon, Pontypool and Bradford (including a brief period selling educational books as a doorstep traveller), he returned to Aberdare in 1903 to take charge of the English-speaking Highland Place church, very much an enlightened congregation with an intellectual reputation out of all proportion to the size of its membership.

As well as possessing a reforming temper, Melchizedec Evans was interested in religious speculation. He was a tall, saturnine man with a pointed face and moustache and beard, lightly-boned, like his daughter and her children after her, an eager, unworldly spirit who, according to Alun's sister, Mair, "used to sit breathing through alternate nostrils while his poor children starved around him. That's how seekers go on, when they really pick up a strong scent — total self-centredness, justifiable because the goal is total selflessness." (The reference to nostril-breathing is to Melchizedec's yogi exercises.) He himself wrote of his conversion to Unitarianism:

> The way from 'orthodoxy' to the broader field, where you are liable to seek what is true and not what is 'safe' is a very painful one, but the freedom of soul that comes when the battle is won is very refreshing, and one is glad there is one body of Christians which is willing to accept men who seek truth and not doctrinal 'safety'.

When she was a young girl, Gwladys often raided her father's top shelves for the books which, unknown to his parishioners, he studied most keenly — books by Annie Besant, Madame Blavatsky and others — and in her time was drawn to the Quakers before becoming an agnostic. Perhaps these books helped distract her from her daily chores, which were considerable. Her mother, Bridget, had died in Bradford when she was fifteen, in the very week she sat her matriculation examinations, and she was left to bring up four younger brothers and sisters, including one difficult boy only a year younger than herself and a baby girl.

While her father went about preaching, Gwladys managed the house with all the frustration of a lively, independent mind, resentful of her mother's death (she was pregnant with her sixth child when she caught a cold which developed into pneumonia) and the endless penny-pinching of having to raise a large family on a minister's salary. Thanks to her fathers's travels, she never really settled in any one place and shared his restlessness of spirit.

Gwladys eventually found her 'truth' in the agitation for women's rights. She became a devoted Liberal (though often mistaken for a socialist by those who didn't know her; perhaps the distinction didn't matter). In Aberdare, she attended the Pupil Teachers' Centre, prevented by her domestic duties from going further afield, and taught for a while. Her best subject was English, though it was of a more aesthetic kind than Tom's, which was based on the language; his literary taste veered more towards historical novels and A.E.W. Mason. When her father moved to Huddersfield shortly before the war, she stayed behind in digs. She had met Tom at a suffragette rally and had been won over by his quiet, gentle manner. He was, as the valley people say, 'close'. Melchizedec thought she was marrying beneath her, but she went ahead anyway. For one thing, she was no disciplinarian and was glad to be rescued from the classroom. In later years, she used to wonder what would have happened if Tom hadn't come along.

Gwladys was regarded by her neighbours as an intellectual and a feminist, ahead of her time. She had the nerve to darn socks on a Sunday. More than that, she was determined that her children would not be forced to attend Sunday school or chapel, both of which could be very repressive, in keeping with the chapel's role as a stabilising force in times of rapid change. They were to grow up free to make up their own minds, though she relented to the extent of allowing Alun to take a temperance pledge when he was four at the insistence of Tom's mother. Preventing the children from attending Sunday school was not only a religious matter, however, since the school was conducted in Welsh and Gwladys didn't speak Welsh. Tom's family argued that at least they could learn the Welsh alphabet there, but Gwladys wanted them to learn their abc in school, not chapel. She thought it was more important for them to roam the mountains on a Sunday afternoon than to be locked up in hot, stuffy vestries. That way they would grow up to accept their moral responsibilities. (Years later, Alun was to reflect: "chapel has no associations for me and I've grown up without it.") Tom Lewis, a believer, would occasionally visit the Moriah Aman Congregation chapel with members of his father's family. No rosy cheeks in God's fresh air for him.

Gwladys Lewis emphasised family before community, an unusual thing to do, and the other Lewises resented the way in which she isolated Tom and the children from them. Relations between them were correct rather than cordial; you could not call at 61 Brynhyfryd unannounced. Even so, Gwladys found life in Cwmaman fascinating after her Yorkshire years. In the begrimed faces, red mufflers and tied trousers of the miners, she discovered "an artistic and impressive sight" which reminded her of the Christy minstrels. Observing the night shift carrying their lanterns in pitch darkness on a winter's evening, she was impressed by their "uncanny human air . . . full of mystery". She was identifying herself with them imaginatively.

War fever reached Aberdare early with the arrival of Belgian refugees and the breaking up of meetings held by the local pacifist M.P., Keir Hardie. Tom enlisted in Kitchener's Army and left home soon after the birth of his second son, Glyn, in 1917. Gwladys was preoccupied in caring for her new child and could not look after Alun as devotedly as she had used to. His personality changed markedly as a result, as she recalls.

> From being a happy contented child, Alun became querulous and difficult; his appetite failed and the plump sturdy little boy lost his rosy cheeks, lost weight and his lively spirit. He refused to go down in his cot at night as he was accustomed to, and cried until I took him in my arms and soothed him to sleep. Our family doctor prescribed a tonic but neither he nor I could remove the root of the trouble.
>
> One morning, baby slept later than usual, so Alun and I had breakfast together and all was as it used to be: cosy, intimate and fulfilling. Then baby cried upstairs and Alun's face clouded with distress. Later as I was bathing baby and Alun was looking on, he suddenly lifted his hand and struck the little one a short sharp slap on the face! I couldn't believe, until I saw positive proof, that a child could be so disturbed. Doctor's verdict: 'A very sensitive child'.

This early sense of betrayal, though common enough, left its mark on Alun. Gwladys had always thought him special, the first fruit of her marriage conceived at her and Tom's first consummation. For nine months she had breast-fed him and established a close rapport with him which bordered on telepathy. "It was akin to the awareness that lovers have to each other's presence in a room, even when separated by a distance," she wrote later. Gradually, the child was won round, but he was never to feel as secure again.

Uncertainty was, in any case, very much in the air. Shortly after Tom joined the army, Gwladys and the two boys moved to Redcar on the North Yorkshire coast to be with him during the summer holidays. With them went Sarah Jane Evans, whom Gwladys employed as a nursery maid when she fell pregnant with Glyn. She was known as "Ajee" to the children (their attempt to pronounce her second name) and Ajee she became to everyone. The summer was hot and busy and Alun had to be distracted perpetually from the army lorries that gathered on the beaches for manoeuvres. In the autumn, mother and children went on to Melchizedec's manse in Lydgate, near Huddersfield, in the Pennines; Ajee returned to Cwmaman.

In March, 1918, Tom was badly wounded in the back of the thigh just above the knee and had to drag himself to the safety of his lines over two miles for half a night. When the War Office telegram arrived, Gwladys shouted, "Hurrah! Tom's wounded!" He would have to fight no more. After a period of convalescence at the Great Western Infirmary in Glasgow, he was discharged from the army in September, 1918 and returned to Cwmaman to begin life with his family anew.

II

Early Schooldays

It was a very different world. The years leading up to the Great War had seen the prosperity of the South Wales coalfield at its height, but by the time Alun was growing up, it had entered a depression that was to last until the outbreak of World War II. The pits that had been sunk so rapidly not seventy years before now began to close with equal rapidity. For a society dependent on coal, the effect was disastrous. In the South Wales mining area, the labour force fell by half between 1920 and 1933. The number of mining companies between the Rhondda and Rhymney valleys was reduced to one. Local authorities went bankrupt, pit villages were adopted by Hampstead and Bournemouth, bags of potatoes featured as prizes in children's raffles. The young departed for Dagenham and Liverpool and Slough. It was the sort of misfortune that breeds stoicism and a compassionate indignity in a people and it made brotherhood more than a word for South Walians, who rallied to the cause of reconstruction with a fervour that was as intense as it was defensive, hoping for the best, fearing the worst. For fifty years or more, Welsh capital, labour and technology had been at the heart of the British Empire; the country's mines and industries attracted immigrants at a rate which, in its heyday, was the *pro rata* equivalent of the United States. This made for a greater internationalism than almost anywhere else in the British Isles and it influenced the politics and literature of the place profoundly.

Alun's parents were politically conscious and he showed an early interest in education, housing and the poor. It was a time when boys went out looking for "a start of work" very early. They were lucky if even the strongest of them could be employed at the pits. The rest had to do at Boy's Clubs, started by the unemployed in tin shanties charging a penny a week. Young married couples looked for shared accommodation rather than houses to rent or buy while mothers of eight or more took in other people's washing. Only railwaymen's children went on holidays, thanks to their free passes. The pits recorded many an injury and Alun and his friends soon learned to read the signs. As Harri Webb writes:

> The victims would be brought up and carried on stretchers through the streets to their homes, covered with the rough brattice cloth used underground. If a man's face was covered as well as his body, he was dead, that's how you knew. Alun Lewis grew up knowing, as a child knows, maimed and crippled men, men drowning in dust, women driven witless by sudden grief, school-fellows without fathers, families without hope, a village living on its nerves, waiting for the hooter.

Alun started school at the Glynhafod Infants School in the autumn of 1920, when it had just begun the task of feeding deprived pupils. "This week", the school log of 4 March 1921 reads, "the number of children fed in School (Mixed and Inf) increased to 75 [out of a total of some 200]. They are the children of colliers who have worked only two days in the week for the last 8 weeks, owing to the industrial depression." Again, on 13 April: "Breakfast and Dinner were provided at the School for necessitous children." There were 258 meals served. The diet was bacon, bread and soup. That summer, the Headmaster reported that the school shower bath (itself a rarity) had proved a great success. "Over 200 baths have been taken [in school time] per week . . . with most refreshing results". The cupboard in his study was filled with mended shoes, not books, and if your father didn't work in the Post Office or the Co-op and wasn't a pit manager or teacher, you were likely to need them.

In 1923, the new Head from Llwydcoed, near Aberdare, complained of poor attendance figures. "It has been very wet and the children absent complain that they are badly shod. The wages are low and the local collieries are are often idle. No child, as far as I have observed, is underfed but there are cases where it is obvious that the children are improperly fed. Illnesses are general." As it happens, Aberdare was the first local authority in the U.K. to have a full-time assistant to the Medical Officer of Health for the inspection and treatment of children (in 1907) just as it was to be the first authority to invoke the slum-clearance act of 1930. It was on one of these medical inspections that Alun was singled out for attention, as his mother recalls.

> As the lady doctor, who was very young, was using the stethoscope, she looked up and said as though speaking of something quite trivial: 'V.D.H. [Very Dicky Heart]. No excitement, no forcing at stool for this child,' and passed him to me as if he were an inanimate bundle.

He had a slight murmur in his heart but it was to vanish of its own accord.

Classes in the school were large — Alun's Standard IV had forty-five, which was about average for the area — but they were efficient, spurred on by the enthusiasm of new teachers teaching in new schools in an area in which the general provision of primary education was itself (as elsewhere) recent. Despite children being called away to help at home and the discomfort and cold of the classrooms, the standard achieved was high. For the rest, the Lewis children played in the streets with their schoolmates or climbed the tips, from which they could slide down using the steel hawsers when the mines were not working. They followed the Nant Aman Fach up to Rhys Weekes's farm (the local dairy) and swam in the pond they built by damming the river. Sometimes they would go further afield, to the Hepste Falls and the Mellte Caves at Ystradfellte, almost a family pastime. "I don't think we knew what a shop was," says Glyn, "just walks and more walks".

There were also visits to no. 10 Railway Terrace, right next door to Brown's pit, where grandfather Job Lewis lived. His wife had died in 1920, so the house was run by Alun's favourite Bopa (Aunt) Jane. She was the only attraction there, says Mair Lewis, who remembers Job as "a Bible-black, God fearing man who never kissed his children [and] whose house on Sundays was like a morgue". Three of Tom's brothers and sisters lived in Cwmaman, the most celebrated being Edward Lewis, a fireman in the pits and founder of the Cwmaman choir, one of the finest in the valleys. In 1935, he was to organise the first Male Voice Festival for the unemployed.

Outside the school term, the Lewises enjoyed an annual summer holiday, partly financed by Tom's evening teaching. In 1922, they went to Broadhaven for a month, the family now including Huw, who had been born in 1919, and Mair, born in 1921. The following two years they went to Llangranog, on the Cardiganshire coast. In 1925, they went to an even smaller hamlet a few miles south called Penbryn, this time with a maid in attendance, and it was to Penbryn that they returned every year thereafter as to a special place of refuge. At first, they lived in a schoolhouse provided by the local Headmaster but, after his death in 1929, they moved to a small mill cottage a stone's throw from the beach inhabited by the miller's only surviving daughter, an old lady known as Nano, who let them have it every August while she retired to one room. Many people visited them there, including two of Gwladys's nephews and nieces, Laurie Phelps and Evelyn Grafton, both of whose parents worked in India. Evelyn has described the scene:

> There were no 'mod. cons' of any kind; water had to be fetched from the outside tap at the neighbouring farm and the lighting was from oil lamps and candles. There was no shop for miles and we went burdened with provisions for a month, supplemented when there by locally-caught rabbits and fish and fruit and vegetables from Nano's wonderful overgrown garden. I remember my aunt performing miracles of cooking on the ancient oil stove in the kitchen of the cottage, a small dark room with a cobbled stone floor and no light except from the always-open back door through which hens strutted in and out. The lack of amenities never bothered the rest of us in the least, as we were there only to eat and sleep and were outside all the rest of the time.

At Penbryn, the freedom of home was projected into an even more enchanted playground of swimming, rock-climbing, rowing, catching crabs, trout fishing, rabbit shooting and walks through the woods above the beach or on the cliff. The high point of the day was teatime on the sands, where the children had a tent pitched for the holiday. Tom and Gwladys brewed the tea on a Primus stove, serving it up with jam sandwiches or home-made fruit cake. There were few other children around; the local ones worked on farms or in town just out of reach while holidaymakers rarely penetrated as far as Penbryn, so they had the place very much to themselves for a month each year. Just to make sure, the children used to turn the arms of the few signposts there were. It was time when, as Gwladys Lewis recalls, they "played and laughed, swam, read and lazed to our heart's content, and when, in looking back, the sun seems always to have been shining, the sky and sea blue and the land shimmering gold."

In 1926, Alun was one of twenty-nine pupils who sat the County Entrance Exam (the old 11 Plus) at Glynhafod school. Three won

places to the County (i.e. Grammar) school and five to the Central
school in Aberdare. Alun won a scholarship of £20 plus fees to the
Grammar school at Cowbridge in the Vale of Glamorgan, having
come top of the list. The decision to send him there was one of the
most fateful of his life.

III

Scholarship Boy

It was Mrs Lewis who pressed Alun to go to Cowbridge, though she was to regret doing so. She was determined that her children should benefit from their education and pushed them hard at their work. She was punctilious about their speech and reading habits. She was always "Mother" to them, not "Mam", while Mr Lewis was "Daddy", even to her. It was she who ruled the household, though her hand could be lax as his was correspondingly strict. Unlike the other houses in the neighbourhood, theirs was something of a lounger's paradise, at least to those brought up on stricter standards of domestic economy, comfortable rather than tidy. There were few gewgaws but many books, mostly collected by Tom Lewis, who could never pass a bookshop without going in. It was Gwladys, however, who won the prizes for Book Society review competitions. She was well-known in Cwmaman for her somewhat unusual appearance, brightly dressed in white (or red) ankle socks and a fillet band in her hair; she was always ready for a chat and served on various committees, including the Women's Social Club with its programme of care for the poor. Tom was her foil and support, gentle and slow, though with an authority of his own, as his pupils were to discover if they failed to learn the lines of verse he had set them. To them, he was "Bull", after his strong, thick-set head and placid air of command, tinged with severity. "[H]elping people, fitting them up, doing something human, useful — she gets much more delight out of it than Daddy, for she's much more of a social reformer than he," Alun later reflected. "He's naturally inclined to the domestic and quiet, the farm gate and the fireside; and don't bother others. I've got a bit of both in me.''

Important as it was for the children to receive a sound education, it was quite another to send Alun to Cowbridge, a boarding school with public school affiliations some twenty miles away, for this only accentuated his separation from Cwmaman and reopened the wounds of his infantile desertion. The coincidence of his going to Cowbridge in 1926, the year of the General Strike, is remarkable. He was more than unusually unhappy there and homesickness was the least part of it. He was, in effect, isolated.

Not that he showed his unhappiness; on the contrary, he was "all fun", quick to take up a dare, easy, sympathetic, a cool, pleasant, self-possessed personality, something of a loner but sociable with it. One master remembers him walking about with a sleepy, half-smiling expression, head thrown slightly back, as if to say, "What's all this for, then?" He was quieter, less academically ambitious than his mother, as if he had absorbed some of his father's silent strength, though he had the sharpness of mind and general eagerness that proclaimed him very much his mother's son.

Cowbridge under its Headmaster, Richard Williams, was in the grip of an iron rule. For the more sturdy boys, this was no more than the inculcation of *esprit de corps*, tough but not unfair; to the more sensitive it was distressing. Williams was a bad-tempered man in charge of a school of few comforts and hard knocks. Games were plentiful, classes taxing if not stimulating, the atmosphere at once more open than in the valleys and more oppressive to one of Alun's upbringing. " 'Obey without reasoning' was the order of the day,'' his mother recalls. "This irked Alun's independent spirit which we had fostered through the years and he was never happy there. He enjoyed the companionship of the boys but he loathed the subjugation of the spirit." No wonder Cowbridge found him "somewhat reserved and seemingly always in a mood of abstraction". Silence, exile and cunning had become the means of his survival.

The school was founded in 1608–9 by Sir Edward Stradling and later bought by Sir Leoline Jenkins, Principal of Jesus College, Oxford, who bequeathed it to the college on his death. Since then, it had had a chequered career, veering between being a charitable foundation and a fee-paying school for the upper classes. However, since these are not numerous in South Wales, it had entered obscurity several times while at the same time avoiding extinction. In 1919, it

1. Wales, showing locations named in the text.

passed to the Glamorgan Education Authority, which provided a number of free places. In the same year, Richard Williams arrived as Head and set about expanding the school. He established a growing academic reputation. In Alun's time, the boys numbered between a hundred and thirty and a hundred and fifty (about half of them boarders) and the teaching staff eight.

On his arrival, Williams found Cowbridge "medieval — or at any rate early Victorian". There was no electricity or water supply and only one bath in the school. Not long after, when Bryn Edwards arrived as French master, he observed "two little old ladies who might have walked out of one of Jane Austen's novels, scurrying past the school, in nodding bonnets and trailing skirts with their umbrellas in the crook of their arms. Farmers on horseback, or driving a pony and trap, were more frequent than buses or cars." Cowbridge was the market town for the Vale of Glamorgan, set in a hollow in the midst of rich agricultural land. The borough had eighty acres but barely a thousand people on them. The town buildings consisted of houses on either side of the main road from Cardiff to Swansea. Several dated from the sixteenth and seventeenth centuries, the church and school (rebuilt in the nineteenth century) set off a little to the south. New industry passed the town by as did the railway when the local gentry opposed it lest it undermine their control of the place. On discovering that other towns were flourishing as theirs was not, they relented to the extent of permitting a spur line to be built to Llantrisant, but too late. Only with the arrival of the motor car did the town's prosperity recover again. The school was connected to the main Glamorgan water supply, oil lamps were replaced with electric lights and shower baths installed. There was also a new boarding house, a Georgian residence donated to the school by Sir Thomas Franklen, after whom it was named. The master in charge was the English teacher, Eric Ainslie Reid.

Eric Reid was a remarkable man. He was an Irishman from Belfast, in his early forties when Alun knew him, a hunchback with partial paralysis of the spine and a bowed back, tall, haggard and with a tortured look and long chin. For six years he had worked as a designer in a linen company before going up to Queen's University in 1912. He arrived in Cowbridge in the same year as the Headmaster and immediately set about reviving the Debating Society, organising the library, producing the school play and editing the school magazine. Above all, he enthused his pupils with a love of literature. In the editorials he wrote for the school magazine, *The Bovian*, he extolled the spirit of idealism and urged his readers to live worthily. "Youth," he declared, "is a time when generous emotions are born and lofty ideals built up", the ideals being those of world peace and the League of Nations, a junior branch of which had opened in the school in 1923. Schools should turn out pupils "with minds tuned to receptivity, robust, vigorous, inquiring", seekers after truth who would fight against war, ignorance and armaments for the benefit of humanity, thus ensuring "that noonday of which we are witnessing the splendid dawn". They would have to put aside the "narrow patriotism and national prejudice" of Kipling.

Reid's editorials breathe a love of learning and repeatedly look to education to break down the barriers of isolation. One editorial regrets that so excellent a volume as Breasted's *History of Ancient Times* is so little used in the library and recalls the thrill of first reading Carlyle's *French Revolution* as a schoolboy ("though not in the classroom") — "a rapture we have seldom experienced since". And it is this "rapture" that is the keynote of Reid's approach, ardent, resolute, ever eager to greet the new day. Progress was his watchword and it led him to praise the Victorians for one quality they possessed even if he could not acknowledge the philosophy they derived from it: "they were in deadly earnest". In Carlyle and Ruskin, Mill, Browning and Tennyson was to be found "the seriousness of life and . . . high destiny" of the race. "We live in a wonderful time," he wrote, "an age of wizardry and magic . . . as wonderful as Elizabeth's. We are indeed but beginning to reap the harvest."

Read in sequence, these exhortations can appear wearisome (sad, too, considering all that was to follow) but they are the work of an unusually vigorous mind grappling with the central issues of the age. They made a deep impression on Alun, and reinforced all the values he had learned at home. Reid's influence spread far beyond the classroom for he was Alun's Housemaster and ran his community on very different lines from the Head. He also produced school plays like *She Stoops to Conquer* in 1930, in which Alun appeared as Kate Hardcastle, though his forte was not so much for the stage as for mimickry, as in mock trials, where he made his mark; it was the sort of talent that was to stand him in good stead in army theatricals later on.

The records of the Debating Society are full of the contributions of Eric Reid and Alun Lewis. In 1929 (when Alun joined), he argued for field-sports and the monarchy but against the Empire or the notion

that Elizabeth I was a great queen or that Britain needed a dictator.
(Barbara Powell, who was in Aberdare hospital with him at a time
when they both had scarlet fever, remembers him asking, "Who or
what" — a characteristic exactitude inspired by his mother — "do you
love best in the world?" Barbara, who had been brought up by her
grandmother, replied, "My grandmother". Alun stood up in bed,
lifted his arms and shouted, "The British Flag!") He also believed
that the power of the press was growing too great. "He said that Shaw
wrote that Journalism was the finest and highest class of writing. He
disagreed with Shaw in the matter."

In January, 1931, he proposed that "the government of India
should be left in Indian hands". India, he said, was a diverse country,
impossible to describe. Nineteen thousand children were born there
every day and it was a huge task to educate them all and give them the
chances English people expected. "The English have always striven
to gain control over an impossible people, and the whole Indian
people are ready to wipe out all the European population of their
country." The attempt to govern them would be "fruitless". They
might be content at first "but soon they would imagine themselves to
be on the same level as their masters and would determine to be rid of
that external pressure." Eric Reid lagged behind on this occasion.
Ghandi, he declared, was "not capable of settling the destinies of
India", though he and Alun later jointly opposed a motion
disapproving of the "Russian Soviet Government". The Russian
government, Alun said, was "worthy of the expense it is causing . . .
The French benefited from the revolution as Russia is going to do."
Master and pupil were together again when they denied that science
was of greater value to civilisation than the arts, Reid reminding his
audience that art and poetry were worthy only in so far as they
promoted "sympathy with other men". It was a theme he was to
return to frequently in *The Bovian*, where he declared that academic
work was valueless unless it was united to "the natural feelings for
common humanity". Such is the noble purpose that saves us from
egotism, "the talisman of sympathy and disinterested service."

This sympathy was duly tested when Alun fell foul of the
Headmaster. He was discovered out of bounds with a girl, either by
prearrangement with a day-school friend in his second or third year
(as his mother recalls) or as the result of a dare in his fifth or sixth year
(as a school friend, Bernard Pile, recalls). Whatever the case, his

parents were summoned and he was threatened with expulsion. This is how Mrs Lewis remembers the crisis:

> Instead of making a clean breast of the affair, Alun said he had been looking for his hockey stick, which was an untruth; and Alun knew that the head knew it was an untruth when he stated it. The glove was thrown down! Alun refused to change his story and the head vowed he would do nothing to forward Alun's career until he did.

This episode may throw some light on the unusual brevity of Alun's time at school. Normally, students sat for their School Certificates in their fourth year, their Higher School Certificates in their sixth year and their Scholarship papers in their seventh. Alun got his School Certificate in his third year, with a distinction in Latin and credits in Scripture, English, History, Geography, French and Mathematics. He came third out of the nineteen boys who sat for the exam. In 1931, his fifth year, he passed his Higher School Certificate with distinctions in English and History and a credit in Latin (taught by the Head). He was placed in the reserve list for a State scholarship, having come second out of six Cowbridge boys. In the spring of 1932, a year early, he entered for an Open scholarship to Jesus College but without success. The examiners were impressed but noted his extreme youth and advised him to try again the following year. He did not do so. Instead, he sat his H.S.C. for a second time that summer, on this occasion gaining only one distinction, for History. However, his first attempt had been good enough to win him the Mold Eisteddfod Open Scholarship to the University College of Wales at Aberystwyth and the second got him a leaving exhibition from the school. He was free to leave Cowbridge at last.

His time there had not been uniformly unhappy. There was little bullying and the masters were reasonable. Photographs of the time show a small, round, full-faced boy, "Lew" or "Baby Lew", as he was called, full of beans, a crooked smile playing on his lips. He was the cheeky chappy, always ready for a dare, like riding a bicycle with no brakes or smoking cigarettes behind a bush. He was a keen hockey player (for which he gained colours), a footballer, a swimmer, a librarian and a house and school prefect. Yet none of these activities could dispel the unease he felt. He had been rendered insecure and his contacts with family and friends broken. The void was filled with, among other things, a profound social guilt. (He was ashamed to go round Cwmaman in his Cowbridge blazer, though in later years liked to savour the prestige of being a public school boy.) It was one thing not having to wake up at five in the morning and walk two and a half miles to the coalface for seven hours' work six days a week, fifty weeks a year, for nineteen to thirty shillings a week, quite another to have to sit down to a lantern lecture at school and be shown how coal is extracted, pit roofs kept up and air circulated.

Alun understood how isolated Eric Reid was, too, both as a man and as a teacher. He was "different", mocked for his accent and physical disabilities (and, doubtless, his "vision splendid"). He had little classroom discipline, being called "Elulora" by the boys (Richard Williams was "skiff dick"). Even his trumpet calls to the young grew fainter as the years passed by. In March, 1932 he begged the boys once more in *The Bovian* to take "a real interest in international affairs". He confessed his disappointment at the failure of the League of Nations to achieve disarmament and the various betrayals of its charter by member states. The advance of the Japanese into China struck him as particularly ominous. Unless the young redeemed the errors of their fathers, they — the very boys he was addressing — would have to pay the penalty with their lives. The irony is touching.

This was to be Reid's last editorial. His health, never very robust, faltered and he took a term's leave during Alun's last term at school. On 16 January, 1933, he died. As his obituarist remarked, "There was a puritan fierceness in him like the sword of an avenging angel." A rare spirit had gone.

It was to his cousin, the novelist Helen Waddell, that Reid turned when he discovered that he had in Alun Lewis a writer out of the ordinary. The best of the stories went into the school magazine and constitute a remarkable body of work, with a poise that is altogether astonishing. They possess an inwardness beyond his years and anticipate all the major themes of his later writing. The only comparable modern example is Dylan Thomas, who filled four notebooks at much the same time, though they contain poems not stories and are more fertile as they are less profound. The theme is isolation, whether symbolised by a dwarf ('The Tale of a Dwarf') or, later, a Reid-like hunchback in the poem 'Vanité', within an advanced perception of the cycle of life and death. "Beware of beauty when it cloaks a harsh design", as one 1932 story has it — whether it is the beauty we observe or the beauty the Muse brings with her when she elects a writer from the very young.

IV

Aberystwyth (1)

At the end-of-term concert in the summer of 1932, Alun wrote and
produced a mock-Shakespearean play and appeared in two of four
one-act plays staged shortly after. With that, he was free of school and
able to enjoy his holidays with a lighter heart than for many years.
With Cowbridge friends, he went camping at Aberporth, just south of
Penbryn, where he was joined by about twenty other people,
including Elonwy Maddox, a Carmarthen girl, and Iris Jones, a slim,
blonde schoolgirl from Tremain a few miles away. She had sad eyes
and a winning smile, somewhat ethereal but with an inner strength,
rather like Alun himself. They spent every day on the beach, dressed
in their new khaki shorts and casual tops. They would climb the steep
steps from the beach to buy fresh buns from the bakery at Glanordu or
stroll along to Tresaith along the coastal footpath or to the beach at
Mwnt. They joined in summer carnivals in Cardigan and Aberporth
and attended the various Saturday night 'hops', where Alun
distinguished himself with his fancy footwork (said to be the result of
dancing lessons). "He was always eager to join in all our activities,"
Elonwy Maddox recalls, "but that lop-sided grin of his gave me the
impression that he thought we were being just a bit childish!"

Alun developed a special affection for Iris Jones. Hand in hand, they
would go for long walks, he with his loping stride, feet thrown in,
trying to interest her in the plants and birds they saw. She thought
him singular and for more than sentimental reasons. She detected a
sadness in him, paradoxically intensified by his winning smile and
bright, kindly eyes, a quality of detachment, as though he were

separate from others and working to a different end. His manner was
cheerful but every now and then he would lapse into a world of his
own, as though he were trying to understand what was happening to
him as much as anyone else. He always carried a paper and pencil and
read her some of his work, including the opening stanza of the
following poem:

> It seemed to me Truth lay at rest,
> In a field of yellow corn;
> I sought her where the black hill crest,
> Turns pink, then gold, at dawn.
>
> It seemed to me Truth was a flower
> Sunwoo'd, rainkissed, asleep,
> Blossoming in a green-leaf bower,
> So lovely the soft winds weep.

The tantalising pursuit of a reality that always recedes is a typical
Lewis theme.

Alun was not the only person who could boast of writing
achievements that year. His mother had won first prize in a one-act
play competition run by the South Wales Council of Social Service.
The play, called *Pleasant Place* (an ironic name for Cwmaman or any
other drab mining town), is written in the vernacular as by one who
does not speak or live as her characters do. It tells of the reactions of
the villagers to the Depression, men such as Jack, a young
unemployed collier, who is fed up with this "damned country. No
chance for a working man while these bloody capitalists have it all
their own way. We want 'Red Revolution' ". The heroine of the play,
Mari, rejects revolution as she spurns the efforts of the Quakers to
alleviate poverty. She looks instead to the next generation of villagers,
people like her son, Alun. "Alun?" a visitor asks. "What a pretty
name! You have such musical names in Welsh. How do you spell it?"
"A-l-u-n," his mother replies, "but 'u' in Welsh is like 'i' in English.
[Mrs Lewis's pronunciation of the name was in fact nearer 'Aleen'
than 'Alin'.] I always said that if we had a boy, he should be Alun, and
he is our eldest son." This Alun has won certificates and prizes on
Speech Day, just as the real one did in 1931 when his story 'The Tale
of a Dwarf' was praised at Cowbridge's Speech Day. Tears of joy ran
down his mother's cheek. "Mari" recalls the occasion:

> And when I saw him on the platform and heard the boys clap, it all
> came over me how poor we were and how could we let him go on and

things like that, and the tears just rolled down my cheeks till I couldn't see at all for the mist in my eyes . . . Well then, I said to myself: 'Here Mari Jones, stop being a fool. Here's one poor boy been and done it, and why shouldn't another?' So I dried my eyes and made up my mind that, God helping me, Alun should go on.

"It's boys like Alun," a young minister remarks, "who are going to settle the economic troubles for us; boys brought up in the midst of the poverty who take up commerce and come to grips with these great world problems. Ignorance screaming from the housetops will lead us nowhere, but knowledge, used with understanding and sympathy, may see us well on the road to a solution." Eric Reid couldn't have put it better.

It was time to decide what Alun should read at Aberystwyth — English or History? The decision was effectively taken by his mother.

Why History when English was the obvious choice? I am afraid I was largely responsible for that. I had a hunch that the edge of Alun's creative gift would be blunted if he dragged his precious English through the stresses and strains of competitive examination work.

Much could be said for her decision, but it was to weigh heavily on him in future years.

Iris Jones left Tremain for London, where she trained as a nurse, and eventually faded from Alun's life. The Lewises themselves were also on the move during Alun's schooldays, from Cwmaman to 62 Cwmaman Road, Godreaman, at the mouth of the valley, half-way to Aberdare, where Tom Lewis had been appointed to a post at the Gadlys school. "I think this was the first step by Mother in winkling Daddy out of Cwmaman where he was born and bred," Mair recalls. "I guess he did not like change as he remained at the same school throughout our childhood". The Lewises were the nobility of Cwmaman Road, the father large and authoritative, dressed in his sober grey overcoat, courteous and mild in manner, very reserved, the mother sharp, quicker, obviously the family figurehead. Alun knew his Godreaman neighbours little, being present only during vacations, yet he impressed them with his gentleness. In a valley where men lived rough and boyhood matured rapidly, not to say discordantly, he was exceptional for the sweetness of his temper. When Huw, his youngest brother, boxed with Thomas Jones next door, he would pace up and down the garden path, upset by their fighting.

Before long, the family were on the move again, from Godreaman to 7 Elm Grove in Aberdare (the same address as that of Wilfred Owen in Birkenhead in 1898), directly opposite the Gadlys school and was again purchased by Edward Lewis, the choirmaster, whose ambition it was to leave each of his daughters a house. Alun now mixed with a new set of friends and fell in love with Mairwen Jones, whom he met on the cake walk following chapel in Aberdare Park. It was there or at Macherpas, the Italian cafe where the young congregated, or on walks on the Graig above Aberdare that they spent their time together. Mairwen, too, was struck by the difference in this shy young boy, a handsome dreamer much too good for this world. He was quieter than before, less impish and round-faced, his abstracted air more pronounced. Eventually, she moved to London to enter domestic service and Alun became friends with a girl called Ruby Griffin. But soon he was immersed in his new life at Aberystwyth.

                                                        ★

> In miles, the run of railway between Carmarthen and Aberystwyth is not long. But its beauty is deep and varied, and you would not get a better chance of appreciating it if you were being pushed through it in a bath chair. This is, without question, the gentlest train in existence, the only railway on earth designed not to disturb the pollen in the lush paradise around.

Thus Gwyn Thomas. Add the same distance again from Aberdare to Carmarthen and you get some idea of the isolation that surrounded (and, to a certain extent, still surrounds) the University College of Wales in Aberystwyth. It was the best part of two hours by bus or train from Aberdare to Swansea, another forty minutes for the run to Carmarthen, skirting the great mountain mass of mid-Wales, a two-hour wait there and a two and a half hour train to Aberystwyth stopping at what seemed to be forty-nine stations in as many miles. Once there, what with the rarity of motor cars, Saturday morning classes and residential rules, you could hardly get away again. Even so, Aberystwyth was a happier place for Alun. True,

> The beach lacks a rich sweep of sand. It is grey shingle crushed fairly fine by generations of holiday sitters. The sea moves very little this way or that, as if cured of all tidal frolics by the markedly earnest town of the town.

True, too, that the University buildings on the sea front (whence its nickname "The College by the Sea") are "somewhat like an Oxford college caught in misalliance with a chapel". A Victorian entrepreneur named Thomas Savin had tried to make the town the "Brighton of Wales" and built the Castle Hotel for holiday trippers. When the trippers failed to materialise, he went bankrupt and, in 1867, sold the hotel to a committee which was trying to establish a Welsh university. This eventually opened as a private venture in October, 1972. Since there was no money to house the students, the men were placed in lodgings in town while the halls of residence were reserved for the women.

Life in Aberystwyth had all the intimacy of a small town. The students numbered about seven hundred and came mostly from the mining valleys of South Wales. No university in England had anything like as many working-class students. Its temper may be judged from a speech made by the Principal of the college at the time of the relief of Mafeking on 23 May, 1900:

> Welsh students detest beyond everything the grasping materialistic temper of some of the gunfire mongering of the day. Their interest in the British Empire is as different from this, and also from militarism, as the east is from the west. The Empire to them is an ideal — and as such is exercising a wonderful fascination — which means broader standards, vaster brotherhood, purer democracy.

In 1918, David Davies and his sisters established a Chair of International Politics to rally public opinion behind the establishment of "a League of Free Peoples" and so promote justice in the world. It was the first such Chair. When Davies became President of the College, he declared: "I should like to see Aberystwyth becoming the centre of study and research for a united Europe, the federation of Europe, as opposed to the conceptions of Imperialism or an Anglo-Saxon alliance." Overwhelmingly, then, Aberystwyth was Welsh, internationalist, egalitarian, qualities as much to be enjoyed as asserted.

The friendliness and informality of the place were reinforced by the fact that Alun's uncle Tim (Tom's brother) was Reader in Celtic Philology and Palaeography there, having narrowly missed the Professorship. The History Professor was R.F. Treharne, recently arrived from the Manchester School of Medieval History at the age of twenty-eight. He promptly set about reorganising the Department on tutorial lines, bringing teachers and students closer together. In 1932–3, Alun read Latin, English, History and French (a special course for

History students), the following year Economics, English and History and in his final year History alone.

Outside the classroom, he became friendly with a number of people, especially Chris Germanacos, a lively Greek boy from Barry. Chris was Alun's best friend, one with whom he could discuss his writing. Through him, he mixed with such society as he did, which was mainly of a sporting kind. They enjoyed boxing bouts in the college gym, bridge or poker sessions every Sunday afternoon, the occasional tennis match and various college 'hops', where Alun was known for the odd exaggerated tango. He played hockey for the College First XI and Merioneth County and contributed song-and-dance numbers to college revues, though he took no part in the Debating Society or the League of Nations Union or any other political club. Indeed, no-one can remember him doing anything other than play sport. He was on the sidelines looking on, reserved but friendly once the barriers were down, serious and delightful, observant and unworldly.

With Germanacos, he joined the Black Angels, a group of drinkers who gathered at the Angel Hotel or the Black Lion pub wearing black shirts and white ties with a black angel motif. Later, at Chris's instigation, they formed the Areopagiticus Club, a discussion group which met irregularly at the old Black or someone's digs. "It wasn't till I got started drinking beer in the old Black Lion," Alun later recalled, "and playing billiards and poker and sharing the rest of Chris Germanacos's opiates and fantasies that I found *myself* at all interesting." His favourite recreation was going for long walks in the country, visiting, among other places, the farm of Dewi Lewis, a fellow student, at Tremain. Dewi had heard about the young writer from y gweithfeydd (the South Wales mining valleys) but hadn't met him until he went up to University. There, he discovered a kindred spirit, one who loved the land and sea as much as he did. The coast around Penbryn, Dewi writes,

> was a home from home for Alun during his youth and early manhood. There he got to know the countryside and the seaside intimately. He loved it all, the place and the people. There he shared the life of ordinary working Welsh people perhaps more than in his own valley where his professional home and boarding school background would have set him a bit apart from his valley contemporaries. At Penbryn he was not only the keen observer but also a participant. During those pre World War Two years regular summer visitors became honorary Cardis. Alun was very much at home in the cottages and farms of

Penbryn. The place and the people became part of him. With his artist's eye he looked and saw with great clarity. Naturally, while he was a young boy, he spent more time with some of the housewives than with their menfolk out in the fields. Some of these Cardiganshire countrywomen made a deep impression on the young boy from Glamorgan.

There was about Alun, the student, a certain sensitivity, an air of languid gentleness, even when tearing up and down the playing field. Some of us rugby team roughnecks thought there was some thing slightly sissy for men to play the girls' game, hockey, even when they were as good and lethal at it as Alun proved to be . . .

Alun's gifts and talents and good looks ensured easy success in all his student activities, including his studies. We often shared a table in the Reading Room of the National Library and I was immensely impressed by the scholarly way he went about things. His collecting and collating were thorough. He was methodical and meticulous, and his note cards and slips were always neat and legible (unlike mine). But there was never any sign of stress and strain. Everything seemed smooth and easy.

Alun was by now a slender, well-built figure, dark but pale-faced and good-looking in his black and white jacket and grey slacks or plus-fours. He would trail his hockey stick onto the field smoking his newly-acquired pipe contentedly. Then "the sound of the whistle would go and in a flash, away would go his pipe, up went his stick and he was charging down the field like the wind. This was characteristic. His dreaming and practical sides were instantaneously interchangeable as circumstances demanded." The former earned him the nickname "Jesus" or "Unconscious" among his fellow undergraduates. He liked to assert that the greatest quality in a person was integrity and defended the Platonic concept of love. In literature, he championed T. S. Eliot and Siegfried Sassoon against the nineteenth-century Romantics.

During his three years at Aberystwyth, Alun contributed eight short stories and one poem to the College magazine, *The Dragon*. None compares in quality with *The Bovian* stories and this may reflect on his absorption in his studies as well as his relative contentment. He was marking time. The theme remains Beauty and Death, though it is occasionally enlivened by folkloric tales in a whimsical mode and stories about sexual awakening, oppressed and yearning.

Alun's relations with women had progressed to a friendship with Bronwen Williams (not her real name), a short, energetic student from Bangor who had come up a year later than he on a scholarship. She revelled in the freedom of the place, so much so that her parents recalled her at the end of her first year. It was at Bangor that he first met her when he was up for a hockey match. He carried for her all the lost romantic associations of Aberystwyth and his slow, quiet charm soon won her over. She was probably better read than he but less confident in expressing herself. For one thing, Welsh was her first language. He spoke in a quiet, trailing voice of his hopes for a better world or about the books he had been reading. Yet he was as quickly gone as come, withdrawn by some melancholy impulse. She was bewildered and tried to protect him from any unpleasantness. Anything — a tramp or blind person — would set him off. Even so, he was avid for experience and exasperated by his own innocence. Activity was for him a form of release and he revelled in it. "He *never* fell," she recalls. "He was always sure-footed crossing mountain streams or climbing rocks."

Alun took her to Penbryn in the summer of 1935. She immediately reacted against Mrs Lewis, whom she found bossy, always trying to do good, like forcing them all to drink milk. She never stopped talking. Bronwen thought Alun irritated by her but obviously adoring and rendered childish by his very adoration. At the same time, she felt he was being forced to share social concerns he did not necessarily feel. He would have much preferred solitude, being one who could not only hear but see the cuckoo, even the drab female. It was this clash between the father's sanguineness and the mother's ambition that she understood to be at the root of the conflict in him.

After his three years of study, Alun was awarded a First Class Honours degree. His course had concentrated on European and British history, his special subject being medieval English political and constitutional history from 1232 to 1272. For his finals, he submitted a thesis called 'The Administration of the Forests', which Professor Treharne judged "an extremely fine piece of work". Alun, he wrote, was a man of "very sympathetic imagination . . . [His] history was always conceived in terms of human personality and character." There was nothing in him of the " 'civil-service' quality of equal interest and achievement in all directions". He had an unusual intelligence, with humour and ideals and an imagination superior to that of most graduates of the day.

'The Administration of the Forests' is indeed a careful study. It enquires into the effects of the forest system: was it a despotism or an efficient form of government? Alun thought the latter and supported his view with a detailed examination of the working of the forest administration. There is, perhaps, less in it of the imaginative character than might be expected from Treharne's remarks (or perhaps there was a sufficiency of it for the author of *The Baronial Plan of Reform, 1258–63*, described by one critic as "an outstanding scholarly book, built to last") but it obviously augured well for his future as a historian.

But did he want to be a historian? He had done his best but hadn't found the subject as beneficial to his writing as his mother had hoped. Rather the reverse: wishing to do his work well, he found he had little time for anything else and lost much of the pleasure that a less factually-demanding course might have provided. It is not surprising, therefore, to find an approach being made through Aberdare's M.P., George Hall, to W. H. Stevenson, editor of the *Daily Herald*, with a view to his becoming a journalist. Stevenson read some of his stories and advised him to stick to his studies. If he wanted to take up journalism, he should try to place his articles in various papers, gaining some experience of the market. "Why sacrifice the substance for the shadow, however glittering?" he wrote. Why, indeed?

The truth is that Alun did not want to become a journalist, either. What he wanted to do was write but there was no modern tradition of men making their living by the pen in Wales. For the Welsh, literature was the activity of y werin, the people, and related to the democratic expression of a mass culture through eisteddfodau. Not being Welsh-speaking, Alun could not share in that. For writers like him, the first generation of Welshmen brought up to speak English to the exclusion of their mother tongue, there were not the financial, cultural or social resources which might have allowed them to make their careers without moving to London or becoming teachers or writing commercially. But what if you didn't want to move to London or teach or write commercially?

There was a further complication: the English-speaking writers of Wales came not from areas like the Gower peninsula or South Pembrokeshire where English had been long established. Nor were they from immigrant families or the anglicised landowners or industrialists. They were from poor mining families and wrote out of a very different complexion of Wales than any that had existed before, their literary dislocation mirroring the larger social and political one. Theirs was an urban world, industrial and increasingly secular, and all they had to go on were the stories of Caradoc Evans and the poetry of Huw Menai and A. G. Prys-Jones. It may be no accident that Alun

himself began by writing short stories, the form preferred by Welsh/
English writers and the one least dominated by English writers.

Journalism seemed a safer bet, though he could not contemplate
launching out on his own yet. His brothers and sister had their own
education to complete and his parents' resources were stretched to the
limit. What with the Depression, it would have taken an unusually
foolhardy man to make the break. There were at this time four
remarkable writers starting out in South Wales: one, in Swansea,
everyone knows about, Dylan Thomas. Several valleys east, in the
Clydach vale (just off the main Rhondda valley) lived Lewis Jones,
author of *Cwmardy* (1937) and *We Live* (1939), one of the most
interesting novel sequences of the period; he died in 1939 at the age of
forty-one. In the next valley but one further east lived Alun Lewis.
Two valleys east again lay the Rhymney valley, home of Idris Davies,
like Lewis Jones an ex-collier but this time a poet, not a novelist.
There were other valley writers — Gwyn Jones and Glyn Jones and
Jack Jones — but the interesting thing about them is that none of them
knew the others. The mountainous geography of Wales was partly to
blame, but they also lacked any magazines, meeting places or common
institutions that might have brought them closer together. Cardiff was
a new capital, unlike Edinburgh or Dublin, and the Depression meant
that there were few resources for any new literary ventures. *The Welsh
Outlook*, a general periodical, printed the occasional poem but it
closed in 1934 and then there was nothing. These were truly artists
working in isolation.

Alun had been away from his valley for nearly ten years and, though
he knew it well, he did not know it thoroughly. This mattered to him,
as we appreciate when we consider the special position of the poet in
Wales. "The poet," Gwyn Thomas has written, "carries the load of
all our stricken and mutilated lives, and seeks, through intensity of
expression, to bring restitution to those who have been too cruelly
denied the gifts of beauty, wisdom and dignity." He might wish to
escape the "messy, ugly, coaly places" but they would not leave him.
This is how Glyn Jones has described the position:

> Let me explain something else about South Wales too, because the
> appalling economic conditions, the poverty prevailing here, the
> suffering, the hopelessness, had inevitably their effect on the literary
> situation. That Great Depression of the inter-war years began to be
> felt in Wales in the Twenties, and the following decade brought to
> our country a period of unparalleled economic decline and devasta-
> tion. Closures, widespread unemployment, emigration, extreme and

long-term poverty were the agonising and inescapable features of the time, with disease, bitterness, resentment and social unrest as the inevitable consequences. Political activity seemed far more urgent to many young people in these circumstances that the 'fiddle' of poetry. This was the period of the anti-war and anti-fascist rallies, of the great hunger-marches of the unemployed, of the staggeringly successful Left Book Club. The party that appeared to have the allegiance of the young was the Communist Party, not Plaid Cymru . . . It's difficult to convey to someone who didn't experience at first hand the intensity of the sense of frustration and foreboding, the despair, the smouldering anger, the passionate rejection, which was then commonly felt by the sensitive young in the presence of such senseless wastage and suffering and human decency. Soon Hitler was murdering his way to power in Germany and Mussolini in Italy; the Spanish government was losing its war to its own Fascists and the end of democratic Czechoslovakia was in sight. The Second World War, which many believed (since 'the Bomber will always get through') was to bring western civilisation crashing down around us, began to appear as an agonising certainty. Whatever I say about the Anglo-Welsh writers of the Twenties and Thirties, their problems and their frustrations, ought to be seen against this appalling background of poverty, misery, terror and defeat.

As Idris Davies wrote, ". . . I walked my native hillsides/ In sunshine and in rain,/ And learnt the poet's language/ To ease me of my pain." Poetry is a refuge from universal suffering but it is also the recovery of values within a larger humanitarian protest.

Alun Lewis had a further burden to contend with. He knew that he was a poet but also that he was as yet incapable of realising his talents. The only poem he published in Aberystwyth, a sonnet called 'The Ladybird Wakes' (*The Dragon*, Summer 1934) describes the ladybird's emergence from "the bonds wintry forges have made". It might be his own poetic awakening he were anticipating. Another poem, published in *The Western Mail* on August 31, 1935, identified Queen Astrid of the Belgians (who had died in a car crash earlier that month) with a majestic figure who embodies the mystery of existence so that, while Astrid is mourned, she is apotheosised as the Queen of Death. Once more, we meet the theme of beginnings and endings.

After his graduation, Alun's uncle Tim suggested that he try for a scholarship to the British School in Rome (for which he had by then developed a passion) but it was thought better that he pursue his studies in this country first so, after much pressure, he put in for the Harry Thornton Pickles Postgraduate Studentship at the University of Manchester, open to all graduates of British universities. He won it

and went up to Manchester in September, 1935. He was barely
twenty.

V

Manchester: Love and Work

In Manchester, Alun lived in Dover Street in Chorlton, the slum district of the city immediately opposite the University. The house (now demolished) was run by a Mrs Cowrie, whom Gwladys Lewis remembers as a broken-down musical artist living with two men friends. He was too poor to move anywhere else. Perhaps he felt he ought to bear it rather than seek refuge in a men's hostel; perhaps it would be the same wherever he went, for he was now in a deep depression. " . . . I used to think every day how simple it is to die. A train passing, a lorry rumbling outside, a train on a platform — so easy. Death was a comforting dark thought in me." When in later years he felt unhappy, Manchester was always his yardstick.

Physically, it was ugly, a sprawling industrial city without the companionship of Aberystwyth or the mountains of Aberdare (not to mention the charms of Paris, which Alun had visited that summer on a grant from Aberystwyth). For one who could be plunged into gloom by the mere sight of a mountain lake, it was purgatory. The faces of the women on the buses made him shudder; the effort of a dandelion to push its way through the flagstones left him sweating; spring gave him an "itchy dirty feeling". Outwardly, he was still the gay young student but inwardly his state approximated the description of his environment in one of his stories from this time:

> It was an evil street. The pavement echoed dull and cold beneath
> the pedestrians's feet, save for the mocking laugh with which

an occasional flagstone greeted the passer-by. How sullen, how inscrutable was the blind stare of its 49 doors, the pain encrusted with dirt that clung in flakes and bubbles like a disease to the rain-warped woodwork. The few doors that boasted knockers stared even more apathetically than their fellows at the silent street, like beggars who have proffered their tin bowls to the passer-by in vain. The windows were coated with grime; some of them had been broken, and cardboarded over to curb the wheezing city wind. In front of the houses stretched a forbidding line of sooty railing which snarled perpetually at any who might presume to break its grim front.

It was his own sense of abandonment he was describing here and there was little, if any, relief from it. He visited friends like Bryan Hopkin, John Habbakuk and Maurice Oldfield (all later to pursue distinguished careers) like a soldier on leave, eager for refreshment.

Despite this, his studies proceeded smoothly. He had wanted to write on a social or economic theme, like an enquiry into the Baron's Revolt but, at the suggestion of his supervisor, E. F. Jacob, Professor of History at Manchester, he decided to concentrate on the activities of the thirteenth-century Papal legate, and later Pope, Ottobono, who helped bring about a peaceful conclusion to the revolt. No sooner had he begun his thesis, however, than Jacob moved to the fifteenth century, leaving Alun in the charge of Christopher Cheney, a lecturer in ecclesiastical history not much older than himself. Cheney at once sensed his unhappiness but felt there was a strength beneath the natural delicacy; if there was any moodiness about him, it wasn't settled. The two became friends, which is just as well since Alun knew nothing about Ottobono (or "Ottobuono", as he called him) and wasn't anxious to discover the rest. Still, he applied himself, if only to distract himself from his loneliness. There was also his obligation to his parents, for the expenses of his course were likely to exceed his finances even after the renewal of Cowbridge's leaving exhibition for a further year (reduced from £45 to £35).

Alun's thesis has since become a standard work of reference. It shows wide reading and manages to gather a mass of information into a shapely chronological narrative; it combines political analysis with an examination of Ottobono's financial activities and his work as an ecclesiastical judge, administrator and legislator. It is dry-as-dust stuff, of course, and even the moderately-interested reader will balk at passages like this:

> The Norwich valuation brought £300 p.a., from Bath and Wells diocese. Yet the clergy of the diocese agree to pay 500 marks for the

privilege of paying £350.4.0½d., a year instead of following the *verus valor*. Moreover, in addition to this the bishop of Bath paid £100 p.a., for his temporalities, so that whereas the Norwich valuation would have resulted in Bath and Wells diocese paying £900, the new arrangement brought £1,683.18.9½d., into the royal wardrobe.

And so we proceed through Ottobono's petitions, constitutions, injunctions, inquiries, electoral confirmations, visits and appointments.

Cheney discouraged Alun's hopes of gaining an academic post. He knew that he was undecided about research and felt he would be unlikely to convince any appointing boards in that mood. Increasingly, it seems as if he would have to fall back on teaching. Bronwen, who saw him every other weekend in Chester (midway between Bangor and Manchester) sensed how much Manchester was affecting him. Whatever their virtues, Mancunians are phlegmatic in comparison with the Welsh and, as the months went by, she saw his misery turn to despair. He wrote every day, pouring out his feelings. She was sitting her finals at the time and was so upset she could not concentrate on her papers, missing her expected first. Alun was furious.

The Manchester University magazine, *The Serpent*, carried five of his stories in 1936. Some offer variations on the theme of death, others expand on the theme of the frustrated lover. During the summer holidays of 1936, after visiting the Public Records Office and the British Museum in London, he wrote 'Interruption' in Aberdare, the earliest story to be published in *The Last Inspection*, his volume of short stories. In Aberdare, he got to know his sister Mair (or "Girlie", as she was called) better and visited Bronwen for a week in North Wales. He pleaded with her to go to Italy with him, saying she could play her fiddle while he wrote. She refused. Her father thought he would go mad if things didn't change; he felt he was being driven more and more into himself. As Alun told Cheney about life in Aberdare:

> I do nothing but look at it all. If I could get stuck into it like Mother, and pother about Unemployment Clubs and get little shillings from all sorts of people for the fathering of skinny little child-legs and expectant mothers — but I'm miles away from them all. They wouldn't have me hanging around and I'm afraid I feel no overpowering call to hang around. I only hope that's due less to snobbery than to a reluctance to associate with anybody at all.

Looking back on this period later, he declared:

> I got lost in [research] and lost to my own age, my own friends. I had
> no politics, no poems, nothing except a vast impossible mass of
> research.

Education had become his enemy.

Back in Manchester in October 1936, it wasn't long before he broke
with Bronwen. They met in Chester as usual. It was raining and they
had nowhere to go. Bronwen had an aversion to drink so they avoided
the pubs and walked along the river, where she slipped and fell in.
They visited Brown's, a local store, to buy her a new pair of stockings
and she irritated him by thinking it too posh for her. Indeed, her very
devotion had by now come to annoy him. She was always solidly,
woodenly *there*. On one occasion, she had waited for him at Chester
for two hours. He had been drinking and when he turned up was both
pleased and infuriated to find her still there. Yet she had refused to go
to Rome with him and was as innocent about sex as he — a fleeting kiss
or embrace was the sum total of their physical experience. Not that he
was importunate; rather, she felt he was trying to prove himself with
her and she didn't want it. Yet he could also be an enchanting
companion, attentive and enlivening, and only this miserable, wet
Saturday to put her off.

When he got back to Manchester, he wrote her his most desperate
letter yet and suggested they break up. He pictured himself as a prince
grieving at his own graveside. She was alarmed and hurt and urged
another meeting. They met soon after but had little to say to each
other. He sent her a poem, 'Fever' (printed in *Raiders' Dawn and other
poems*), explaining his feelings and reprimanding her for her sexual
backwardness. As another early poem, 'The Desperate' (also in
Raiders' Dawn), has it, love without lust is ache — for the soul's sweet
sake, "Release the seed".

In May, 1937, escape of a different sort was at hand when he visited
Pontigny, in France, for nine weeks at the invitation of Professor
Jacob. Pontigny was an abbey near Auxerre, in Burgundy, taken over
at the Revolution. It had become a centre for study run by Paul
Desjardines under the title "Anti-Babel". Desjardines (then in his
late seventies) was a teacher, writer and Christian philosopher anxious
to encourage an exchange of ideas between students of different
countries. He feared the destruction of Europe, particularly after the
outbreak of the Spanish Civil War, and had founded the Union pour

la Verité (The Union for Truth), in the first instance to bring Catholics and non-believers together. When so much of French religious life was going to the right, he offered a counterbalancing emphasis, attracting leading intellectuals like Gide, Roger Martin du Gard and Jacques Riviére. The first student conference was held in 1937. It was a twelve-week affair in which students were separated into "intellectuels" and reéls" (those who were educated and had read Virgil and those who were in contact with reality). Alun was one of the two British students.

Pontigny should have been a relief to him; instead, it was his "adolescence's Golgotha", as he put it. Placed together with students from Sweden, Norway, Ireland, France and Germany studying Benjamin Constant and John Stuart Mill, discussing topics like 'The meaning of Waterloo' or 'Pascal as a rationalist' and generally putting the world to rights by the Socratic method, he felt himself floundering. His French was insecure, he disliked academic argument and, much as he would have liked to talk about the League of Nations or Trades Unions or the forty-hour week, he was too tongue-tied, "amiable but dumb". As he prepared a paper on 'Liberty in England', he felt his ignorance increasing and verged on "complete atrophy".

In a panic, he wrote to Cheney, who telephoned him urging perseverance. Thanks to Jean Gilbert, Pontigny's librarian, he stayed. Gilbert, an older man, took him on bicycle rides to Chablis and Vézelay and Avallon and the crisis passed. The students were attracted by Alun's dreamy appearance and gentle manner, especially when he read them Shelley, his voice soft and cadenced, with a touch of sadness.

Pontigny brought the suffering of the last few years to a head, a feeling "when everything seems not merely inexpressible and congealed, but worst of all completely evaporated. I've lived too introspectively," he told Cheney, "and I feel just as though I've been feeding on myself until I've eaten myself up. And then when it comes to arguing and opinions and theories I realise with a shock that I've got very few. The only true mood is when I'm not communicating with anything or anybody, almost not with myself. And I'm afraid to break it up by writing then." Introspection had become his enemy, too. He told Gilbert (in a passage translated from the French):

> I am still aspiring to follow 'the huge cloudy symbols of a high romance' even if I could not translate them into words. I've not got enough individuality to be able to live the details patiently and I've

not got enough inspiration to penetrate them . . . Thus I've both fear
and joy . . . I must read instead of talking, speaking, dreaming, things
which turn their faces inwards without creating the honey that I'd
like to give to the seeking bee which will come, which will come,
perhaps, but perhaps. But I've a treasure of sweet things in there now
and sometimes I believe that I'm the bee myself or the tree eating my
own fruit.

Alun's mood at Pontigny is reflected in an unpublished story called
'The Novice', which tells of a young Englishman who spends a year as
a novice in Burgundy. The peace he feels continually threatens to
dissolve into a "chaos of fear and doubt and ignorance, from whose
anguish there was no relief but apathy . . . he was in terror lest his Joy
should be smothered in the black slimepit of apathy and disorder and
despair."

It was just as if everything suddenly shattered into fragments,
leaving no order, no certainty, no peace. Books, thoughts, beliefs,
principles, people and ways of living and death — all grew confused
and unreal and meaningless. And when he tried to master them, they
evaded his recollection, so that from all his frantic search he could
find nothing but his misery and his desolation . . . He was nothing in
himself but an awareness of moods — moods that came and went of
their own volition and over-rode his will and his reason. He could see
no plan, no purpose; yes, it was true, no God. He knew nothing,
nothing — except that Joy and Pain were inextricably entangled in
his very roots.

During his last year at Manchester, Alun published a number of
pieces in *The Serpent*, including 'A Pattern', a poem in four parts. It
has a familiar burden: "How lovely evil things may be". The world is
alive with the joy of creation but it is also fraught with pain "as of a
wooing girl and boy/ Who want, and know not what they want, and
ache/ Insatiably". Beauty is in the frog-infested lake as much as
"blue-tit Spring", in nightshades and briars and rats that go "Soft,
sneaking-paw'd,/ Fearing the ever threat'ning blow".

After Manchester, he tried to join the Civil Service. He thought it
unlikely that a candidate like himself with a mild Welsh accent would
succeed but there was no other choice, so he entered his name only to
discover that he had got the closing date wrong. He canvassed a
number of other possibilities (including tutoring in Pontigny for the
winter) before eventually deciding to apply to Aberystwyth for a
teacher's training grant. "How nearly I could do all things well!" he
sighed.

Mrs Lewis helped steady his nerves by upbraiding him for his despair. She would rock him till he stopped weeping and talk him out of his troubles; "then I'd wake in the morning with no recollection at all of the terrible despondency and nothingness of the previous day." He had been reading Gibbon and like him felt he had "achieved nothing, absolutely nothing, all he's done was study coins and Roman history — and I felt the awful horror of having achieved nothing, never so intensely as then . . . [I] hated research more than anything else and had no purpose at all." One day, just before lunch, he blurted out, "I'm no good, mother, no good at all." She rounded on him and they drifted into a discussion which lasted until the small hours of the morning.

The flavour of their discussion is caught by 'The Tunnel', an unpublished play from this time. (The title refers to the tunnel the young must enter before they reach the light.) It is set in a small mining village in Glamorgan and revolves around Gron Roberts, a twenty-three-year-old student, son of a colliery undermanager, who "seems to live inside himself — as if 'is thoughts won't let 'im be". He envies Harold Watkins, a young collier who has a reputation as an "agitator" and rails against ruthless businessmen and introspective intellectuals alike. "Live, that's what. Live. All of us. Live like we ought to live. The world's big enough and rich enough. If only we stopped being selfish and worked together instead." Gron would like to do this but cannot. He is lost in his tunnel, where he has discovered the "germ of death".

> When a baby is born the only certain prophecy about its future is that it will die. Sooner or later. The germ of death is always in us, ripening in its own time. And sometimes the soul encounters it, in the darkness, and is bitten by it and is then like a flower turned into china.

Alun had been reading Rilke and borrowed this idea of death ripening from him. He traces Gron's failure to live and his sexual sterility to the same cause: "Oh, I'm dried up, somehow, Mam, and barren and cut off from everything."

Borrowing an image from his story 'Chestnuts', he argues against forcing things. Gron's mother warns him that he is "[a]ll in a fever to make the world clean through and through, wanting to make everything new. And you're all politics and poetry and worry — as if every day was the day of Judgment." Gron complains about the way children are brought up to suppress their natural desires, they are told to be good "as if they know what good means unless they've been the other thing" (a coy circumlocution) and to work hard "as if they were machines, not strange sensitive live things" — a Lawrentian admonition. When his parents die shortly afterwards, he feels "purified somehow": "something seemed to flame inside me, running through my veins. As if I'd wakened to my own power. I've still got the same feeling now — as if I can do anything. *Anything.*" Free of his parents, like Paul Morel in D. H. Lawrence's *Sons and Lovers*, he is bold for life at last.

VI

Aberystwyth (2)

Alun's holiday mood at Penbryn in 1937 was unusually relaxed. He was writing a little, though he didn't think what he was doing was much good. "The time hasn't yet come," he told Jean Gilbert. "Instead I feel now that if I do find expression, it will be in prose. I am growing again familiar with the nuances of people and things. Conversation rediscloses its subtleties and if only I could find the essential plot and form I would write well." It is what he had hated most about research, the way it cut him off from his subject matter.

His holiday came to an abrupt end when his father sent him home for being "ingrate and foolish". Tom Lewis wanted him to get a secure job and had been particularly disconcerted by the half-hearted way he had gone about applying for the Civil Service as well as his apparent lack of enthusiasm for any other course of action. He thought Alun was "an unbalanced little enthusiast", fired by conviction one moment, utterly despondent the next, never steady and resolved. As late as July, he was applying for librarians' posts, travelling down to Cardiff to polish up on the Dewey decimal system of classification. But it was writing, as ever, that most absorbed him. That summer he completed several pieces, including 'Atropos to Ophelia' (included in *Raiders' Dawn*) and a short story, 'The Miner's Son'. The hero of the latter is Meirion, a milder version of Gron Roberts, two years down from college and still without employment. He is "[d]ark like his race, but not sallow, brown wavy hair and pale cheeks hollowing beneath high cheekbones, full-lipped mouth falling in a bitter slant at one corner" — an excellent self-portrait.

Apart from fretting about politics (he thinks the capitalists ought to be turfed out of their "damned feather beds too — with a pitchfork rather than a bayonet though"), Meirion worries about his inability to write; all he can do is brood, like Hamlet in 'Atropos to Ophelia', "in whose dark mind/ Huge tortured thoughts lie fallow". He has moments of trance-like union with nature but each time feels as if he has lost part of himself. Thinking is rotting him away: "I no longer know what people would say in a certain situation. I can't conceive characters — if such things exist — and I can't make plots — for life seems to me haphazard and shapeless." Even his facility for the short story has gone. "I'm shallow and — and undersexed — I don't *feel* anything." This despair is answered by Rilke's 'Letters to a Young Poet', which teaches him "to endure the empty years without losing hope".

Meirion's affections are divided between Muriel Benson, a recent arrival at the Social Service Settlement (from whose point of view the story is told) and Menna, his old girl-friend, to whom he gives *Sons and Lovers* to read. She tells him, "You've got something of Paul Morel in you. The way he fell into a carelessness about himself and his opinions — I've seen you like that." So have we. Meirion's ailing mother reminds us of Mrs Morel while his father has something of Mr Morel's mixture of roughness and sympathy. When Muriel taunts Meirion for not really wanting her, he replies, "I've never properly wanted to. I couldn't until I feel whole inside myself" — a typically Lawrentian complication.

Meirion's divided affections may reflect on Alun's relations with Bronwen Williams and Marjorie Walters, an Aberdare girl who was then studying in London. They had met during the holidays and become friends. They shared an interest in the arts, nature and ideas in general. Marjorie was a clever, pretty girl and she and Alun made a familiar pair about town. Their friendship was intellectual rather than emotional, though with an element of personal attraction mixed in, more strongly on his side than on hers.

Alun later came to regard the summer of 1937 as marking his recovery from the nadir of Pontigny. Writing was his rescue: two plays, 'The Tunnel' and 'The Visit', a short, humorous piece developing the vernacular touch of 'The Wedding' (published in *The Dragon*, Michaelmas, 1937), four short stories and a dozen poems. To these was added 'Squibs for the Guy', published shortly after he returned to Aberystwyth in October. Aberystwyth was as he remembered it, friendly, busy, boozy, playful, argumentative. He himself helped the arguments along by calling a protest meeting against the Japanese bombing of Manchuria and urging a boycott of Japanese goods. He even thought for a while of going to Spain (Chris Germanacos' parents were ships' chandlers and he hoped they might get a ship to run the blockade there) but before long he was lapped in the beauty of Dolgellau, a small village some thirty miles north where he spent four weeks practice teaching. It was here that he wrote the five 'Poems from the Chinese', inspired by Helen Waddell's translations. Three were sold to *Time and Tide*, where they appeared the following year. The finest of them, and Alun's first distinctive achievement in poetry, is the fifth, 'The Poet'. Mrs Lewis remembers him writing it while he was still a schoolboy, returning from a walk on the mountain breathless with excitement with the poem in his hand saying, "Look, mother, I can do it!"

> Five slender birches grouped in peace,
> Five silver boles at the end of the wood, lifting a green head.
> The thunder breaks across them in the pent-up sky.
> And I, uncomfortably feeling the sky's need,
> Cannot sense the slenderness of the five birches.
>
> Then the liberation of rain on the parched leaves,
> On the cracked thunder lips,
> On the scorched breath of lighting,
> — Ceasing —
> And leaving to me the five birches.

Alun's four weeks at Dolgellau were serene. Surrounded by mountains again, he was at peace with himself and delighted in each moment, "each thing justified by its existence, its being — and we fortunate enough to be able to look at them, like them, try to alter or improve them." His teaching however did not go well. His supervisor thought he was "the worst bloody teacher" he had ever met and went so far as to cast doubt on his grip of the subject. Alun, stung, took his case to his Professor and got some satisfaction. Even so, everyone, including his father, with whom he shared a class back in Aberdare just before Christmas, urged him to put more vigour in his voice. He couldn't. He thought his course "piddling stuff" and found pleasure only in his special subject, which was painting. Nevertheless, he had success of a kind when his friend Nansi Price read 'Birthday', a short story, at an end-of-term concert. This tale of a boy's thoughts concerning his mother's death reduced the usually noisy college to silence when she read it.

Alun still nursed hopes of a Welsh fellowship to Rome, or, failing that, a job with the London County Council. That September, he began an article on Roger Leyburn, whose military expeditions after the Barons's War he had briefly touched on in his master's thesis. (It was eventually published in *The English Historical Review* in April, 1939.) Soon, however, he was distracted by an affair with a tall, willowy girl called Dilys Western (not her real name). By the beginning of 1938, this had come to grief, though she still clung to him and caused him a great deal of pain. At the same time, he was ill-at-ease in his digs, shared with five others in Commerce House. They were bemused to find him reciting his poems from the Chinese or sitting up half the night in his pyjamas in the castle grounds in freezing weather cleaning his head for the poetry he said he wanted to write. He was desperately poor and used the four guineas Christopher Cheney sent him as a gift to pay his examiner's fees. The meanness of it all was nervewracking and exhausting. Struck by flu, he took to bed in February and found himself "wandering down an avenue of horror and I got convulsions for five minutes".

In March, he went to Newtown, Montgomeryshire, to teach gymnastics. The town was near Ottobono's ford where the Peace of Shrewsbury was signed. "I'm not much luckier than Orestes," he told Cheney. The teaching went badly again. Nonetheless, good news came when he heard that his father had been appointed Director of Education in Aberdare (the administrative head of elementary and intermediate education in the area). This meant an extra £150 a year on a salary of £500, a considerable sum. The appointment came as a surprise to some but Tom's long years with the National Union of Teachers had obviously stood him in good stead. Mrs Lewis was as excited as if she had won the post herself. "Mother's full of ideas for getting shoes and milk and things for the slum schools," Alun told Cheney, "and Daddy says he's not going to have any Assistant Directors; but she's insuppressible." Another honour followed when Mr Lewis was made President of the Glamorgan Teachers' Association. In his inaugural address, he declared that children should be taught to approach all questions with an open mind "but with definite loyalty to the great truths of life", individual liberty and "the equal right of all to develop naturally".

Alun's unhappiness with Dilys drove him into a gloom reminiscent of Pontigny. There were anxious recriminations and reconciliations. He even contemplated marrying her out of a mixture of guilt and sympathy. "She's ever so nice," he told Cheney, "but quiet and always somehow obsessed." Then there was his trouble with Marjorie, "who is always awake about books and people and poems and problems — and Marjorie wants most of all her independence and so keeps her *self* aloof." Cheney felt sufficiently alarmed to propose a meeting in Shrewsbury in March. They took a train to Wenlock and walked along the Long Mynd to Church Stretton and Ludlow, repeating the pattern of a weekend visit they had paid to York the previous summer. It was mild and misty, curlews flying over open ploughed fields, and Alun seemed to recover his balance, enough, at any rate, to feel he could contend with the chaos in his classes. "They would not stop talking. They would not listen. They objected at the top of their voices to being hit on the head" he told Cheney.

At Easter, he was back in Aberdare recovering from a writing block that had seized him ever since Dolgellau. He spent his time listening to conversational exactitudes:

> Very cold, yes!
> Aye indeed mun.
> Where arrre yew now?
> Oah, Aaaber.
> Home on olidays is it?
> Aye mun.

He typed out a radio play in four scenes called 'Taliesin' and finally decided against applying for a fellowship to Rome. He tried once again to break with Dilys but without success; there was further fear and weeping. At the same time, he prepared applications for various teaching posts. Since there had been only thirty-three history vacancies the previous year, he went about it more in hope than expectation. He wrote to Bristol, Bedford, Beckenham, Cardiff, Cockermouth, London, Sutton and Wednesbury — all to no avail. Not even his Division I pass in the written exam for his Diploma and Certificate helped. "I apply and Echo answers. But as I try not to hear myself applying I don't hear the echo either."

His failure to gain employment remains something of a mystery. Graduates from the (quasi) public school system, let alone first-class graduates, could expect an appointment as a matter of course, yet he was repeatedly unsuccessful. Perhaps it was the unfavourable impression he made with his abstracted air, quiet, withdrawn, "daft" even. Perhaps, too, his indifference to the posts he applied for showed. Yet this does not explain the infrequency with which he was called to interview. Still, he pressed on. He approached Professor Jacob about a post on *The Daily Telegraph*, went for an interview with the Editor of *The Western Mail* in Cardiff (who suggested he try for a six-month apprenticeship with *The Aberdare Leader*) and was told by the BBC that they "promised to consider" him.

With such encouragement, he put in for another travelling grant to France from Aberystwyth and toured Normandy for two weeks in August with a college friend, Richard Mills, a serious, reflective North Walian (from Dolgellau, as it happens) who appealed to him more than the usual boisterous South Walian types. They walked from Le Havre to St Malo, Alun secure in the knowledge that his university days — and with them the tension between learning and writing — were over.

VII

The Mountain over Aberdare

The summer holidays of 1938 were scrappy. Alun was revising his
Leyburn article and "diddling about with reports and funerals and
pretty weddings, galas, police courts" for *The Aberdare Leader*, where
he was unofficially employed by the editor, Glyn Prosser. He thought
his work there "little better than a dog's" but took it seriously enough
to learn shorthand. In his spare time, he worked in his father's office
examining records of eduction in Aberdare in the nineteenth century
and printed the results in a series of articles in the paper in July and
August. After Normandy, he wrote some plays and stories born of his
relations with Marjorie Walters. He spent as much time as he could
with her but felt she would prefer him to keep out of her way. No-one
wanted to publish his work though he broadcast a selection of his
poems for the BBC in Cardiff in October. He paid several visits to
London, enjoying the various pleasures of a large city, and met
Christina Foyle, of the famous bookshop, who agreed to act as his
agent. She thought his stories lacked commercial qualities and
advised him to try publishing them in book form instead. He wrote to
Robert Lynd of the *News Chronicle* and W. P. Crozier, editor of *The
Manchester Guardian*, who published three of his stories in 1939. He
also took to lecturing briefly for the W.E.A. on International Relations
and the Left Book Club on Chekhov. He felt "a bit flummoxed with so
many irons stuck into an empty grate".

Of the poems published at this time, the most ambitious is
'Mortuus', published in *Time and Tide* on 23 October, 1938. This
reflects his anxiety at the Munich agreement between Chamberlain

and Hitler. "Complete agreement: War Averted". Alun could see only disaster ahead.

> Oh Death, oh Death do you
> Know aught of birth?
> Or will a great and irrigating Good
> Fertilise fields now choked with blood?

As he told Dick Mills in a letter, "I think I imagined many kinds of death and renounced many lives [after Munich]. I felt sure it was my individual end and I lived intensely." He wrote letters to the press (none published) advocating the Plan of Peace proposed by *Le Fléche*, a paper of the Popular Front in France. In *The Aberdare Leader*, he published 'If War Comes — Will I Fight?' and 'Munich and Peace, The Significance of Re-Armament'. *The Dublin Magazine* printed 'Anschluss', a poem which appears, in revised form, in *Raiders' Dawn*.

'If War Comes . . .' argues that, while he was capable of anger and hatred and had hit a man with his fists, "I do not think I could stick a bayonet into him. Nor could I bomb an open town." Yet, if instinct could not be relied on as a guide to behaviour, what about principle — patriotism, say? He thought not. All men were patriots, but that should make them friends, not enemies.

> The way to cure Germany of her Jingoism is not to fight her, but to make a reasonable settlement with her . . . how many of us are willing to give our lives — our LIVES — for the defence of British capital? Let the government put our Colonies under supra-national mandate and give every nation access to our untapped wealth of raw materials. And then, if the Third Reich still continues its self-aggrandising policy, we know that we will be fighting for the preservation of something worth defending.

There was another argument: the government had acquiesced in the Japanese invasion of Manchuria and the Italian capture of Abyssinia while following a policy of non-intervention in the Spanish Civil War: "I for one object to dying on behalf of a Government with such a record of bungling and error." (On 28 May, 1938, nearly 10,000 Aberdarians rallied in protest at government policy on Spain; later that year, 5,000 attended a meeting in Mountain Ash commemorating the dead in Spain at which Paul Robeson sang, so the issue was a lively one in the valleys.) Finally, he turned to the nub of the question: would it not be worth fighting for democracy and freedom?

"Socialists and Communists speak often of the Fight against Fascism. Let them beware. The French Revolutionaries in 1789 fought for Liberty, Equality, Fraternity. The result was the Napoleonic dictatorship. And why? Because war demands a strong, ruthless Government whose policy is conditioned not by Justice or Equity, but by expedience. Such being the case, Democracy is more likely to perish than to thrive on a European war." The only danger war could avert was a German hegemony over Europe.

> And are we to throw away the remainder of our years when the sacrifice will produce no redeeming gain for humanity or civilisation? The young man losing the chance of a wife and children, the artist and writer and scientist leaving undone the tasks that have burgeoned in their hopes and in their thinking . . . ?

It was a question that was to haunt him for the rest of his life.

In 'Munich and Peace', published on 19 October, he attacked Chamberlain's attempt to "re-build peace by establishing a compromise with the Totalitarian States". The only result of this would be the emergence of Germany as the greatest power in Europe. The abandonment of Czechoslovakia was morally indefensible "and if Mr Chamberlain [that "determined dogged septuagenarian", as he called him] considered a test case for liberty and democracy not worth defending, then he can hardly expect us to defend with our lives the purely selfish interests of British Imperialism." Even so, if the settlement were not to be merely expedient and selfish, it should be followed by a conference to settle all outstanding grievances.

The argument is not altogether clear, but its hesitations are honest. As he told Jean Gilbert, "I wanted people to live and still couldn't justify the capitulation." Prosser encouraged him to air his views, struck by the flair and elegance of his style, but he found the restraints of newspaper writing increasingly irksome and withdrew. The notion of working to a deadline was anathema to him. Prosser found in him the same kind of feyness as his mother together with a countryman's reserve, a touch of austerity (not to say severity) borrowed from his father — "my very pragmatic and tantalisingly sober father", Alun called him. It was the same "difference" everyone noticed now that he had returned to live in Aberdare for the first time in twelve years.

*

Aberdare is a compact town lying at the head of the Cynon valley. The ground there is broader than in most of the valleys, the pits tucked away in the surrounding hills, giving the town the look of a market centre, solid and virtuous. Flanked by the Rhondda to the west and Merthyr to the east, it was the quiet one of the western valleys, a centre of cultural life, sometimes called "the Athens of Wales". Alun now began to write about it. "[I]f you want to think," he commented later, "climb the mountain and look down on the quiet little town." The poem he wrote, 'On the Welsh Mountains', dates from the war years but is interesting to consider in this context.

> To note precisely all I know
> From this high mountain ledge:
> The drab streets hacked across the cwm,
> Red ruck or rails, abandoned shaft,
> Grey Hebron in a rigid cramp,
> White cheapjack picture-house, the Church
> An old sow stretched beside the stream,
> My uncle's house in Milton Street,
> Black gardens row on row,
> Old thorntrees stunted by the wind,
> The new building of the Labour Exchange:
> All moving me more, oh much more,
> Than the pigeons cleaving and furling
> And all traditional beauty . . .

It is, in fact, Cwmaman he is describing and the need to take his bearings from it rather than from nature determines the simplicity of the style, very different from his pre-war verse. The stance is Audenesque but there is in it none of Auden's quick, witty notation, as if fixing a scene before preparing to leave it. Instead, we have a patient, steady, oddly-sad itemisation of a once-known reality. The strategy is intentional:

> Deliberately to understate;
> To pare down to the quick
> Reality; to be
> In love articulate.

The poet views his home from his mountain ledge which he is never to leave for his attention is soon distracted by a mermaid swaying before him in an imagined sea-surge and the scene dissolves. The Cwmaman Alun knew was a blankness yet happy, too, an out-of-doors place yet stifling, where a thunderstorm, a sheepshearing or a fielding of pit ponies was an event and family occasions (of which there were many) the sum of daily life. Yet how to reach out for the larger existence that lay beyond when so many ties prevented, when indeed, you could not say precisely what it was you were reaching out for? The nearest you could come to it was up in the mountains, all vague and yearning.

Alun's escape eventually came through poetry, but the more his imagination urged him on, the more his humane instincts restrained him. The compulsion to imagine the sea-surge breaks over him like a wave and removes the drab scene by throwing him into an embrace with his mermaid/muse. "I am forced to imagine," he writes. In his "little peace", he is splashed with "heavy brittle tears" and views the "stubborn foreheads of these hills" as his tears mingle with the rain this "wet evening, in a lost age". We sense a vast feeling of waste.

"I'm getting more materialist in my conception of History," Alun told Cheney, "— i.e. history ought to have been more materialist than it has been, and then art wouldn't have been built on such an ignorance and insouciance of poverty". He himself felt unloved and avoided his friends. Artistically, he was as uncreative as ever. All he had written was "a mistake, a very delightful mistake for me, but still." He went for long walks in the Brecon Beacons or to Penderyn, where he took a room in the vicarage to do some writing. "It must have been like having a cross angel to stay," a friend remarks. This is how his mother remembers him at the time:

> Alun in the easy artistic, slightly Bohemian, style he observed in civilian dress — grey blue worsted slacks: more blue than grey; grey blue sports coat, more grey than blue; a deep blue soft shirt with turn-down collar and a bright red tie. And above all, his radiant laughing face and fine head with its wavy hair. Do you remember the Portrait of A Young Man by Van Gogh? . . . It breathed the very spirit of Alun as we knew and loved and laughed with him.

It was the gay inconsequence all who knew him loved him for, confessing his belief in the goodness of things, a goodness so signally denied him and his world.

There was a major attempt to gather his concerns in the autumn of 1938 in a poem called 'Threnody for a Starry Night' (published in much-revised form in *Raiders' Dawn*). In 1943, Geoffrey Bullough described it as containing "some of the finest lines in recent poetry" even though he thought it lacked "the explicit lines which would make it a unified whole". Then, in the third week of November, Alun's solitary, restless life was broken by a telephone call from the Lewis School in Pengam, a county grammar school, asking him if he would deputise for a sick teacher. "Damn," he said, and took it. It was "my first meeting with WORK and WAGES and it's rather interesting," he told Dick Mills. His father thought he was living at last, his mother merely that he was earning his living.

The Christmas holidays that year were spent struggling with "a mort of stories that wouldn't come right". He thought Aberdare full of "frigid exteriors, or politeness, or foolishness" and was determined to try his luck in London but, as fate would have it, the master he was deputising for had been diagnosed a diabetic and sent to a sanatorium for rest and observation; he was likely to be away a long time. In "normal and sensible" mood, he found the teaching enjoyable and threw himself into the life of the school. He started a debating society and contributed to the school magazine, *The Ludovican*, but nothing was worth a single poem to him. He tried reading an hour before bed every night and was particularly impressed by T. E. Lawrence's *The Seven Pillars of Wisdom*, which he found "a solace and a help". "I have grown attached to it," he told Christopher Cheney, "— his long journeys through the desert with the nomad Arabs impress like the legendary trials and torments . . ."

Ever hopeful, he typed out his "elegant sufficiency" of stories and poems and submitted them to various publishers. (Chatto and Windus thought the former "quite slick, but very short, very varied, and quite unsaleable"). He also sent examples of his work to Gwyn Jones, who had begun the periodical *The Welsh Review* in February, 1939. An earlier magazine, *Wales*, had been started in 1937 by Keidrich Rhys. It was dominated by Dylan Thomas and the impressive if eccentric quality of its editing, slapdash but with a keen appreciation of good writing beneath the knockabout fun. The literary desert of English-speaking Wales had suddenly begun to sprout an oasis and round it gathered a number of writers — Thomas himself, Glyn Jones, Idris Davies, Lynette Roberts (the last two published by T. S. Eliot at Faber) and Emyr Humphreys among them. Of the pieces Alun sent Gwyn Jones, it was the poems that meant most to him. "As for the poetry — the heart knoweth its own saviour, and the stranger shall not meddle with its joy."

There was one story, however, in which he did "devoutly believe", 'The Housekeeper', and it returns us directly to the argument of 'On the Welsh Mountains'. The main character, Myfanwy, is trapped between looking after her unemployed husband, his quarrelsome mother and her two children and finding her own freedom. Hers is a bleak, narrow world of poverty and pit closures.

> The back garden was about four yards wide, and as the house was built against the side of the hill, the garden sloped up steeply to the shed at the top. It was fenced off from the gardens of the next door houses by a hotch-potch barrier of old zinc sheeting, rusted iron bedsteads, and tin advertisements of Colman's Mustard and Brooke Bond's Tea. There was no door to the shed, and the tarred felting which covered the thin wooden front hung over in flapping folds, like the crippled wing of a black vulture. The garden itself was a patch of rubble and ash, holding nothing but a few rows of rotting beansticks, a line of seed cabbage, and three bare currant bushes. Next door up had a line of washing out — long workman's pants pegged up by the legs, the wind blowing through the holes where the darning had given way, a pair of patched sheets, three tiny frayed vests — flapping and beating in the gusty weather.

That is very well done and captures the ambiguity of the narrator's position perfectly, repelled by the ugliness before him yet savouring it as an artist at the same time as he identifies himself with those imprisoned by it. Hence Myfanwy's own recourse to the mountain ridge. 'The Housekeeper' shows all Alun's gifts as an observer. Although it derives from his own tensions, it is perfectly objectified and deserves to be regarded as his first considerable achievement in prose.

Alun remembered 1938 and 1939 as a time when he was "abominably lonely". At weekends he would walk over the Graig to his Bopa Jane in Cwmaman, who offered him the warmth and simplicity he craved. During the half-term of winter, 1939, he visited Oxford to see Christopher Cheney and Marjorie Walters (then studying there) and at Easter called on friends in London, including Barry Davies, a fellow student in Aberystwyth and Manchester with whom he went on a bicycle tour of Essex. This was made memorable by the accidental discovery of Edward Thomas's Childerditch (mentioned in his poem 'If I Should Ever by Chance'). From Childerditch, just south of Brentwood, they went to Codham (also mentioned in the poem) and back again to London. There, all his old wretchedness returned and he had to struggle to restrain himself from dissipation.

At Whitsun, he took a bicycle trip to Somerset, jotting down his thoughts as they came, a habit he had begun at least as far back as his university days; he hadn't been as happy since Dolgellau. Then, at the annual Three Valleys Festival in Mountain Ash at the end of May, he met a young teacher from the local grammar school, Gweno Ellis, a native of Aberystwyth. As it happens, she had been at college with him but neither had noticed the other, though they had both served on the Student's Representative Council (with Dick Mills) in 1934–5. Alun wrote to her asking her to go for a ride on the Brecon Beacons but she had been invited by a teacher friend, Ethel James, to the family farm at St Dogmael's near Cardigan, for the weekend. Remembering Alun's invitation, she called on him en route to explain the position. He had just returned from Pengam and was having tea with his family and some visitors. As she spoke to him, Ethel ran up to the front door and cried out, "Why don't you come too?" He did. ". . . it wasn't like it might have been before the Fall," he told Christopher Cheney. "But it was memorable, mon dieu, and the sea blue and the water deep round the rocks, and the corn all stooked and warm." They were, Gweno recalls, "humpy" with each other but attracted.

Later that summer, she went to Porthcawl with a teacher friend who advised her to think carefully about offers from men like Alun, so she wrote back accepting his invitation for a ride on the Beacons. No sooner had she replied than he was on his bicycle to her digs, only he had got the number wrong and was knocking next door. She thought, "Oh, let him knock and let me get on with my own thing!", but eventually relented and let him in. She was glad she did, for she found him what the valleys called "near", someone easy with all kinds and temperaments. Whether arguing with her Left landlord about politics or chatting with her collier neighbour or local grandees, he was always the same. By now, he was a square-shouldered young man with a good head, soft, silky hair, big forehead, smooth skin, deep-set hazel eyes and long lashes with a characteristically dreamy look. The nose was smallish, slightly retroussé, and she thought that if he'd had her father's or brother's nose, he'd have been a "smasher". He carried his head slightly to one side, as if to avoid his own pipe-smoke. His expression was diffident, the mouth rather the worse for wear following various hockey accidents. (A front tooth had been removed at Manchester, leaving him with a plate and a scar.)

At Penbryn that summer, he pondered the next step in his abortive literary career. Solitary as ever, he would go off with a Penguin book (then a new thing) and climb up into the rocks, debating with himself whether to pay £50 to have his poems published. He nearly did, but

Huw's college expenses forbade it. Besides, he was now embarked on a novel about life in a mining valley and the times seemed unpropitious. "I will probably join up, I imagine," he told Dick Mills.

> I've been unable to settle the moral issue satisfactorily; when I say *I imagine* I mean I have a deep sort of fatalist feeling that I'll go. Partly it's because I want to experience life in as many places as I'm capable of — i.e. I'm more of a writer than a moralist, I suppose. But I don't know — I'm not going to kill. Be killed, perhaps, instead.

Again,

> It's making a mess of life *when we have it* that I hate. But death is something I have more than once, in the climax of past agonies, imagined completely. And so it may come when it may. Meanwhile I live. [There is] a worse battle than war or peace to fight — the heart is my battleground, a bloody place.

More and more he was being called from home and more and more he was growing anxious about the cost. This is reflected in the novel he was writing, about a young boy who grows up "through poverty and love to disenchantment and wisdom". It engrossed him. "I eat it, dream it, sleep with it. It is very thrilling & exacting and sometimes disappointing — like my girl!" It was as if, like Edward Thomas before him, the greater disturbance of war had mirrored his inner disturbance and released the writer in him.

Morlais, as the novel was called, is an attempt "to synthesise two lines — that of the industrial novel and of the intellectual–aesthetic novel. It's my own life, really, I suppose, & that's why I find it so difficult to be honest." Morlais Jenkins is a miner's son, "a baby, a cleckerbox" (sneak); he would prefer to be a gang-leader but feels "desolate, soft" inside. At school, he befriends David Reames, the new pit-manager's son, who finds it difficult to mix with the colliery children. Morlais himself admires the vitality of the miners but is seized with a "spasm of revulsion" when he sees his sister in close conversation with a boyfriend in a back lane one lunchtime. As he turns from them, he meets two girls from his class who make advances on him and runs away, demoralised and ashamed.

Morlais entertains two images of woman, the first identified with his mother and sister, the former mild and exhausted, with furrowed skin and bony shoulders, the latter dressed in soiled vest and red knickers who scratches a spot between her breasts as she looks for blackheads in the mirror. She is akin to Winnie Morse, one of the girls in the lane, a club-footed, squint-eyed creature in a torn frock whom Morlais dreams of "thrusting her naked deformed body into his face and making foul accusations about his parents and foul demands on himself." On the other hand, there is his teacher, Miss Meredith, whom he idealises as a creature from another world. She is like David Reames's mother, a cold beauty who soothes all her son's troubles away, poised and detached, learned, refined. How different from his own mother! In an extraordinary episode, he moves from the one to the other when David is killed in a pit-head accident. Mrs Reames comes later the same night to ask his parents if they will allow him to come and live with her. They wake him up to ask him and he sleepily agrees. He is promptly packed off. The fact that this occurs on the day of his scholarship exam encourages us to interpret it as Alun's own view of his removal to Cowbridge in 1926.

One night shortly afterwards, Mrs Reames visits Morlais in his bedroom.

> He woke under the touch. Not her physical touch. But he knew she was in the room, in the pitch dark. He felt her presence, tingling in him. But he didn't move. His eyes opened, that was all.
>
> She sat on his bedside, softly, carefully. Her hands touched him, his hair, his ear. He closed his eyes. Her fingers touched his eyelids. He could hear her breathing. In a whisper she spoke.
>
> 'I loved you, Atthis, once, long, long ago;
> You seemed to me a small ungainly child.'

It is the moment of election, a fearsome rendition of what it might be like to feel oneself being chosen by the Muse.

Four years later, Morlais discovers that he is a prisoner in the Reameses' "dungeon", envious of the life of those who have gone down the pits, like his old school contemporary, Bob Linton. His mood is queer, numb and weary, as after much suffering (as so often in Alun's writing at this time). Morlais finds relief by climbing the mountain. Here again is the haunting presence of Cwmaman (called Glannant in the novel):

> His eyes saw [the valley] intensely and the sight of it made his heart pound. It was so narrow and deep; the mountains possessed it, overpowered it. It was theirs, this narrow valley with its straggle of grey streets, its ruck of railway sidings where the timber was stacked and the coal trucks waited, its tips and its colliery whose great wheel seemed so tiny. The mountains had mastery, the vast power of

> silence, the huge upward sweep of fern and rock and swart grass.
> Scanty pasture they gave to the skinny sheep and the wild ponies;
> great silent misers hoarding their silence through the centuries.
> Build walls on their tremendous flanks; the walls crumble . . . The
> farm down there, half way up the mountain; that was older than the
> pit or the village. Yet how insecure its tenure, clinging with its
> whitewashed cowsheds and muddy yard in poverty to the mountain.
> And the perpetual flux of people, coming, going, meaning less than
> the farm, less than the pit, less even than the sheep that found shelter
> among the green rocks in wild weather . . . So he found that the
> mountains held in their silence the secret of love, and their love was
> for the blue sky, the infinite, intangible feminine, the termagant, of
> winter.

As in 'On the Welsh Mountains', the observer is lost in a realm above
human history or purpose, the "infinite feminine" — like Mrs
Reames' house. In comparison with it, valley life dwindles into
insignificance.

In acknowledgement of his new allegiance, Morlais flings his arm
round the twisted bole of a thorn which stands at the very brim of the
mountain. "And he saw how dwarfish and stunted it was, all its
branches bent in the direction the wind blew, the wind that was the
temper of the silent strife of mountain and sky" — the wind, we might
say, of his own inspiration, though the tree reminds him of his father's
stubborn life, misshapen by poverty. He recalls being taken to school
by him, having been dressed against the cold by his mother, and leaves
the reader to infer the difference between their care and his present
isolation, the direct result of their endeavours to "improve" him. Like
the thorn that "stood alone against all the long assault, and put its
leaves out in spring and held its silence", his existence is tenacious,
fruitful, deformed.

Mountain and valley continue to contend for Morlais's allegiance.
Eventually, he decides to leave Mrs Reames and return to his parents
but his mother refuses to have him.

> 'It's the only reason I'm not sorry you're living in the big 'ouse.
> You got a chance to get out of it all.'
> 'No, I haven't,' he said, clenching his teeth with the strife that was
> in him. 'I'm here, *here*.'
> 'No, you're not, not for good,' she said sharply, stamping her foot.
> '. . . No, keep at your lessons now, and go to College, see?' She stood
> in the path and commanded his eyes with her burning ones. 'You go
> on, see? You'll be a teacher or a minister, something where you can be
> yourself, see?'

'I want to come home with you, that's all I want,' he said quietly.
She caught her breath; he sensed her hardening.
'Don't be daft,' she said curtly. 'We don't want you.'

It is the crucial rejection. Mrs Jenkins imagines that he will become
"himself" by becoming educated but he knows that individual
identity without love or community is no identity at all. Mrs Reames
repeats the point when she cautions him against the "terrible power"
of his sensitivity. "Your struggle must be first to find yourself. You
must become yourself first of all. It will take all of your courage and
sweat to do that." It is what D. H. Lawrence taught. Yet, how to
become "yourself" when the very condition of your wholeness —
family and village and friends — has been taken from you?

At this time, there is renewed agitation in the pits and Morlais
senses the conflict in him coming to a head. After attending a miners'
meeting, he returns to his house and pauses over Mrs Reames' Keats.
He sees two lines swim into focus:

> actually a voice, a frantic deadly earnest voice. The words were
> concentrating all their slowly-accumulated intensity upon him. He
> saw them; two lines.
> 'When I have fears that I may cease to be,
> Before this pen has gleaned by teeming brain.'

He goes upstairs and looks into the bathroom and sees Mrs Reames
trying to kill herself with a bottle of pills. It was *her* voice he had heard
coming to him, the muse's voice, we might say, a displaced expression
of his own.

On his last day at school, Morlais pauses on the mountain top and
wonders whether to go to Tredur, where the colliers live, or home
with the Reameses — "which path to renounce?" We notice the
phrasing: it is not a choice but a renunciation. His father has been
sacked from the pit by Mr Reames on the orders of Head Office and in
the rioting that follows, Bob Linton is arrested and given a ten-day jail
sentence. The Jenkinses now move to Mountain Row, a notorious line
of wood and iron cottages behind the steep slope of the mountain
where children and gamblers play. At this point, Morlais goes to ask
his father permission to return and gains it. His father arranges a job
for him as a library assistant at the Workmen's Institute at seventeen
shillings a week. He warns him:

> you can't fight the boss class with your fists — they got the soldiers
> and the magistrates be'ind them. And they're not too soft-'earted to

string you up by the neck, neither. Same as they did with old Dic Penderyn and Lewis the 'untsman when they led the attack on old Crawshay's castle over in Cyfartha . . . It's an old cause we're fighting for, my lad. An old cause. I don't reckon I'll see the end of the struggle in my lifetime. It's like the old tree on top of the quarry. I didn't see it planted and I won't see it die. But I see it putting out its leaves every year.

Morlais is embarrassed by the colliers' ready acceptance of him.

And it was something deeper than the usual discomfort that the sensitive introvert experiences when meeting people. It was a complex that had matured slowly, in the seclusion of the Elms [the Reameses' house, echoing the Lewises' house at 7 Elm Grove]; that had been fed by the daily evasions of contact with village, by the choice of empty back lanes or lonely mountain paths in going to and from school, by the perpetual feeling of shame at this shrinking from his own people as though he were diseased or hunted. He knew he had gone outside the community, broken their law and forfeited their familiarity. It was the hardest thing of all, this humiliating petition for reinstatement. The pain of it frightened him.

Another fine passage. Ironically, Bob Linton has decided to leave the valley but Morlais decides to stay and learn "how coal is mined, how the winder works, how wages and hours are fixed, and who's behind it all. I want to read about other countries, too, and about government. And the *reason* for it all."

He also wants to write — that is his silent commitment — but he cannot do so yet because he lacks his natural subject-matter, the classic bind of the Welsh writer educated out of his community and language. There is a further bind, however, for even if he were reunited with his people, he still could not write about them convincingly because he cannot to commit himself fully to them. All he can do is dramatise the tension within himself. So Morlais settles down with his parents again and teaches boys like Bob Linton. It is a resolution devoutly to be wished.

VIII

The Gathering Storm

The holidays in Penbryn in August, 1939 were cut short by war. Ever since the family heard of the German-Russian non-aggression pact, consternation reigned. Tom Lewis, a billeting officer, was plunged into planning for the arrival of evacuee children while Alun applied through Aberystwyth for liaison work. "I'm not a pacifist at heart," he told Christopher Cheney. "At least it's doubtful, and therefore I'll give the British Army the benefit of the doubt. I don't know what else I can do, decently." Nothing came of it, so he reapplied for non-combatant work. Dick Mills had taken a commission but Alun was not prepared to go as far as that yet. "Plunge in? Into what? Socialism through bloodshed? Or fall in — into line?" Should he join a fighting machine or try to make the war an occasion for building a better world?

He wasn't made a permanent member of staff at Pengam until November. Being under twenty-five, he was of military age and he thought that this might explain the hesitation since the authorities would not want to pay his salary if he were called up. He took digs at King's Hill, Hengoed, a few miles from Pengam, and stayed there during the week, travelling home at weekends. He had grown used to Pengam by now. Like Cowbridge, it was one of the best-known schools in South Wales, two hundred years old and with a highly-selective entrance. Like Cowbridge, too, it had passed into the hands of the local Joint Education Committee and was under the headship of Stanley Knight, who had been appointed in 1926. Knight liked Alun, though he understood him to be preoccupied with other things. He thought Alun an inspiring and conscientious teacher, probably the most popular in the school, one who encouraged the boys and took an interest in them, helping them to keep scrapbooks and maintain a weekly exhibition display. In class, he used a good deal of source material — aerial photographs, extracts from chronicles, blown-up postcards and the like. He favoured imaginative descriptions of historical situations, such as a report from a Roman commissioner inspecting British fortifications, but he also emphasised the "scientific accounting" of cause and effect, loss and gain. In the senior forms, lessons became discussions involving Dickens, Marx, the French Revolution, Germany and Industry. He could not hide a preference for Gladstone over Disraeli and a marked antipathy to Bismark.

At first, he turned up to school in an old cloth cap and suit pushing his bicycle or ambling up the path the cross-country runners used. If he were early, he would take a stroll in the woods. The Headmaster was quite prepared to see him returning late offering his humblest apologies. At lunch, he would lie out on the grass, just like the boys. (At twenty-four, he was not that much older than his sixth-formers.) With his soft, light, sing-songy voice and gentle — not to say lethargic — manners, he attracted the nickname "Dopey", though he could be considerably animated in discussion.

His idealism was well-known and in any case suited the general temper of the staff. Some feared the effect on him of such intense humanitarianism. He seemed vulnerable to the strains of war, though none doubted his determination. There was a litheness of purpose in him. Nevertheless, his vacant air and hollow cheeks suggested a lack of confidence, a shyness reflecting tension as well as a natural reserve. There would be an occasional play of the mouth and a jerk of the chin as if he were pulling himself together. His writing, too, seemed to lack vitality, though he tried to make up for it by plain description coloured by lyric feeling, as in 'The Housekeeper', watchful, subdued, undramatic. He realised that his work was "too much of myself" but had nothing else to go on yet. The trick was to make the "self" interact with his surroundings in a creative manner.

He was seeing a good deal of Gweno now. As he told Dick Mills, she was "a fine companion . . . full of life and broad of mind". A poem he wrote at this time, 'Destruction', shows something of his feeling for her as well as his broader concerns as a writer. The poem has a vague lyricism in the manner of Dylan Thomas but this vies with a more documentary approach:

This is the street I inhabit.
Where my bread is earned my body must stay.
This village sinks drearily deeper
In its sullen hacked-out valley
And my soul flies ever more rarely
To the eyries among these Welsh mountains.

A nice mixture of resignation and revolt, recalling Myfanwy in 'The Housekeeper'. Two styles merge to produce a concluding passage which anticipates the mature Larkin by a couple of decades.

And the train that took her roaring towards the dayspring
Is rocking her through the dawn down empty sidings
Between dark tenements in the neutral city
To the street she must inhabit.

Here is a colloquial ease and an alertness to the pinched misery of everyday life which points the way his writing was to go.

It was not easy getting to know Alun. He had recovered only slowly from Manchester and the previous spring's anguish when "I lived on the margin in more senses than one". Gweno herself wasn't given to easy confidences and the wariness on her part matched the caution on his. Truth to tell, they were both somewhat solitary. Apart from Chris Germanacos, he had no close friends at Aberystwyth while she, as a town girl, missed the friendship of the hostel girls. The freemasonry of "Aber" thus passed her by to a certain extent, especially since her subject, German, was taught in a small department. Moreover, she lived right at the top of Constitution Hill, directly across the road from Alun's Uncle Tim, as it happens, and one needed ardent suitors who were prepared to face the steep climb with equanimity. She was a devoted daughter and sister, member of a family of three boys and two girls headed by a "Viking" of a father, an ex-sailor and something of a local celebrity who stood "against all the elemental powers" in the Victorian house he had built called the Château. She thought Alun interesting and intelligent, like her brothers but bringing a freshness of outlook. For his part, he found Gweno "a fountain of joy, very lively. We live together tempestuously". She was his "little highnecked colt".

One evening, when she was leaving Hengoed station after a visit, she expressed a doubt about his feelings for her which he described in a letter written a year later.

> I remembered how you refused to believe, and how once on Hengoed station, you said it was all meaningless, and how personally hurt I was, that you wouldn't believe, but seemed to question my sincerity, and the sincerity of love. I wondered why you were so unwilling to believe, and why you never speak of those things, but keep silent, silent: and how little of you I know: and, horrible doubt, whether you thought that the inexplicable deaths of me, when I felt nothing, responded to nothing, valued nothing — whether you thought 'he is inconstant, unreal, deluding himself with false affirmations which he regrets sooner or later and tries, subconsciously perhaps, to disclaim and deny.' . . . All the time I've had to struggle against your silence, and refusal on your part to believe, to be free, to take the risk of life. Do you know that I've always felt that mistrust of yours? From the day I first talked to you.

The mistrust never left her. His "inexplicable deaths" involved his withdrawals from her under pressure of his "old nervous strain", moments when he became "cold and out-of-worldly". Nothing meant anything real to him then. When they visited Llanthony Abbey, an hotel, shortly afterwards, he experienced "a horrible black twisting"; he begged her to believe he couldn't help it. "I'm like life — capable of going terribly wrong, capable of dying; it's in the nature . . . — birds aren't all song." Nevertheless,

> although we've shied and reared like colts in the dark or in a storm, the impulse has been clear and consistent and deep and good in us, I know, for it's a power in me for ever, giving me courage and faith and a joy nothing can destroy. I've always had intense longings to live up to some standards, some imagined quality; and now it's simply resolving itself into writing what I know is good and loving you, being Alun to you as you are Gweno to me. Those two things.

Just after Christmas, 1939, he rented a cottage near Port Eynon, at the southern tip of the Gower peninsula, to try to finish *Morlais*. The thought of being called up gave him nightmares and the writing, though engrossing, was yet not the "real thing". Something in him broke. As he told Dick Mills, in Keatsian vein:

> . . . I've been worse, in the past. This has only been a reminder of my mortality. Not the absolute & final thing. There may still be time to profit from it. I *must* go on writing, sometime. But it must be real. It mustn't be a dogged persistence. It must be natural. And in nature nothing is fixed; it's organic. Society has tried to fix itself . . . But [we] ourselves are a tremulous balance, a delicate equation. I've lost my balance — chaos. And I don't want to recover it by going into the shell of habit, by returning to schoolmastery. I hate Mr Chips. I want

a deeper sincerity, a profounder humanity. And that spirit must be in
my flesh & blood, not only in my intellect, my wishful thinking.

The question of joining the army continued to preoccupy him; he
found himself "sweating like a pig half a dozen times a day". "The
world doesn't get better through that sort of heroism," he remarked.
"1914–18 showed that. I've a terrible feeling that I shall be unable to
answer that question. I don't want to kill. Is it then a victory over
myself, to go and kill, to do something terrific like bayoneting a man?
Really I am uncivilised. I don't accept, in my soul, the implication of
being British, or believing in the League. It's funny that to believe in
the League you must be willing to bayonet a man. A highly civilised
soul would *feel* the connection . . . It's always been my trouble, this
slipping away of individuality. It is my character to have no
character."

Before ceasing publication with the outbreak of war, *The Welsh
Review* carried a number of Alun's reviews together with a short story
called 'The Wanderers'. It was to prove one of his most popular,
though he professed not to think much of it. By 1940, he was working
on another autobiographical novel concerning the adventures of
Adam, a student at Aberystwyth who has just finished two years'
research in London and feels "only relief after the cruel barren
anguish of last year and the year before, when his soul had been an
ooze of black putrefying matter inside him and he had been alone,
alone; God, yes, alone". He tells his girlfriend about a recurrent
dream he has had of something "slimy and irresistible" pushing him
into a tunnel, "a sort of sewer, through which you've got to crawl if
you want to reach the sunlight on the other side. And it's so narrow
that you're terrified of getting stuck there for ever." (We recall the
"black slimepit of apathy" in 'The Novice' and Gron's feeling like a
corpse in 'The Tunnel'.) After London and the ending of an affair
there, Adam fears he cannot feel anything. "I can never decide
anything. I can't simplify." This may be a Keatsian quality (Alun had
been reading Keats recently) essential to his imagination. His
girlfriend, however, tells him that he can't leave well alone; he is
always trying to discover the significance of everything. He replies by
taunting her with her principled refusal to have sex with him.

What with his weary thoughts and enforced chastity, complicated
by a quite fierce Puritan sense of shame, Adam falls prey to depression
again. He feels irrational moods of despair and joy, like the songs of
thrushes, sudden, ecstatic. For men of his generation, the world has

always seemed to be in shadow: first the Great War, then the collapse of the Twenties and Thirties and then the threat of war again. There never has been a time when the possibility of life *not* being a struggle has been real. As Alun himself once remarked, "[I]t is difficult to plan intelligently for the future when one is only conscious of the helpless hands and aimless mind, and the dead hours in the queue outside the Exchange. Apathy and impotence sterilise the will, clog the glands of hope and vitality, degrade and disintegrate the personality. I long to be a dead soldier." More than that, "I don't foresee any more Peace for Europe for perhaps a century — longer than our time, anyway . . . It will need a great and violent effort to win back the liberty that we have perhaps never really had."

Adam senses within himself the presence of "a capsule that was breaking, leaking, a black drop each year of his puberty, his adolescence, his young manhood"; it is "like drains of a poison he had unconsciously secreted, sullying and sickening his individuality." Trying to embrace his sweetheart, he finds himself impotent.

> [H]e knew almost at once that he had done the wrong thing in attempting to respond physically to her. When he covered her with kisses he hated himself; and hated himself more and more as his lips became more frantic. And . . . revulsion dried up all his seed, all his vitality, and held him as if he were a dead fowl and choked him closer and closer the more his lips writhed to find the impossible release.

In his diary, he confesses: "The last thing we learn is that we cannot love." Bitterly, he regrets the poems, music, paintings, ideas that might have been his. Drunken binges and perfunctory sex offer no more than momentary relief. He would prefer to think of others — if only he could love. Alun though of using Adam's story as the starting point for a longer novel dealing with "secondary and university education in relation to the economic situation" but nothing came of it.

On Friday, 8 March, 1940, he suffered an accident at school. While preparing to show his fourth form slides of medieval cathedrals, he plugged in the epidiascope machine. There was a blue flash and he found himself stuck to the wire with a jerk. One boy tried to pull him free but was stunned by the current and had to let go. Another, Huw Thomas (who had been carrying the slides) pulled the wire from the wall and released him. After resting a few hours, he sat his St John's Ambulance exam as planned later that afternoon despite a burning hand and twitching body. (He was thinking of entering the Royal

Army Medical Corps.) That evening, he visited Gweno at Mountain Ash with his arm in a sling. They discussed the possibility of his registering as a conscientious objector. Gweno, who had visited Stuttgart on exchange service in 1936–7, had many German friends and loved all (non-Nazi) German things. She advised him, "Take your chance with the rest". After that, he went home and fell into bed. Hot fomentations were applied six times a day but the wound turned septic; the burn at the root of the thumb had been particularly severe. Ten days later, he suffered a delayed collapse which precipitated a depression almost as bad as the one he had experienced at Manchester.

On the night of his accident, he began writing 'Last Leaves of a Civilian Journal', a mixture of reminiscence and reportage recalling various childhood episodes, including his first day in Cowbridge: "At the door of the Headmaster's study mother was torn from me. I can remember the hurt of it . . . I felt utterly, utterly betrayed." The next day, he registered at the Labour Exchange for military service. Until now, his search for himself had come before everything else. "[E]ven when the left unfurled its thrilling red banner before me and my loneliness, my incompleteness longed to enter into the brotherhood of man. I preserved my integrity then by standing aside". This was no longer possible so, in negative mood, he decided to enlist. There was no choice between being a soldier and seeing "white bodies writhing under the whip and the smashed milk-teeth of children" (a detail borrowed from 'Threnody for a Starry Night': "By the mutilated smile,/ By milk-teeth smashed,/ Love is outcast.")

On 1 April, he went to the Drill Hall in Pontypridd for a medical inspection and asked to be put down for the RAMC, failing that, the navy. "But the navy intends to take life," the interviewing major told him. "Yes," he replied. "But there's less chance of sticking a man in the bowels."

> Sometimes when I cannot sleep black silent columns march on me and trample me down — the black silent column of poverty, the quiet streets of the derelict villages in which I live and teach. I flesh myself for having done so little. At various times I have restrained the impulse to fling myself into social service, the Spanish war, slum missions.

It was the first time he was able to sound so confident and outward-looking. Despite his own failure, he had decided to sacrifice himself to the future. *That* is what had been wrong with him. Before now, his life had been full of objectives — essays or sports teams, essay prizes or love. In 1935, all that stopped. He was no longer interested in academic research and he could not love. All he wanted was silence, "not as Rilke wanted silence and aloneness [he had been reading Rilke again that January]; I wanted it like a dying animal." Now, he had an objective again. "We feel each death personally, each death of the innumerable deaths in Spain and Poland and Finland. Our own death. But we are no longer morbidly preoccupied with death as we were in our youth. We have overcome death."

For all his *soldat malgré lui* valour — socialism through bloodshed — Gweno noticed how depressed he was. It was as if a glass pane had descended between himself and the world. Before, he would return, mysteriously refreshed and strengthened; perhaps it was only the chemistry of the brain, perhaps only the frustrations of the times or his effort to become a writer. Whatever the case, he was soon his old extrovert self again, laughing, walking or swimming. But now he was more distant from her. At Aberystwyth, where they were staying with her parents, she taxed him with it and he reassured her, "You never come between me and the light." At her suggestion, they took a walking holiday in North Wales in the hope that it might cheer him up, but the condition persisted. He would wake up in a mad turmoil, agonised by his thoughts. Yet he could also rise of a morning with a handstand and knees-up as if to say, "How's that!" It was the same scrambling over mountains and cliffs, when he frightened her by his refusal to look where he was going, landing with a sudden jerk or stumbling down a path. Then again, sitting in the kitchen, he would suddenly say, "You won't be hurt if I go off for a while?", pick up his rucksack and disappear.

In May, 1940, just after a Whit holiday with Gweno and Mair in Gower, he decided to leave his reserved occupation and enlist. It was the sort of impulsive thing he could do, the obverse of his depressions, and no-one was more astonished than he. Perhaps it was the formation of the new National Government under Churchill earlier that month or perhaps the invasions of Scandinavia and the Low Countries. In 'Last Pages of a Long Journal', he wrote:

> We do not need banners fluttering against the sky, no Fahne Hoch, Union Jack and Stars and Stripes, Red Flag. But courage, honesty, hard work, and the imagination alive with goodness. It is a slow and endless mission. Often it will be too much, as the 1914–18 war was too much for Wilfred Owen; there was too much against him, and he

was too much alone with his love of humanity and his hatred of the
authorities who legalized the crucifixion. But slowly, this is my
fantasy, we are achieving wisdom.

Owen's fate was a warning to him and it was with a brave hope — the
"imagination alive with goodness" — that he prepared to leave.

The basis of my faith is that those people who do not care about
politics, who do not bother about education, who are simple,
affectionate, patient, want the same things as I do.

It is part of his "radical humanitarianism", a simple declaration of
faith.

At Gweno's suggestion, he thought for a while of going to sea and
had been introduced by a friend to a merchant navy man during his
Whit holiday. On 15 May, in the middle of the week, he left school
suddenly after reporting to the Head with the intention of joining
Gweno's brother, William, second mate on the *Anglo-Saxon*, which
had recently arrived at Victoria Dock in London. However, the ship
wasn't signing off for another nine days and he did not want to work in
the stoke-hole, the only job open to him (fortunately, for the *Anglo-
Saxon* was torpedoed on its next journey in mid-Atlantic with only
one survivor). The next day, he tramped round the shipping agencies
until a clerk in the Seamen's Mission pointed out a poster asking for
dockers to serve in the Royal Engineers. He thought they might need
checkers, so he went down to Tower bridge and signed on. Two hours
later, he left Waterloo for No. 1 Railway Training Centre at
Longmoor, Hampshire. His war had begun.

IX

Longmoor (1): Death and Beauty

Alun thought that, by volunteering as a docker, he could support the war without compromising his refusal to kill a man. His trade on enlistment was given as tally clerk (that is to say, one who checks lists of cargoes on loading and unloading a ship). He hoped that he would be given non-combatant work in directing traffic transport later on in France. This may have been what the recruiting officer at Tower Bridge told him, though he himself may not have quite believed it and returned the big lie with a little one by allowing himself to be inscribed as "C of E" on induction.

At a stroke, Alun Lewis became 1883697 Sapper Lewis, one of about eight hundred men who arrived in Longmoor every week. He was posted to the A1 Company, the 8th Motorised Transport Battalion of the Royal Engineers at Bordon, a few miles away, with a pay of 14/- a week. "My job ought to be fairly safe and reasonably congenial," he told Gweno. It wasn't quite like that. Even before familiarising himself with the routine of camp life, he was thrown into fatigues for the British Expeditionary Forces retreating from Dunkirk and had to spend six hours from four in the morning scrubbing and cleaning floors, peeling potatoes and onions and serving bacon from spluttering vats to upwards of 3,000 men. The scene was dominated by endless queuing for meals and inoculations and sleeping on spring beds with twenty-five others in barracks rooms where "the adjective dominant is f-ing".

The beds were soon given up to the Canadians training at Bordon (Bordon was a Canadian ex-World War I camp) and the recruits put

through three weeks of basic military training, including bren gun and
bayonet drill and platelaying, which consisted of dashing down the
rail track, breaking or blowing up the line and then relaying it before
the next train was due. "All very hectic stuff and interesting for the
first dozen times," recalls Albert Harden, a fellow-recruit, "but
thereafter very boring. When this palled we would be given large
hammers and sent down the lines to bang in the 'dogs', huge nails
which held the lines in place. This was unbearably boring and
something neither Alun nor I could stomach". Alun escaped by
walking through the hilly country round the camp following the chalk
paths as they wound among the woods of fir and birch and cypresses
and along the heather. He was especially drawn to a nearby lake where
he went swimming every evening. Friends from home sent him books,
most notably *The Collected Poems of W. B. Yeats* from his Form IVA
at Pengam and *The Collected Poems of Edward Thomas* from his Uncle
Tim. The Yeats bore the incription, "He understood us." Both poets
have left a marked influence on his work.

An hour each day was spent on the firing range amidst the trees.
Alun passed the time watching the linnets. Even so, he got the highest
aggregate in the company of five hundred men: "It's ludicrous to
know one has such talent," he wrote. All the instructors seemed to
him "illiterate and foulmouthed", the men (mostly Welsh stevedores)
even more so. "*Terrible ignorance* on politics, socialism, religion, oh
anything. It's astounding. I think of the philosophers in the North
Welsh quarries and social democrats in the south Welsh coal mines to
strike the proper (?) balance." He was put on a charge for leaving his
bolt and magazine in his rifle and grew to learn how to live in a tent
with nine others, diving into the underground shelters at two in the
morning whenever the alarm sounded. Otherwise, it was cleaning
latrines or running errands for "snooty little office clerks" or joining
fire pickets (the heather was always flaring up). He was also
discovering something about the etiquette of troop life; any news
must be shared, though he was disinclined to talk yet.

He and Dick Mills met regularly at weekends in Farnham, midway
between Bordon and Sandhurst, where Dick was training as an
infantry officer. Ever since their holiday in Normandy in 1938, he had
found Dick an "ideal travelling buttee" and turned to him for
sympathy and encouragement, though their present meetings were
strictly out of bounds since Dick was on commission and Alun a
sapper. They talked about Gweno and the war and whether or not he

should follow Dick into the infantry. "I didn't get further than stating the problem — the selfishness of being unselfish (going into the front) for the ideal and for peace of one's own mind and honour, and the unselfishness of being selfish (save myself for what I might be able to do in the future, the people I might give delight to by living and working with them my biblical three score years and ten." Again the question is posed: what survives?

A poem from this time, 'The Soldier', shows us a a man gripped by the excited fear of a "climax of disaster". He turns from his fellow-soldiers to nature, in particular a pair of finches he observes sporting blithely in a beech copse in a chalk pit. They may not be as harmonious as they sound nor experience the emotions of human lovers in their "holy mystery":

> Yet still
> I who am agonized by thought
> And war and love
> Grow calm again
> With watching
> The flash and play of finches
> Who are as beautiful
> And as indifferent to me
> As England is, this Spring morning.

This isolated calm, so deliberately different from the melodramatic opening of the poem, is repeated in 'The Public Gardens', another of the "very quiet poems, like Rilke's Bilder [Pictures]" that Alun was beginning to write now that poetry was at last flowing in him. "Poetry is becoming my mainstay now," he told Andrew Davies, one of his fellow-teachers from Pengam. "I sit and remember poems, during air raids and duties and meal times — all times." He approached his experiences through careful literal description (his best poems have the clarity and precision of prose), noticing the difference between what is seen and and his own intense, sometimes wayward emotions. He is the accidental juncture between the world and all "turbulence and time". The form is loose, quite different from the derivative, metrically dainty earlier poems; "the problem is, I think, a new one — to be in the Army and write," he observed. "So little has been written during service: mostly it comes out years afterwards." What was needed, he thought, was something "Impressionist, pointilliste, spasmodic, spontaneous", and this is what we get from the poems of this time, "approaches to the truth, little glances at corners of the prism".

In 'The Public Gardens', the poet has only to watch the people sharing the park with him on a spring evening to observe the drift that is separating him from them this "glittering" summer (the adjective is omnipresent in the poems of 1940). This threat of death so quietly done here is repeated in 'Raiders' Dawn', which depicts the fall of civilisation with a lightly-rhythmic menace, epitaph-like, grieving but restrained. The lovers lie dead (a repeated image), the young are buried in pits of lime (smashed milk-teeth again). Ronald Blythe has called it "a poem of such feathery valediction that it is like the leave-taking of ghosts":

> Blue necklace left
> On a charred chair
> Tells that Beauty
> Was startled there.

A conclusion of almost Imagistic compression. Interestingly, the prose gloss of the poem which Alun gave in his journal is more optimistic than the poem (as his prose regularly tends to be), seeing in the lovers "the seed of humanity" that will survive the war. The poem emphasises the more sinister conjunction of Beauty and Death.

Another poem, 'Parable' presents Death as a "sabre-toothed shaggy hunter" which inspires "primal terror,/ Regret and fascination" among its victims. The language is over-excited, as so much of the verse of this time is, but the mood was understandable and, in any case, widespread, "the ear half-catching/ Rumours of rape in crumbling towns". Fortunately, Alun was able to survive it.

> the stench
> Of breath in crowded tents, the grousing queues,
> And bawdy songs incessantly resung
> And dull relaxing in the dirty bar;
> The difficult tolerance of all that is
> Mere rigid brute routine; the odd
> Sardonic scorn of desolate self-pity,
> The pathetic contempt of the lonely for the crowd;
> And, as the crystal slowly forms,
> A growing self-detachment . . .
>   ('After Dunkirk')

Exactly.

The inspiration of his love for Gweno led him to write a poem for her beside his lake. It opens Rupert Brooke-like:

> If I should go away,
> Beloved, do not say
> 'He has forgotten me.'
> For you abide,
> A singing rib within my dreaming side;
> You always stay.

The sentiment is as sweet as it is truthful and once more it is expressed in a quiet voice. The biblical imagery so frequently employed in Alun's poetry lends the flexible, musical rhythm a simple but grave seriousness, lyrical and dramatic. Death succumbs to the lovers, whose soul withstands its terror "And has its quiet honour/ Among the glittering stars your voices named."

After Bordon, he went for advanced military training to the 15th Technical Training Battalion at Weaver's Down, about half a mile from Longmoor. The camp was on a bare, flat-topped hill so that the amount of black dust kicked up was prodigious. After a while, the boredom of twelve hours drill *ad nauseam*, digging trenches and going on 15-mile route marches (including crawling through bog-land on bellies) began to tell. Army life, he thought, was like the Communist millenium, all obedience, uniformity and tedium. "One suit shall clothe us all; our faces shall be identical for we love no one more than another, and therefore do not consider each other's faces, nor our own." At his own request, he was sent to Bordon for a three-week course in P.T. instruction. The evacuation of the Channel ports had put him off "clerking (so-called) in France" and he hoped this might be the first step to his gaining a commission, which he now began to think was preferable to being "a supernumerary R.E. with a bit of a rifle and field training who might be flung into any breach". He wanted to give his *own* orders and do what *he* thought best, "like the intelligent moth, attracted & revolted by the fire".

Gweno visited him for ten days in August and stayed in a rose-grown cottage in rolling woods at Greatham, two miles from his "ashtip" at Weaver's Down. At first, he arranged that she should share a room with a sergeant's wife but she would have none of it, so the sergeant's wife had to move. For the past three months, they had existed solely by correspondence: "Letters are my proxies, my pigeons," he wrote. "They bulk hugely in the soldier's life." Now, they got to know each other better, staying out in the fields from four until nine every evening when he would return to camp, his big boots sounding on the road as he went.

Army life was his "durable expedient", a continuation of his political struggles as a student. ". . . I'm fighting as I fought before the war," he told Gweno, "— against evil — poverty then, murder now. Not for Churchill or Kenya." "War first. Reconstruction afterwards." — that was his motto, "I'm full of love and work." 'Lance-Jack', a short story, first published in *Life and Letters Today* in November, 1940, is his fullest account of what the army meant to him. It is part of his war diary, "my diary of soldiers without a war". As it happens, the diary suited him well, as he himself noted: "One does things in bits here. I think I'd better give up the attempt at being consecutive: . . . the diary form and the poem are the only two ways of writing." At Weaver's Down, he visited the lake at evening to watch the wild white-and-gold water lilies and blue dragonflies whisking and flashing beneath the northern pines and larches. It was here that he realised how near-allied were the impersonality of the artist and the different impersonality of the soldier — how, in a way, the army was the best place for him to be. From the moment he had landed at Longmoor, he had begun to write with a new fluency and seriousness, indeed, may be said to have become a poet at last. Previously, the seclusion of the mountainside (or, rather, the contrast between it and the valley) had energised his imagination. Now, the army allowed him to go further, not always in command of his rhetoric but testing it against appropriate subjects for, when you become a soldier,

> Conventions go, respectability, narrowness, the suburban train and the Sunday best. Those who were trapped are forced to be free of old routine. Those who were happy are forced to be unhappy, conscripted into a new way of life. Everyone will realise sooner or later that nothing is fixed, nothing inevitable. They will realise the possibility of change. Many long-standing abuses will no longer be able to conserve themselves.

That is the optimistic construction of war, and we know it is what happened. Many abuses were removed, radical change was promoted.

But there was another side to the soldier's freedom and it comes closer to Alun's notion of the artist's impersonality: "The soldier doesn't bother. He is a migrant, an Arab, taking his belongings with him, needing surprisingly little of the world's goods." When he goes home on leave, he finds it difficult to readjust and feels "out of it" save with his wife or sweetheart. Even then,

> when he is utterly alone, utterly impersonal, on guard at night at some outpost, somewhere, he can only envisage the human past, the great centrifugal force of the heart which draws into its orbit and unites in love all differences of people, mother and sweetheart, friend and pauper, employer and baby daughter, I say he can only envisage this great power of life as a swarming of bees on a bough, of flies on a fallen damson, a noisy, slightly indecent congress. A complex, if you prefer.
>
> And if you ask why a man appears to prefer what is casual, rough, hazardous and incomplete to what is warm and personal and loving, I suggest you read Edward Thomas's poems again. It is, if you like, curious that the idealist should live casually with regard to himself and the preservation of himself, that he should find the haversack, the trench, the journeying most suited to the pursuit of high ends. Christ had no home. Women dislike even hate this quality in their men. It is the overturning of all that was so hard and slow to win, the gradual building up of friendship, love, mutual knowledge, home, children, the rooted beauty of flowers, budding and opening in petal and colour and curve *in one place*. But it is a fine quality, in the best men. And there is always, it seems, some suffering. There is Beethoven as well as the nine symphonies.

This is an extraordinary passage. Gone is the affection for people, the ideal of brotherly love and the image of lovers transcending time. In their place is another, colder, "orbit" down which the soldier voyages, in trench, with haversack, "casual, rough, hazardous".

In the third and final section of 'Lance-Jack' (Alun's rank at the time), some soldiers are heard talking near the lake. *In propria persona*, he wishes he could write a poem about the dragonflies and thinks of Gweno and friends like Dick Mills. A heron circles the mere slowly, "which it sees as I see it, a mirror of rest, a breast for the dark and silent visitant. But it is deterred by the laughter of soldiers and girls, and goes, as I am going, elsewhere." This sense of a journey just beginning provides the theme for Alun's career. It is a constant in his work, defined by the conjoined imagery of lake and water.

If 'Lance-Jack' represents his most developed apprehension of what the "horrible cul-de-sac days" of Longmoor meant to him, his poetry explores different aspects of soldiering. In 'The Odyssey', for example, the men returning from Troy with Odysseus lament the loss of the "simpler things" of peace when they went to war, "the common satisfaction/ Forfeited when we answered wrong with wrong". This is the view from the ranks, decent, humane, but it is countered by 'The Sentry', which expresses a contrary fascination with the dark.

> I have left
> The lovely bodies of the boy and girl
> Deep in each other's placid arms;
> And I have left
> The beautiful lanes of sleep
> That barefooted lovers follow to this last
> Cold shore of thought I guard.

Evidently, the outer landscape has been fused with an inner one where the sentry surrenders to the "black interim" of youth and age (coldness and darkness running closely together here as they do in Alun's poetry hereafter).

> I have begun to die.
> For now at last I know
> That there is no escape
> From night. Not any dream
> Nor breathless images of sleep
> Touch my bat's eyes. I hang
> Leathery-arid from the hidden roof
> Of night, and sleeplessly
> I watch within sleep's province.

A new conviction of destiny in the poetry, sombre and beautiful. The composure is intimidating.

In 'A Soldier's Journal, Prelude to War', Alun wrote,

> [W]hat I fought for is alive in me, though some of me is dead. I am still alive. That is the divine miracle I now discover. I know why I died. I know now to what end I must strive. My life is the world's. My life is for Life. If I had hidden away, avoided death, I would have no knowledge, no authority. But now I can speak, and slowly my words will take body, as spring grows into leaf and flower and birds.

That is a positive way of viewing the army. But 'The Sentry's' flower is the flower of "fury", "the folded poppy,/ Night", something altogether different, "poppy" playing on the notion of enchantment and the shedding of blood World War I-style. Moreover, the soldiers' knowledge (as 'Lines on a Tudor Mansion' makes clear) is one of violence, sexual betrayal and inhumanity. Even so — and curiously — it is preferable to the long-lived and peaceful, something fulfilled by the fleeting forest sun as by dragonfly's blue flicker.

At the beginning of October, a friend in the cookhouse mentioned Edward Thomas's house at Steep a few miles away and Alun decided to take a walk there. It was to have momentous consequences. By now he had shed his last reservations about becoming a soldier. "I'm not a pacifist any more," he told Gweno. "I'll be sorry to my dying day, but I won't shirk it."

> You must see that Hitler is wrong and is still wrong even when France shows that her core is rotten. All you hate now — hypocrisy and inflamed nationalism — and the rest — all that's superfluous today. It's a pity, but we're back to the fundamentals — attack and self-defence. . . It's a new world to me, this world where war has entered the dream world of poetry.

And the man who taught him about it was Edward Thomas. Like Alun, he had joined up for reasons that were other than patriotic and, like him, had begun to write poetry only after he had done so. In his 'Post-script: for Gweno', Alun described Gweno as a "singing rib" within his dreaming side. Now that the war was in him, too, the poetry began to flow.

> Thinking back on my own writing, it all seemed to mature of a sudden — between the winter of 1939 and the following autumn. Can't make it out. Was it Gweno and the Army? What a combination! Beauty and the Beast!!

It is what 'Lance-Jack' had tried to say, pointing to the two sides in him: the man who suffers and the mind which creates. Secure in love for the first time since childhood yet drawn away from it by the war, he began to write seriously and the walk to Edward Thomas's house marks the occasion.

Alun admired Thomas more than just as a poet, more even that a sympathetic personality. It is not too much to say that he was possessed by him.

> Climbing the steep path through the copse I knew
> My cares weighed heavily as yours, my gift
> Much less, my hope
> No more than yours.
> And like you I felt sensitive and somehow apart,
> Lonely and exalted by the friendship of the wind.

The tone is modest, but the emotional intensity is not difficult to detect. These lines come from 'To Edward Thomas' and they are spoken above Thomas's memorial on the hill behind Steep. The

wind, Romantic symbol of the imagination, unites two isolated men,
one following in the footsteps of the other. "I have been garrisoned for
six months in Edward Thomas country," Alun wrote in a review of
Thomas's poetry for *Horizon* shortly afterwards. ". . . I have read his
poems often and often in tent and hut." And now he was to take
shelter from the rain in the house he used to live in, walking across
from Longmoor by Liss and Steep accompanied by a stray dog. He
passed some children collecting conkers and filling a pram with
brushwood and asked the way of an old man at Steep church. Then he
climbed the winding path through the trees to the white stone that
bears the inscription, "To Edward Thomas, poet". "He was still
there," he told Andrew Davies. "He is more than ever my friend." A
few paces on and he was in Cockshutt Lane, which runs along the crest
of the hill, where he met Bill and Leslie Sykes, the present owners of
the house, who were busy inspecting a motor-bicycle they had just
bought. They invited him into Thomas's house (called The Red
House) and were immediately attracted to this quiet, reserved man
with handsome features. He promised to return as often as he could,
charmed by their friendship and the remote peace of the house, set
high above the Sussex Downs. By happy chance, he had returned to
his mountain ledge.

The day after, he was confined to his tent by a great gale that had
blown out of the sea. He told Andrew Davies about it.

> . . . all day I watched the grey rain swirl and creep along the heather
> outside my tent, & the acorns pattered onto my canvas & the pine
> needles. Then the marquee we mess in blew down & we got soaked
> thro', grappling with the mad flapping things. Then nothing to
> change into, nowhere to get dry. Blankets damp. Darkness early. No
> lights. No desire. Sleep in warm moist blankets and dirt. Itching but
> tired, tired.

The poem he wrote out of the experience, 'All day it has rained . . .'
directly recalls Edward Thomas's 'Rain':

> Rain, midnight rain, nothing but the wild rain
> On this bleak hut, and solitude, and me
> Remembering again that I shall die
> And neither hear the rain nor give it thanks
> For washing me cleaner than I have been
> Since I was born into this solitude.
> Blessed are the dead that the rain rains upon:
> But here I pray that none whom once I loved

> Is dying to-night or lying still awake
> Solitary, listening to the rain,
> Either in pain or thus in sympathy
> Helpless among the living and the dead,
> Like a cold water among broken reeds,
> Myriads of broken reeds all still and stiff,
> Like me who have no love which this wild rain
> Has not dissolved except the love of death,
> If love it be for what is perfect and
> Cannot, the tempest tells me, disappoint.

This is one of Thomas's finest poems as it is one of his most terrible and it turns on the identification of rain with a longing for death, here regarded as a cleansing act, one which draws the poet away from his loved ones. The same feature appears in the poem Alun now began to write (I quote from the manuscript draft):

> All day it has rained & we on the ridge
> Of the Down Moors
> Have sat ^sprawled in our tents groundsheets ^moody & dull and
> ^as boors blankets laid spread unrolled on the ^circle of dirty ground ...

The tone is relaxed, gently rhythmical, as he itemises his surroundings with an effect that is anything but documentary. The long-spun lines flow on, lulling, hypnotic.

> And the rain has rolled & glided wave & mist & dream
>   in waves a wide & sandless stream
> Of gossamer gliding waters misty as a dream
> Rolling & gliding, wave & mist & dream
> Drenching the heather & gorse in its gossamer stream.

So the poem finds it way through softly-cadenced repetitions to its watery conclusion. The soldiers reading the Sunday papers think about the war and girls and home,

> Yet thought softly, morosely of them &
> as indifferently
> As of ourselves & those whom we for years have
> loved & may perhaps
> And may tomorrow (learn to) love again

It is the Thomas recoil from people.

> We are ~~no more than~~ ^{as passive as} the ^{grey} drifting rain
> Or the acorns that lie in hundreds under
> Whiter where their gnarled cups held ^{sodden} them . . .

Throughout, the lilting rhythm persists, making of the soldier's boredom and futility an enchanted languor. This is not how army life "really is", as Cyril Connolly put it when commending the poem to readers of *Horizon*, but a register of its alienating power. The monotony, that is to say, is a medium that reveals more than just the petty irritations of service life (though it does that too, as Alun himself was fond of remarking when pointing out the civilians were more likely to face fires and bombs than soldiers sitting about in camps far from the action). It discloses the poet's melancholy, like Edward Thomas's before, their sense of waste and frustration. The poem, then, is not a social commentary but a psychological and imaginative enquiry.

> The darkness creeps through us all, all thru'
> the dark the rain
> Soaks & insinuates itself — oh when
> Will I love a living woman once again ^{love wake in its anguish & in my heart again?}
> ~~And I long for the shout of alarm, the bursting shell~~

A natural irritation at the delay of training merges into an impatience to live and love again, to face action, which then yields to a vision experienced at Edward Thomas's memorial stone instinct with an apprehension of death.

> Where once a poet sat & brooded ^{where Edward Thomas brooded long}
> On Death & Beauty — till he was fell
> till the darkness took) his song. ^{And he lies}
>   broke)

When Alun published 'All day it has rained . . .', he added a regular rhyme scheme (the first such employed in his mature verse) and divided it into two long paragraphs, the first describing the enforced idleness of the soldiers, the second his walk to Thomas's house and the fate he discovered there. The connection between the two is subtle and has been overlooked by some. Even so, the poem made an immediate impact and remains his best-known work. It is a "study in disintegration" (as he called his Longmoor period), one uncannily

like the experience described by Thomas in the following passage
from *The Icknield Way*:

> I lay awake listening to the rain and . . . before I fell asleep it had
> become a majestic and finally a terrible thing . . . It was accusing and
> trying me and passing judgment. Long I lay still under the sentence,
> listening to the rain, and then at last listening to words which seemed
> to be spoken by a ghostly double beside me. He was muttering: The
> all-night rain puts out summer like a torch . . . the splendour is dead,
> the summer is gone . . . Even so will the rain fall darkly upon the grass
> over the grave when my ears can hear it no more . . . I am not a part of
> nature. I am alone. There is nothing else in my world but my dead
> heart and brain within me and the rain without. Once there was
> summer, and a great heat and splendour over the earth terrified me
> and asked me what I could show that was worthy of such an earth. It
> smote and humiliated me, yet I had eyes to behold it, and I prostrated
> myself, and by adoration made myself worthy of the splendour . . .
> The rain has drowned the splendour . . . The rain denies . . . There
> never was anything but the dark rain . . . It chants monotonous praise
> of the order of nature, which I have disobeyed or slipped out of. I
> have done evilly and weakly, and I have left undone. Fool! You never
> were alive. Lie still . . . There was life and there was death, and you
> chose. Now there is neither life nor death, but only the rain.

This fascination for the promised release, awed and chastened, is felt
by one who is "half in love with easeful death", as Alun brilliantly
divined in his review of Thomas's *The Trumpet and Other Poems*
(published in the same number of *Horizon* that carried 'All day it has
rained . . .'):

> . . . as war poet, say that he did not suffer as Sassoon, Owen,
> Rosenberg, and was not embittered beyond bearing, but felt it as a
> profound and serious experience, a voice in him — Death, the
> ultimate response that he, despite himself, desired.

This view is elaborated in the blurb he wrote for his first book of
poems a year later:

> Whereas men like Owen and Sassoon were severed from home by the
> continuous horror of the trench massacres he has been with civilians
> in the bombed cities as well as with the soldiers in their isolated
> camps. The continuity between his poems and those of the last war is
> most clearly expressed in his 'Lines to Edward Thomas', for like
> Thomas the war has become an integral part of his life experience,
> not a violent thought-slaying wound as it was to Owen.

To the soldier's anticipation of death, then, is added the poet's
appreciation of it as his natural, even fitting, end, an escape from the

"wet, shabby slums of misery" Longmoor represented, both internally and externally. "Being heavy-headed and Longmoorish" is how Alun defined the mood, "when the heavy superstructure of despondency keeps its load fixed on my head." It was worst on waking up, he said, recalling the wet, black sense of decomposition he had experienced at Manchester, when he had first experienced a love of death, and it is this emotion which the rain touches off again.

There was a second poem of appreciation to Thomas in the autumn of 1940, 'To Edward Thomas'. It employs the same dreamy, semi-automatic manner to describe the "voice" that called Thomas to the "dream beyond the fact and farther still/ The final fact beyond the final dream". Like Virgil and Dante in the second section of 'Lance-Jack' the poet has gone ahead. In a striking passage, Alun describes the view from the memorial stone almost as Thomas himself might have done:

> I sat and watched the dusky berried ridge
> Of yew trees, deepened by oblique dark shafts,
> Throw back the flame of red and gold and russet
> That leapt from beech and ash to birch and chestnut
> Along the downward arc of the hill's shoulder,
> And sunlight with discerning fingers
> Softly explore the distant wooded acres,
> Touching the farmsteads one by one with lightness
> Until it reached the Downs, whose soft green pastures
> Went slanting sea - and skywards to the limits
> Where sight surrenders and the mind alone
> Can find the sheeps' tracks and the grazing.

As Ian Hamilton has said, "a superb moment in Lewis's poetry". No wonder Alun confessed that *The Story of My Heart*, the autobiography of Thomas's mentor Richard Jefferies, was "the nearest expression of my religion that I've read". This passage represents the view from the mountain top again and it repeats the absorption in solitary moments in nature Alun had experienced before, but now done with unaccustomed firmness of line, offering an analogue of death as the sight surrenders and the mind continues alone.

A journal entry of this time reads:

> In my hands are four threads of Death. When I talk of death I am talking of life. The first thread is love of death. It is a mood and seasonal as rain. Listening to music one seems to be lying midway

between the actual pleasure one feels with the senses like an embrace, and the profundities one apprehends. It is love of those profundities that is love of death. It is the poetic source of Edward Thomas's last poems —

> There is not any book
> Nor face of dearest look
> One would not turn from now
> To go into the unknown
> I must enter and leave, alone,
> I know not how.

In that quotation, we recognise the source of the lightly-pointed, flexible verse-forms Alun preferred at this time. Once more, the eye dies and the mind wanders off into the distance. Here is the "hinted land" of 'To Edward Thomas' and Thomas's own death in 1917:

> . . . I knew the voice that called you
> Was soft and neutral as the sky
> Breathing on the grey horizon, stronger
> Than night's immediate grasp
> . . .
> Till suddenly, at Arras, you possessed that hinted land.

An ending that recalls the ending of 'All day it has rained . . .' in its sharp syntactical arrest.

All this passed in something of a daze. Indeed, what prevents 'To Edward Thomas' and 'All day it has rained . . .' from being fully achieved is the sense we have that neither poem has experienced. That is why the latter can still be mistaken for a documentary account, despite its Romantic associations of setting, rhythm and language ("dream", "gossamer", "wild south-westerly"), while the former continues to be ignored in Edward Thomas criticism. Nonetheless, they are fine poems, Alun's first important poems. We might call them 'war poems' in the same sense that Thomas's are and the relation between them emerges in a curious detail at the end of 'All day it has rained . . .' where Alun describes Thomas's death as being caused by a bullet. In fact Thomas died from a heart attack occasioned by a shellburst; the body itself was untouched. A death by bullet wound was yet to come.

X

Longmoor (2): Taking the Plunge

At the Red House, Alun met Howell Davies and his wife, Becky. By coincidence, both Howell and Leslie Sykes had been students at Aberystwyth, where Howell was editor of *The Dragon* before becoming a journalist in London. Some years before, he had read and admired 'Attitude', a short story Alun had published in *The Dragon*, and was now delighted to meet its author. Alun was equally pleased to meet a conversationalist of the greatest vivacity, purveyor of the higher gossip, literary and political.

With the Sykeses, he talked about himself and his family, in particular his mother, whom he described as intelligent as well as interested in things domestic. In 'Last Pages of a Long Journal', he saw himself as acting for her even in the army: "When I was a little boy I used to run down the village to the grocer's shop after morning school to get mother a tin of corned beef for dinner. Now I am running down into the world to get her those things she wanted her children to inherit when she brought them first into the world, but which, for a variety of reasons, have been made more difficult to obtain than they need to be."

Increasingly, he grew restive at his job as P. T. instructor. He thought it was too soft to keep or want to keep — organising company sports days and inter-brigade cross-country races wasn't his idea of fighting a war. He half-hoped for a transfer to the Intelligence Corps or the newly-formed Education Corps and toyed again with the idea of putting in for an infantry commission. "I've always known I'd have to take the plunge one day," he told Gweno, who was down with him at half-term in October. They roamed the fields together until midnight, roasting chestnuts over a fire of fir cones in his helmet. They were now unofficially engaged, but had agreed to delay marriage at her father's request. "She's a brick of a girl," he told his parents. "My writing & my living seem to thrive on her comradeship, and I feel that it's a perennial root, not a phase."

After she had gone, he felt unsettled: ". . . it's very hard to be as Gweno & I are, so much apart, so passionately (& rarely) together". Burdened by a number of family commitments, she could not visit him as often as he wished and he complained loudly. He felt her parents could do more to allow them some time together. For her part, she found it impossible to drop everything but continued to visit him at camp, suffering all the tedium and discomfort of rail travel in wartime. Apart from the Sykeses and his brother Huw (whom he had seen twice that autumn), Alun lacked for company. Dick Mills was in Blackburn with his battalion while Bill Perry, another friend, had been posted to the War Office. The prospect of another month's "technical training" depressed him still further. "Mere boredom isn't the total emotion by a long way," he wrote. "Disgust, anger, contempt also; and apprehension." He had been put on a second charge for allowing his men's kit to be slovenly and for not reporting them and was returned to barracks after enjoying the privacy of a bunk and his own fire. This only added to his disenchantment. He felt the offence, was trivial and could have been overlooked. If his C.O., who knew he wasn't a slacker and called on him to organise concerts, debates and the like, had wanted to reprimand him, he could have done so as between equals instead of reducing him to the status of a shivering third-former. Going into a pub in Farnham earlier that year had taught him the lesson in a different way. Only the Canadians there were friendly to him. "The English, poor creatures, all had their duty to society to perform, they couldn't even dream of wanting to talk to a sapper. This country is being crucified by class. Not that the *people* mind or envy. But those who pass each other in the lift, or live on opposite sides of the square — they divide the house . . . [The artist's] integrity isn't a class integrity. But it isn't ivory. He's in jail, & in concentration camps; in the army." When Dick gained his commission, he wrote to congratulate him, adding: "the officer who is friends with his men is doing constant and real good to the army and the cause. Of that I'm positive."

After a drill cadre course and a fortnight as a railway or docks clerk spent memorising forms for handling cargo, he managed to talk himself out of technical training ("the zero of absurdity," he called it) and went instead as a guard on the Longmoor railway. Paradoxically, he had even more time on his hands as a result, so he started learning Welsh; "there are heaps of things in Wales I want to discover: and a history book to write: and perhaps a BBC job or something after the war. So now's my chance." At about this time, he met Jack Aistrop, a journalist, who ran a duplicated magazine called *The Bugle* on a machine provided by Bill Connors, the legendary Cassandra of *The Daily Mirror*. Aistrop encouraged him to write for it and he responded with reports, letters and stories in the manner of *Men Only*. In the same spirit, he wrote sketches for company concerts and acted in them.

Aistrop was won over by Alun's modesty and admired the quality of his mind and turn of phrase. They would show each other their stories (Aistrop shied away from the poetry) and discuss technical problems like the need to report dialogue accurately. On their walks to Sheet, Alun would fall into silence, lost in his thoughts, while any liberties the *Bugle* personnel enjoyed in gaining access to N.A.A.F.I. quarters failed to interest him. As at Aberystwyth, he was remote, inspiring affection from those who knew him but remaining pleasantly withdrawn. "I'm finicky, aren't I?" he told Gweno. "There are heaps of nice chaps here, but I choose none of them as friends."

After his period in the loco sheds, he moved again to the 7th Railway Battalion at Longmoor as railway clerk, reverting in rank (as was normal) to sapper. His application to the Education Corps had not been successful and he was posted to his own Brigade Education Staff as Assistant Instructor lecturing recruits on world affairs and teaching them French. He had his own office, fire and typewriter again and drew up a syllabus on "19th–20th Century world politics — Liberté Egalité, Fraternité & after. Scheme carefully laid aside in O.C.'s desk for further consideration! Debating Society first meeting tomorrow: Topic 'We are fighting for vested interests' (!!!); hopeful." And then not so hopeful; ". . . I *can not* accept all we are asked to accept today." The army, he thought, "uses discipline to silence true patriotic criticism." Nevertheless, he organised a mock peace conference to discuss a "New World Order, shifting populations, adjusting frontiers and restoring democratic liberties to enslaved people" — fighting talk in an army trained to think of itself as defending those same liberties. In the battalion newspaper, *The Sandpiper*, he published an article arguing that the Engineers shouldn't spend all their time on technical training but form a volunteer Demolition and Rescue Party to respond to calls for help from any neighbouring municipality. (He was thinking of the bombing of Southampton early in December.) "Let's do *something*, for God's sake." The over-emphatic quality of his pleading at this time should be seen against this background of tedium, waste and official indifference. (The O.C. demanded a right of reply and reprimanded Albert Harden, the editor of *The Sandpiper*, for printing the article without showing it to him first.)

A great fillip came when John Lehmann accepted 'Farewell Binge', a short story, for publication in *New Writing*. Alun admired Lehmann for making precisely the contribution to the war he would like to have made himself. In a letter to him, he wrote:

> I find myself under a regime which is hostile to everything it is fighting to preserve. It's odd, the mixture there is in the Army. Centralised & socialised in distribution & production of goods, monastic in its celibacy and its veto on private property, communal as hell: and yet absolutely crucified by repressions, regimentation, precedence and the taboos of hierarchy.
>
> I have been trying incessantly to humanise & free the unit I'm with: I've started a weekly magazine, a debating society . . . : I've put forward a scheme of lectures in 19 & 20 century world affairs: and all I have earned is suspicion, resentment, a petty charge & reduction to the ranks. Tiens!

'Farewell Binge', written in December, 1940, hints at the human quality lost by such regimentation, the friendship of the men squandered in all the chatter, booze and lust of camp, life and the "vague feeling of great danger" summoned up by the possibility of service in the East. (Alun could be very pious in his treatment of his fellow-soldiers: ". . . I don't mind the men being swinish after their boozings. They are alright, in their own way, under the circumstances.")

Three lectures a week hardly occupied him, so he asked to be put on the P.T. staff during the day. He established a reading room for the men, making all the shelves himself and filling them with records and books, but not even the commendation of a visiting general for having the best education department in the country cheered him up. "Awful!" he complained. "Not a hint of war. I feel as if I've been

cheated . . ." Again, "My life is the soft core of indolence in camp. I
read & write stories and argue & the days go by & I don't know when
my spirit will get the hardship it craves." More and more, he felt he
would have to put in for an infantry commission. Nobody wanted him
in the services he wished to join and the one he had joined denied him
all purposeful activity.

By the New Year, various editors were asking for material following
the success of 'All day it has rained . . .' Graham Greene, literary
editor of *The Spectator*, wrote praising his work and regretted that the
taste of his readers would not allow him to print any of it.
Tambimuttu, editor of *Poetry (London)*, agreed to publish three
poems in his March-April number and three more in the next,
including 'To Edward Thomas' and 'Post-script: for Gweno', while a
reader of *Horizon* was so impressed by 'All day it has rained . . .' that
he sent in 3/6d. Alun was reluctant even to accept payment for
publication let alone this additional donation but Connolly pressed
him: "[G]et yourself some nice books with this, if you have everything
else," he wrote, waspish-sensible. Others had noticed the poem for a
different reason. The papers had been asking, "Where are the war
poets?" (thinking of Rupert Brooke) and 'All day it has rained . . ."
seemed to fit the bill. At least it described the war truthfully. It was
patient, humane, sympathetic, with an honest disenchantment suited
to the times, anti-heroic yet not without a certain longing for action of
a sacrificial kind. The death of Edward Thomas provided an
additional pathos to the growing number of readers who were
discovering his poetry for the first time following the shock of Owen,
Sassoon and the rest (the reset *Collected Poems* were published in
1936). The irony is that, though Longmoor was inimical to Alun's
"loving self", it was nonetheless beneficial to him both as a man and as
a writer, as 'Lance-Jack' had predicted.

> I've often called this place a quarantine. It's like a T.B. sanatorium in
> some ways. You are enclosed, out of the world, obeying a fixed
> discipline that can't touch your mind. Rather it frees it, and gives a
> chance to consider all that has happened, all that may happen, to
> examine emotions and values and beliefs, to verify and reject. It's like
> every other turn in fortune — it can be used for good as well as bad.

Reginald Caton, owner of the Fortune Press, offered to publish his
poems but Alun did not like the "distant manner" of his letter of
acceptance (signed "The Fortune Press"). He thought it lacked
evidence that the poems had actually been read: "you give no sign of

criticism or suggestion regarding the selection and order of the poems." Rarely can a publisher have received such a rebuff; rarely can a poet have had the high-mindedness — or confidence — to offer it.

The short stories written at this time include 'The Last Inspection', Alun's frankest exposé of the hypocrisy of Longmoor. He expected "a stretch of clink or a voyage to Egypt . . . a ticking off at least" after it appeared in *Horizon* in February, 1941, but he got none of these, probably because (as he wrote) "the old Brigadier has left — as the story said — and the new one was responsible for chucking him out . . . So maybe he'll agree with what I say." Howell Davies thought he was protected by his position as a writer.

In the spring of 1941, Alun was visited in camp by Lynette Roberts, wife of Keidrych Rhys. He had been in correspondence with her and her husband before *Wales* went under but hadn't published anything in the magazine. Lynette wrote early in 1941 asking for some poems for an anthology Keidrych was editing and he and she exchanged poems. She sent him 'Poem from Llanybri' (where she lived) and he replied with 'Peace', a poem that came to him, he said, as he went across the camp to queue up at the cookhouse. "I found I was singing quietly — words and music" — the same kind of compulsive quality we find in 'All day it has rained . . .'. He thought she would not like the poem: "you seek intensity, . . . my words fall softly all the time, like snow, although I feel like hell, like HELL. It's the same in all my poems. Reading them over last week, reading them really for the first time, tidying them up for the publishers, I felt as if I'd failed. They're all so quiet. But really it's the quietness I seek . . . I don't seek war and the clash of people. I try to resolve always all things."

Lynette made a considerable impression on him. She was on her way back from London, where she had seen Keidrych, a gunner on coastal defence, and, dressed in her red cloak, worn habitually and in style, she arrived bearing a record of Gigli's 'Una furtiva lacrima' from Donizetti's *Elixir of Love*. It was a romantic descent. "She's an exciting and strange creature, very vivid and Welsh and restless . . . a strange uncontrollable simple living being," he told Gweno. Perhaps because she was the first poet he had met, with "a world of disaster and courage" in her like himself, perhaps because of his present irritation with Gweno or perhaps because of her own full-faced beauty, he was drawn to her and decided to admit her into his charmed circle. In the field where they met, he held up a stick for her to pass under and showed off his skill in practising falling, a secret, he said, hidden from all but herself and Dick Mills. When she got home, she wrote to him, "I like your letters Alun but I should be frightened if you came too near. I might be disillusioned. Of the two I prefer the first. The second is horrible."

The writing of 'Peace' moved Alun greatly. He had been at home at Easter for a week and found it more than usually difficult to adjust. "*I couldn't feel* what I touched," he complained. "Its partly because of Army life: but this time more because of a very strange and disturbing spiritual excitement I suffered last week in camp . . . it's very difficult to write of: suffice that I wrote a poem last Monday which so completely took possession of me that I've been nothing but the images which these words, repeating themselves day and night in my mind, *evoked*. Beautiful ice cold death images of perfect poetry. "Can't you see? Can't you SEE?" they were saying — and I could see high upland pastures with white milky waters falling in foam-fans over the green rocks. And those pastures and those waters falling have been everything." It was a vision which continued the argument of 'All day it has rained . . .' and 'To Edward Thomas', gathering death, poetry, water and highland views into an image of perfection.

He gave a fuller account of the event in his journal:

> [S]tress in the soul exhausts you like old age. You feel worn out by the struggle of life — and the struggle has been simply that poem . . . these words came *out of me* and they came *up into me* . . . Gradually, in about three days, I came to see a vision — rather like a climbing valley in North Wales on the south-east approach to Snowdon . . . On and on, up and up into the horizon of hills and skylines and clean black flow of rock against a dawn rain, red sky soft as snow. But a silent land: I know the hills, and wet bog's rough water well: it had none of their crunch, their reality. "Can't you see?" the words said. "Alone — come alone." This is the home of the soul, its freedom to wander, alone and released — released from the body and the situation. A spirit world . . . I grew lonelier and more blessed, more rapt than I have ever been. And I thought, I can write wonderful poetry now I have the way to poetry — the vision.

It is a signal experience, as if he had been taken out of his "body and the situation", though no-one could guess so from a reading of the poem. Once again, the mountain-top liberates the poet. And once again it prompts an equal and opposite reaction in him.

> I find it essential to fight my way back to the simple things, home, friends, love. If I had stayed there, I would have hurt too many people. . . . I have grown in the people — I must rise above them,

climb into the literary hierarchy and be wonderful and lost like Yeats.
But I must stay in the barrack room, in the ranks, in Cwmaman, in
Naffy and pub, in the third class compartments. I've worked out
something simple, intense and simple, in social politics, and it's for
the people. I must tell them of it.

The same thought informs 'They Came', a story which won the
Edward J. O'Brien Short Story Prize for 1941, and which once more
seeks to find an answer to the question, What survives? The reply, as
in 'Raiders' Dawn', is love and memory, the human values, but this
version is more than a little touched by morbidity of a sentimental
kind.

Another visitor to Longmoor in the spring of 1941 was John Petts, a
Londoner and graduate of several arts schools. He had been
impressed by 'The Wanderers' when he read it in *The Welsh Review*
and meant to write to Alun telling him so. He was greatly surprised,
therefore, to receive a letter from him at Christmas, 1940, expressing
his admiration for the illustrations he and Brenda Chamberlain had
done for various magazines. Brenda and John lived in Llanllechid,
high up in the slate-quarrying district of North Wales, where they had
fled the machine to follow D. H. Lawrence's creed of free love. They
inhabited a stone cottage above the village with a haybarn attached;
nearby stood a stable, a cartshed and a pigsty. They were moving in a
different direction from Alun but he felt nonetheless that they were
responsive to "all that is inarticulate, all that is potential in ourselves
and Wales — not in us alone: nor in Wales alone."

Petts had registered as a pacifist at the outbreak of war and
volunteered to do agricultural work, turning up at Addlestead Farm (a
nice Edward Thomas-sounding name) at Headley, near Epsom, early
in 1941. It was there that Alun visited him, arriving after a four-hour
bus journey. He ambled slowly down the lane quoting Edward
Thomas in honour of Petts's work as a cowman. Petts was
immediately struck by the incongruity of this gentle man in rough
khaki. His dreamy expression and droopy air seemed at first to be
signs of tiredness but he quickly understood these to indicate the
presence of a poet, and an unusually contemplative one at that, one
who carried his lines with him in his head. (The stories seemed to
come from a different level.) Alun helped him carry buckets of milk,
weigh them, sweep up and swill out after the cows; they caught a cow
that had escaped and pitchforked sileage. On a walk together
afterwards, Petts observed Alun's long silences, broken only by the

odd remark and snatches of poetry. Quoting the refrain from one of his poems, he murmured, "Now where did that come from, I wonder?" Yet he could also be lively and humorous, more like the social being he wanted to be, tried to be. Not that there was anything assumed about him. There was a beauty of character in him, sincerity and integrity shining through.

Petts sent him an engraving of himself after their meeting and Alun asked him if he would do one of him, too. Petts agreed and visited Longmoor a few weeks later for the purpose. Alun met him at Petersfield and gave him a brief guided tour of the area beginning with his favourite bookshop and going on to Steep church to show him the war memorial there. Petts, observing the difference between himself in civilian clothes and Alun in uniform, was suddenly struck by a sense of occasion, as if Alun were showing him not just various sites of interest but everything that moved him most deeply. As he indicated Edward Thomas's name on the stone, Petts had the impression that Alun was pointing to his own name as well. "Oh dear, you too!" he thought. Thereafter, they walked to Bedales school and up the hill to Thomas's memorial stone and on to the Red House, where Petts was staying.

The engraving is a signal document, valuable not only for its own intrinsic qualities but as an unbiased contemporary record of the man. It had to be done quickly and was done first time off on boxwood with a sharp burin — a hazardous enterprise. Fortunately, it came off. Alun told his parents, "It's a very learned serious face — not a bit like mine, I feel", a view they naturally enough concurred with. However, he told Brenda Chamberlain, "He's made a very serious study of me — very true, though I don't know how he found me out!"

It is precisely what Gweno had discovered at Hengoed, his "inexplicable deaths", the "old Adam in me", as he put it, "'closed', not feeling properly". The portrait captures the essence of the man. It is grave, sombre, even, the head looking down, delicately outlined, the eyes lidded, the face fixed, tranquil yet intent, all energy spent, the heart stilled.

Alun went up to London later that spring to meet Cyril Connolly. He couldn't help noticing the distance that separated him from the "strange nervous *Horizon* gang". They were so susceptible that he felt "as if my khaki were much too rough and my boots much too heavy to be near them: Spender's long fingers and tall restless body and head high up in the air above his sloping shoulders he was like a mixture of hawk and dove. I don't think they'll ever lead the people to a new world. I feel satisfied that my work is sincerely valued by them, though; they were very thoughtful in speaking with me, not patronising or off-hand, and Connolly said he hopes to go on printing my work for a long time yet."

The belief that it is the business of the poet to lead his people to a new world evidently made Alun sympathetic to Spender and the other poets gathered around Auden but there was something in them that distinguished, as he could not, between the imagination and goodness. The cause lay in more than the personal factor which led him to tell Gweno afterwards that he felt like the only bull in the china shop. There was something cultish about them, dandyish, and it suited ill with his earnestness. If, as has been said, English intellectual life between the wars was marked by the political divide not so much between left and right as between commitment and detachment (a view exemplified by Connolly's editorials for *Horizon*), then it was a commitment Alun could share, leaning as it did towards "a general radical revolutionary leftism vaguely identified with such ideas as socialism, Communism, artistic responsibility, and political commitment". It was a leftism both conscience-stricken and playful, urgent and fanciful. Yet, at the same moment that Alun began to emerge as a writer, the left lapsed from their commitment. Their influence had been at its height during the Spanish Civil War, but the disillusionment bred by that conflict, together with events like the Nazi-Soviet pact of 1939, dampened their political ardour and led to Orwell's denunciation of progress and reaction alike as "swindles". "Seemingly," he wrote, "there is nothing left but quietism . . . give yourself over to the world process, stop fighting against it or pretending that you control it; simply accept it, endure it, record it." There followed the essays on picture postcards, boys' weeklies, Dickens and P. G. Wodehouse.

For Alun, however, this was precisely the time to try to regain control of the world process. "We must go into Life." he wrote in 'Last Pages of a Long Journal'. "Self-perfection will come of that, we must not seek it as the main end. What is unhealthy in a man comes out in sweat as he runs" — a Lawrentian perception. True, Spender could still declare, "We are living in a political age . . . With few exceptions, the incisive, penetrating, daring, imaginative, and therefore poetic minds of our time are materialist, for better or worse, because the outstanding problems are material ones", but by 1946 he was lamenting the fact that young writers were no longer concerned with the "ideology of British Democracy. They have abandoned the hope of an integration of their own higher interests, their own humanity, their own personalities within any politically organised society." That was because the war had robbed them of political purpose. Alan Ross argues that a Lewis-like preference for rapportage, short prose sketches and "poems containing rough segments of raw experience" was appropriate because the war was "a flight into Nowhere in face of enormous odds, and at the end of which there would perhaps be only debris." Such nihilism is echoed by Connolly's advice to artists to seize the opportunity of war and concentrate on their own work, in the spirit of Auden's recent pronouncement: "Art is not life and cannot be/ A midwife to society". E. M. Forster agreed. "Art for Art's sake? I should just think so, and more so than ever at the present time . . . It is not very dignified to be a rat; but all the ships are sinking, which is not dignified either". At this very time, however, Alun was insisting: "Life isn't for art's sake." It should represent "the marriage of poetry and society, goodness and business, culture and civilisation", a strange echo of *Howard's End*.

In his correspondence with Brenda Chamberlain, he urged her to turn to "the quarry, the pit, the slum streets & the bench in front of the Workmen's Hall" for her compositions. Thinking over his own concern for poverty and politics, he declared, "[T]here are two urgent needs for me: — one, to write for: the other, to educate *The People*. In practice, they work together — my writing is an expression of all the comfort, all the hope & faith & despair & love that is humanity." Accordingly, he proposed a new venture: the publication of broadsheets like the chapbooks pedlars used to sell, each with a ballad and a woodcut illustration. He had been struck by an engraving John Petts had done which bore a similarity to his poem 'The Sentry'. Perhaps they could join such poems and engravings together and sell them for a penny or two; he offered to pay the initial cost. Keidrych Rhys had attempted something similar with a wartime broadsheet (the only one issued) after the closure of *Wales* consisting of a series of poems, including one by William Empson, but Alun wanted something less recondite, "universal poems, not obscure modernities", designed to reach the people "with beauty & love".

Brenda Chamberlain doubted the practicability of such a venture in wartime but he persisted. By the middle of May, he was announcing publication of the broadsheets at the Caseg Press, the publishing concern run by Brenda and John named after the river which ran near their home. The poems were to come from a variety of Welsh writers, mainly living: "[I]t's entirely a friendly project," he told Gwyn Jones, "not a business racket". Its purpose was to show the "continuity, almost identity, between Wales sixteen centuries ago & Wales today", its subject "the peasant, the soldier, the land. It's for the people, to show them the continuity and courage of the race, see?" Jones responded enthusiastically, inadvertently suggesting the title by which the publication came to be known, the Caseg Broadsheets. (They were, as it happens, printed by the Gomerian Press in Llandysul when Brenda and John's little Adana duplicating machine proved itself to be unequal to the task.) The artistic community so signally lacking in Alun's prentice days was slowly coming into being, albeit in the most disadvantageous of circumstances.

By now, Alun's period of service at Longmoor was drawing to a close. He had been posted to an officers' training course (OCTU) at Heysham, in Lancashire. Delivering the first of his Saturday morning lectures on the war, he was interrupted by the Colonel of the battalion who shouted, "It's a lie. Tell the truth or I'll stop the lecture." Alun replied, "Stop the lecture if you wish, sir. I've told no lie." The Colonel insisted. "You've been listening to lies," he told the men, "I call the meeting closed." Eventually, after an interview with the Brigadier, he apologised to Alun and asked him to conclude his lecture, which had sought to explain (amongst other things) that "Japanese imports were restricted into British colonies by the Ottawa agreement". He had dared to suggest that the enemy might have grievances. Thus ended "Alun in Blunderland". Nevertheless, he had to submit his talks in typescript to the Colonel in future and felt he was almost being forced to toe a particular party line.

Soon after, he began a five-week course of field works at his own request, a heavy programme involving demolition, wiring and trenching. He then prepared his farewells with heavy heart. He remembered his times at the Red House and meeting Howell Davies with particular affection. Howell, he thought, had "said many sharp and illuminating things as well as helped me to find a general sense of purpose and direction." In mid-June, he left for the Infantry Training Centre at Gloucester. On his departure, he found he had one one garter, so Jack Aistrop had to lend him his. Having joined the war to avoid killing others, he had chosen a course much more likely to bring him near that end — and all because he had found life behind the lines so wasteful. His own high sense of purpose had defeated him. "Every true soldier is true," he had told Gweno when he enlisted. "It's just his bad luck."

> You know how the army is — like any other mass of people, noisy, selfish, vulgar — I don't feel any kinship with that sort, I'd fight them if they attacked what I treasure. Do you see why I must fight then? I who love peace and creation so much. Don't say I'm wrong — we've got to decide ourselves whether to be always passive and accept, or make a bid to preserve what is good. The National Trust fights to save beauty from jerry-builders. I to save my own freedom. If Hitler wins, I'll always be in the clutches of the bully and the dolts, his minions. I'm in their power now — the corporals — but I only signed myself into slavery 'for the duration'. That's what I surrendered. And it's worth it. Buying my future by a mortgage on the present. Or buying someone else's future by mortgaging my life. Chance will decide which.

Out of the blue, he received a letter from Philip Unwin, of Allen and Unwin's, asking him if he had any material to submit. Unwin had heard about him from Clifford Makin, business manager of *Horizon*, and was impressed by the sympathetic humour of 'The Last Inspection'. Here, he felt, was the authentic voice of the ranks. Perhaps he might have a novel in preparation. Alun sent him a list of all his published work, omitting the short poems published in *The Observer* just before the war and pointing out that the poetry was likely to be of more interest since it was mostly recent whereas all but three of the stories were pre-war. Unwin agreed to consider the poems and passed them on to his reader, Bernard Miall. Shortly before Alun left Gloucester for Heysham, he received a letter of acceptance and an advance of £15. He was "breathless with delight".

XI

Marriage and OCTU

The first night of Alun's visit home at Whitsun, 1941 was a disaster. The weather was glorious and he had been looking forward to visiting the Gower peninsula with Gweno over the weekend but a bomb fell nearby, killing two families and blasting the doors, windows and ceilings of her house. He was plunged into another of his depressions and made no effort to check whether she had been hurt. It was, he confessed later, a "sort of fatalism, a shrug of the shoulders, and disbelief in danger". The next day, having repaired the damage and made air-raid blinds for her and his family, he suggested they resume their planned holiday but she refused on the bus: "something immediately froze in me and I became horrible and dead". He had felt the mood creeping up on him at Longmoor the previous week and hoped she might help him avert it, yet here was the crisis he had feared. Empty words of recrimination, failure and confusion followed. "It's up to you to decide whether I'm worth giving an insurance policy to," he wrote when he returned to Longmoor apologising for his behaviour. "I'm never like this with Girlie or Mother because they aren't so innate in me as you are. You'll always have to suffer it when it comes, if you choose me . . . Forgive me for not being a nice young man — the neighbours may think I am, but I'm not. Perhaps I don't want to be, either. Do you want me as I am, Gwen?" It was the nearest he had come to telling her about his trouble and the uselessness of commonsensical palliatives in alleviating it: "nor will the advice of neighbours or the rule-of-thumb maxims of teachers for settling with refractory children be anything but a curse and a hindrance to be cast away before they fuse the whole circuit of trouble."

"Dear Gweno," he wrote,

> you know how much I need you when I'm like this (for I'm still not myself, something falls across my mind all the time so that I can't feel properly, can't feel freely and generously as I was made as a human being to feel) I can't help it either — I'm as cruel to myself as to you. But I wish it weren't so. After you'd been so brave and practical all Friday night and Saturday morning and endured such a shock, it would have been cruel beyond words for me to strain you further at all. Yet I did, with the dead weight of my wretchedness. And now I'm wondering whether you have had enough of our life, and are trying to say finis. But I don't believe you can, any more than I can; but don't try to, darling, *please*. I've told you often that when my tongue is like a salted lash you must help me then most of all — and I think your help will be by *patience* and by *losing* everything as I lose everything. Not by saying 'Oh it's only a mood, a tantrum — and leave him alone and he'll come like Bo-Peep's sheep.' Something *fetches* me back each time, comes seeking me and finds me and stays with me till I'm well enough to return. I feel sick, having to talk and think of this. But you, if you do care — do remember and do love, really — then it is bound to live and survive innumerable deaths. I invoke love with such humility, Gwen. I am asking so much, and I know it can be as agonising as it can be beautiful, it is the most dangerous and incalculable thing in Life, it is like a gift of Life itself . . .

He confessed that he was "a slave to some capricious demon" and came to her "more humbly than a beaten dog" for salvation. She was frequently hurt by letters he wrote to her "in bad moods" and there had been further arguments about her family commitments. He would call her a "reactionary" and "an enemy of the people" for wanting only him and her brothers to survive the war and that her parents should grow younger every day. She, in turn, would tease him with his stock "character" of the collier-cum-student-cum-socialist and then they would burst into laughter.

His waywardness continued to puzzle her. On one of their walks above the tree line behind her house, he fell into an "atrophy" and this was repeated several times in their meetings. Through it all, however, their affection deepened and he bought her a piano that spring in lieu of an engagement ring; the ring followed, at the insistence of his mother. She lost it two years later. An ill-omen, she thought. There was another; a photograph of him on her bedroom mantelpiece fell, smashing into the fire grate one night, no doubt on account of the vibrations from the nearby colliery.

In mid-June, on a visit to Llanthony Abbey, Alun proposed marriage. She refused because it would mean losing her job. Glamorgan County Council had ruled that married women could not be employed during the war. He sent her a number of telegrams and letters from Gloucester and so urgent were they that she decided to visit him there. He met her at Bristol and they travelled back together to Gloucester, where he found her a hotel room for the night. He proposed again and she hesitated for two minutes.

> And then you thought 'Well, he'll be worse still without me', so you said yes, rather doubtfully. Only somehow or other I didn't doubt at all. Because I was so positive it would have to be so. Even when you 'didn't know' at Gloucester in that little hotel, I knew . . . you took my hand as I stood on the landing, saying it doesn't matter a bit, darling, and you said we *will* get married tomorrow.

What did it matter anyway? Her Headmaster and her parents couldn't eat her.

The next day, Saturday 5 July, he was like a little boy who has washed behind his ears. As he went by a narrow, cobbled alley to the hotel, he picked her a few white flowers and, after watching her eat breakfast, toured the shops with her and bought her a brown floral costume with accessories to match, including a dark straw hat with turned-up brim. Pressed for time, they chose the first ring in the first jeweller's shop they saw and hurried off to the registry. En route, he stole her another spray of flowers for her, some roses hanging over a wall. The wedding, in the Food and Registry Office, was witnessed by two army friends, David Gunn and Maurice Gilford. By chance, the officiating registrar was also called Lewis; they laughed so much that they nearly left without paying him. As a wedding gift, Alun bought her a gilt-framed detail of Botticelli's 'Birth of Venus'. The next day, they visited Tintern Abbey and Chepstow, where they said goodbye. As he stood by the window of the crowded bus, he gave her a penny "for being such a good girl".

Four days later, they met again in a field in Wenvoe, just outside Cardiff, for a few hours. From there, he wrote to his parents telling them about the marriage.

> I think Gweno and I will always be happy together, if the world gives us a chance. I know her well now, and I know she's a girl who reveals deeper and deeper secretions of wisdom and courage, and she loves the real things, home and family and the little ways which make people so worth loving . . .

Mrs Lewis was disconcerted both by the suddenness and rapidity of the news; there was neglect and rough-riding in it, she felt, but gradually she was won over. Contemporaries of Gweno and Alun were surprised too. They had not guessed there was anything between them, remarking the difference between his personality, very much that of a wandering spirit, and hers, more down-to-earth. (Alun was later to compare his mental strain with Gweno's "admixture of healthy cynicism and rather grudging confidence in people and events.")

When he got to Heysham on 11 July, his first task was to prepare his poems for publication and complete the long poem he was writing inspired by his marriage, 'War Wedding'. He thought this his best poem to date. The most important revisions made were to 'Threnody for a Starry Night' and 'On the Welsh Mountains' (retitled 'The Mountain over Aberdare' — somewhat confusingly, since the view it describes is not that of Aberdare but Cwmaman). The major part of the poem is now the description of the valley, from a position even more detached than the Welsh mountains. Where before the poet's attention was divided between the village and his rainy fantasies, now everything is subsumed under the former and a profound sense of waste communicated, one greatly strengthened by the intervening experience of 'All day it has rained . . .'. Having left Cwmaman, he goes to fight a war which he hopes will ensure that it will never again suffer as it has done yet also registers a sadness which has more to do with his destiny than its own. Accordingly, he prepares his farewells to a place he has never really belonged to with "brittle tears".

Heysham Towers, the site of Alun's OCTU, was previously a Butlin's holiday camp. Situated two miles outside Morecambe, it greeted the cadets with signs like "Cast Care Aside" and "Buy the Official Camp Song". In a welcoming speech, the Officer Commanding urged them "to cultivate the officer mentality, and not hold our wives' hands in the street and not look for ways of avoiding work as the common soldier does". (After the first month, passes were made available every weekend and married cadets had sleeping-out passes.) This was the first time Alun had been separated from the "the common soldier" — the Welsh soldier, too, for he was the only Welshman on the course — and his reaction was characteristic. He thought his lot were decent but with the wrong ideas in their heads. The atmosphere filled him with unease. He expressed his views anonymously in an article called 'The Creation of a Class', published in *Horizon* in September, 1941:

> Men may never be born equal. Alone the Army and the public schools go on re-erecting the collapsible ladders of inequality. [At OCTU, v]oices begin to be lowered, that wonderfully quiet way of talking sets in . . . They are never in a hurry. Or they are never *seen* to be in a hurry. Their enunciation begins to slur and blur. It is already a lot of trouble talking.
>
> [The] moustache — what a symbol and a hope! Never have I seen so many of so many colours and textures and shapes. They are great blooming yellow haystacks and drooping fuschias, sad ones and gay ones, fierce little bristling black ones on very small and fiery cadets, and the common coarse hairbrush that still lent its owner a stability he would never have had when shaved . . .
>
> Here could have been a great and grand opportunity for building a class of men, designed to bear responsibility, in the spirit and shape of things that are coming. There is no hint of such a thing in the Octu system. There is no glimmer among the staff that things must change and things are changing. On the contrary, thousands of young men are being moulded without their knowledge to believe that things *will never change at all* . . . There is no conception of a society based on the welfare of the many.

Alun enjoyed his work, which was far more intellectual than at Longmoor, but still found that he had to "live in blinkers all the time", holding himself from "drifting into the great undertow that my mind has become". He was now "really morbid". Even so, his instructors though him "quiet but definite", hard-working and capable. He was considered particularly good in section training and tactics, where his command of principles was judged "sound" and his theoretical work "outstanding". Even the stabbing of dummies with bayonets failed to disturb him.

Fame of a kind reached him when *Lilliput* published an article on the English Poets in December, 1941, featuring Spender, MacNeice, Plomer, Day Lewis, Empson, Dylan Thomas, Anne Ridler, Laurie Lee and himself. He was also one of seven co-signatories (including Orwell, Koestler and Bonamy Dobrée) to Connolly's *Horizon* plea for writers to be given similar status to war artists. "It's all very comic," he wrote, "for I feel almost as unique as a grain of sand in Libya."

Gweno came up to stay in August for three weeks. They went to the Lake District for a delayed honeymoon, as Mr and Mrs Lewis had done many years before; it poured with rain. There was further dissension when the time came for her to leave. He felt she hadn't stayed long enough while she fretted about the strain on her parents of keeping a house full of visitors (they had recently been ill). After she had gone, he met Bronwen Williams in a tea-shop quite by chance. She asked him how long he had been married. "Three days, three weeks or three years," he replied. "You can guess [Gweno]," he told Christopher Cheney, "when I say we'll have lots of quarrels over personality — she retains her integrity by freehold and assets immunity from . . . all the . . . rights the flesh is heir to."

By October, the months of training had taken their toll and he felt his black moods deepening. He travelled to Carnforth and walked for miles through stormy woods to Silverdale, a village by the sea fifteen miles north of Morecambe. "Well, what is it that keeps on being proved to me? This — that I'll never be bought over as long as I live. Every time there is an attempt I shie away like a wild horse. It's instinctive. I observe it as a natural phenomenon. I won't even write to Gweno as Mrs Lewis; I know we're married, but I've told her that I'll never make love to her indoors." Reading John Llewellyn Rhys's *England is My Village*, he saw how the army could persuade him to follow the same course as the hero of that book, "with a romantic assignment with Death . . . always dépaysé, without Wales or England, like a . . . travelling booth man, love and hope on one side, stalking men in uniform on the other."

He now decided that he did not want to publish *Morlais*, despite offering it to Philip Unwin at a meeting in June. He felt that it had dated, like the stories, and was "symptomatic rather than complete"; he hoped to come up with something "valid for more of Welsh life than the small section it covers now" after the war when he would be a man and not "an excited and troubled lover of existence". The only new piece he wrote at Heysham was 'The Prisoners', a story printed in *The Last Inspection*. He tried emulating D. H. Lawrence in its composition, rewriting each version completely each time, though the result failed to satisfy him. Unwin had agreed to publish the stories if the poems sold well but Alun felt he needed more time to revise them as well as see the poems through the press. He also wanted to attend to the broadsheets but there would be little time in the seven days' leave allowed him before joining a battalion, so, with Unwin's support, he applied for an extension and got thirty days.

> Now why, with such a prospect, with so many things to be lucky about, should I feel this deep-rooted yet utterly sane presentiment of nothingness? Because I grieve in my soul for the Russians? [Hitler's

invasion of Russia, like the Italian invasion of Greece the previous autumn, had disturbed him deeply.] Because I see things going ineluctably the wrong way? Because I feel the proximity of that familiar of men — Death? Because of all these . . . So I say to myself 'Stick it out for another fortnight — Only another fortnight. And then for a month you will have *joy*, such joy, pure as snow. *And after that you will go away*. But is not a month of joy more than you could ask of Life? Why then this sadness in your heart of hearts? And are you so selfless that you still grieve that your death won't mend the world, and the old miseries, by plaguing those who survive, plague your dead spirit also? Are you really as selfless as that, Alun? I would like to think you are, but I do not believe it.'

And this problem, of why I feel *so* unhappy when I know I am sane and lucid, is one I cannot satisfactorily resolve.

He prepared to leave Heysham on the 31 October. He had passed with flying colours. In his report, his C.O., Lt. Col. Goff, said that he thought Alun would make "a good officer. He has worked hard and has shown the ability to lead . . . a valuable cadet." On his way home, he stopped at Bangor, where he met Brenda Chamberlain and John Petts and travelled by mare and gambo up to Llanllechid. He then went on to Dovey Junction, where he met Gweno and the two returned to Aberystwyth, where she was staying for half-term. Gwyn Jones met him there for the first time and has left this record of him:

> He was dark and lean, with a long Welsh head narrowing downwards from a noble forehead to a sensitive mouth and strongly moulded jaws. In height and colouring he was the very symbol of the Valley folk he loved so well. He had that slightly 'foreign' look which many handsome South Walians have, both in their own and others' estimation, but was native to the nail-ends . . . as a person he was remarkably mature for his twenty four years. He was a man of great enthusiasms, freely expressed; but I remember the droop of his eye at certain enthusiasms of my own. He approved, but his sense of humour was keen.

The next day he travelled to Llandysul, where he spent the morning choosing paper for the first of the broadsheets featuring his own 'Song of Innocence' and 'Raiders' Dawn'. It was, perhaps, unfortunate, as he himself realised, that his should have been the first poems chosen but necessity dictated: John Petts's 'Debris Searcher' was the only engraving ready at the time. In any case, 'Song of Innocence', with its praise of "simple words" and simple truths, and 'Raiders' Dawn', with its pity for the innocent victims of war, make an apt introduction to a series aimed to illustrate "the fortitude with which Wales has faced centuries of war and adversity".

Back in Aberdare, he slept at Mountain Ash during the week and Elm Grove at weekends, spending the day with his mother and the evenings with Gweno. (Curiously, he continued to address all his correspondence from Elm Grove.) During his first weekend at home, his parents held a party to celebrate the reunion of their children. It was a happy occasion, though Huw had a premonition that this was to be the last time they would all be together. Shortly afterwards, Alun and Gweno visited Lynette and Keidrych Rhys at Llanybri. This is how Keidrych remembered him:

> You felt in him a burning idealism, and that sense of isolation and austerity of spirit you feel in the poet, the lover of solitude and the sensitive artist — and you loved him for the unexpected bubbling sense of fun that came from him, and made him a very human being at the next moment . . .

During his leave, Alun received a proof copy of *Raiders' Dawn* and sent it to Dick Mills, then bound for India. "What will [the war] do to you?" he asked. "To me? I know I'm going to meet some tremendous experience in the next twelve months. I would like to survive it, to write about it in poetry, I hope, not prose."

A new correspondent at this time was Robert Graves. In a radio talk earlier that year, Graves had explained why the war had produced so few poets. For one thing, no-one disputed the justice of the cause; for another, there was no volunteer pride, no need to stimulate recruiting (or, later, to warn those back home) and no large-scale engagement with the enemy. Indeed, the soldier's life was relatively safe. Moreover, the army was increasingly professional and mechanised. "The sort of soldier who in World War I would naturally have become a 'war poet' now feels a mist the colour of khaki blanco rise between him and the world of his imagination." If he did write, it was to mark the difference between himself and his fellow-soldiers, and here Graves quoted from John Waller's 'Aldershot' and Alun's 'The Soldier': "But leisurely my fellow soldiers stroll among the trees./ The cheapest dance-song utters all they feel." Graves repeated his views in an anonymous review published in *The Listener* shortly afterwards of Keidrych Rhys's anthology *Poems from the Forces*, in which he said that the editor had "given us one real poet and one only, Alun Lewis" and that he wrote "movingly, decently and truthfully, that his 'influences' are accepted because of spiritual kinship and not grabbed because of fashion, that he writes uncompromisingly about a life which is like a gauze between him and his vision, and that he is not afraid to say of his comrades: 'The cheapest dance-song utters all they feel.' "

Alun wrote to Graves on his return to Aberdare complaining that he had been quoted in support of views he did not share, "to wit, the isolation or *difference* of the poet". If there were isolation, it was "not that of a cultured gent timidly roughing it with a blunt gang, but the simple cosmic loneliness that is natural to a man today as to the old Ecclesiast". He continued:

> I don't theorise or belong to schools more than I can help; apart from knowing where I stand in politics and in love I take what comes. I've never felt lonely in the Army, in the ranks anyway, (I'm just going as a Subaltern to the South Wales Borderers), because I've never lacked comrades: wherefore I feel it necessary to state my position to one whose poems I place second to Yeats . . . If you do read my poems or collected short stories when they appear you'll mark them, as perhaps you mark this letter, as immature. But I hope you won't find them precious. I'm stuck right into this world mess and haven't much patience with the isolationists, — though half my friends are C.O.s! And I don't want to be quoted as proof that the élite of letters should be allowed to travel 'first'.

Graves replied: "To feel cosmic loneliness I think means merely that one is short of friends who also think cosmically." The serious poet, he thought, always found the friends he needed. As for liking Yeats, that *was* immature. "Test him again, by all the maturest tests you know, and see whether his glamour is really the reflection of poetic fire and not a piece of post-druidic magic, cast by a little man, who made friends with demons, over young minds." He ended, "Let the élite of letters travel 'First'. They will be with the General and Black racket Bosses & why not?"

Alun tried again.

> If you read any of my work, please know beforehand the source from which my writing comes. *Humility*. A dangerous thing to have in one, but without it one is useless to do good.

Once again, we notice the poet's assumption of responsibility for the lives of others. In a further passage, Alun emphasised that humility was

> the source of all my long struggles, for it brings me into conflict with self-pity and pity for the world, with authority and presumption on the part of those who are not humble, with intolerance and cruelty,

and with submission. Because of it I have never joined any party or school, but recently I have been able to identify myself with many men I have met in the ranks, who have their own integrity and willingness to endure. And that is why I say I know where I stand in politics and in love, and have no desire to travel first . . . The only thing I fear is that I won't outlive this war, or rather live long enough to do something positive towards realising for others the miracle that I know is possible.

— life being, as we know, perpetually a miracle, especially for those who have fears that they will cease to be. In response, Graves noted that the Welsh were characterised by "over impulsive warmth" and "humility", the latter shared with poets in general, "but I think it is important to make the humility something that one puts between oneself and one's impossibly high standards, not between oneself and others."

Alun's leave was soon over. On the 29 November, he caught a train for Woodbridge, in Suffolk, to join the 6th Battalion, the South Wales Borderers. (By coincidence, Edward FitzGerald, translator of Omar Khayyam, had been born there.) His month with Gweno had been wonderfully solacing and, despite his disappointment at not getting the Royal Welsh Fusiliers or the Intelligence Corps, he was in good spirits. They were not to last long.

XII

Second Lieutenant Lewis

The Borderers plunged Alun into the deepest depression he had known since Manchester. Being "so easily upset, like a wrist watch by a bad jolt", he was distressed by "the barren ugly coarse loud life of the army" as never before. "[T]here is & always has been something that shackles and jails me," he told Brenda Chamberlain. "It was worse once. Now it is mainly circumstance that assails me; and sometimes it grimly gets the better of me." His melancholy was so acute he could neither eat nor sleep.

> I've had no time to look at a tree or a book since I got here & all my energies have been consumed in a struggle to endure the ugliness and loudness of this life & these people. I won't enlarge — it's a petty nightmare, which I suppose will hang over my eyes till the war or the world pass away and I become something nearer myself . . . Life is hostile, & grins at me like a Jap.

Being separated from Gweno was an agony, "like a jab in the stomach", and, as at Pontigny, his sense of his own inadequacies compounded his misery. He seemed not to possess the knowledge that everyone else possessed: how many rounds there were in a Bren gun, how many shovels per section, how many inches long was a sandbag. Going to meals in the Officers' Mess reduced him to a state of nervous anxiety, "literally *sweating* with uneasy silences and being exhausted by shop talk and the sharp words of company & battalion commanders . . . I've got the enemy of life inside me."

> I shouldn't have taken a commission. It was a mistake. Now I have to pay for it in a thousand ways. For I see now what made the army

tolerable was the way one could retire from the world, and be anonymous and do simply what one is told and not think or partake in it at all . . . these days have re-opened old wounds and I can't think without a cold sweat of the terrible anguish I lived in once, when I was 19, 20, 21.

The recruits who had joined the 6th Battalion, the South Wales Borderers in June, 1940, when it was raised, came from the South Wales valleys. They were men after Alun's own heart, but he was now obliged to share the company of officers. "I have to make conversation in the Mess, assume anger or dignity to the men; I can't lounge about listening to the natural & earthy talk of barrack room & pub any more. There is a whole world of caste and stiff traditions fencing me off." 'It's a Long Way to Go', printed in *The Last Inspection*, gives the flavour of his distress perfectly. Second Lieutenant Greening (aptly named) goes to his room.

His wife's photograph looked at him from the medley of pamphlets and files littering the trestle table. (Darling, I'm so sorry. I'm so useless, so worthless.) He opened his diary and looked at the list of tasks he'd made out before breakfast. 'Phone M.O. *re* 18 Harris's medical board. Check platoon ammo. Collect range card. Paint gas detectors. Toilet paper for billets. Write to factory for 27 Evans's wife to be released during his leave. 'Phone P.R.I. — can newspapers be bought for men's billets? Prepare A.B.C.A. lecture.' He'd ticked off three of them. The others he hadn't done. What a marvellous achievement! Actually three things done!

God, how he bullied himself. Never let himself alone. If only he could get into action, he knew he'd be alright. But this endless waiting, this normality in an abnormal life, letting things slide, lacking conversation in the Mess, knowing no dirty jokes, excusing himself from beer-crawls, never reading Jane in the *Mirror* or his horoscope on Sundays, eating more meat meals than his wife, doing less work that his collier father — oh Christ, the weariness of it!

His wife smiled at him. (Darling, I'm sorry I can't write to you. I wish I was more of a husband to you, more of a man. Especially now the baby's coming. It used to be alright, didn't it, when I was teaching in the Settlement and taking evening classes in the Boys' clubs, and we had wild roses for our wedding, and there was the constant active fight for a better world, for the pits to be reorganised and money coming into the grimy streets, and books and playreadings and hiking for the pale boys?)

He stood up, suddenly realising he was an infantry officer.

Alun's Commanding Officer, Colonel V. J. F. Popham ("Pop"), took one look at him and asked the company commander, Captain O.

A. Evans, to give him a report within a month. Evans thought him "the complete village idiot with a drawling Welsh accent and stupid grin", a "crude type of left-wing socialist and alien to the refinements expected of an officer." The Colonel told him he wasn't much use, the Adjutant just looked through him. There was in the battalion in any case a division between the senior officers and the junior ones, the former regular army men, the latter commissioned ranks, and each viewed the other with mixed feelings. Popham and his second-in-command, Major I. O. Moon, were disciplinarians, as much with the officers as with the men. They had been entrusted with the task of forming a new battalion and discipline was their way of welding it together — that and sport. The first intake consisted of young married men from the eastern valleys of Wales, fit, eager types with a lovely sense of humour and a strong comradeship that survives to this day. They were colliers, mostly, in their late twenties, used to hard work, co-operation and danger, and the combination of men like them with officers like Popham and Moon was outstanding. The young officers, however, felt that the thinking of their superiors hadn't advanced much beyond the First World War so that intermingled with their admiration was an impatience with tactics and an idiom derived from the Northwest Frontier that seemed unlikely to help them in any war they might be called upon to fight. The rigidity extended beyond military matters for, if you did not have a sense of caste or colour (and the men from the valleys did not), then you were a marked man.

Eventually, Captain Evans gave Alun a favourable report. He thought that, as platoon commander, he had shown he could look after his men. It was, perhaps, unfortunate that Evans should have been Alun's company commander. Alun thought him "a rotter". Nicknamed "the black adder", he had a streak of harshness in him. He was a warlike man, coiled like a snake, and it was unlikely that he and Alun could get along. His friends were men like Alun Gwynne Jones (the present Lord Chalfont), Dai Martin Morgan, Cliff Vivian, Teddy Coles, Tony Lewis, David Drummond, Selwyn Evans and Jack Gush. Gwynne Jones remembers him as very much the Englishman's idea of a Welshman, small, lean and dark, slightly cadaverous, with a suggestion of a snubbed nose, intense and with a deep, mysterious air about him, faraway, fey (perhaps the look mistaken for vacancy by Popham). He was generally considered the men's Trojan horse in the Officers' Mess, dogsbody of the battalion at the beck and call of everyone. "Boy, shut that window!" might come the call from a senior officer. From time to time, he would withdraw from his surroundings and everyone came to accept this. He inspired affection and respect and an appreciation of his endearing shyness and friendliness, a rare quality of depth.

In his public activities, he pushed himself to the point of foolhardiness, as if to make up for an element of insecurity. He was the enemy within whose own weakness he had to overcome. As Brenda Chamberlain has observed, his "moods of black frustration [were] only to be expected from a writer forced into a life totally against his nature, yet it must be remembered, he had chosen to become an officer. He had been withdrawn, was withdrawing himself, further and further from home." Certainly, the men thought him much too good for the army. He was a scholar and a writer, a "gentleman", kindly and understanding. As for his writing, it was considered "rather rum" by the Mess, "a harmless pastime, so long as it didn't interfere with his efficiency as an officer. It was generally hoped, however, that India would knock all that nonsense out of him." If he had to be in the army at all, the squaddies thought he should have been in welfare or education, not in an infantry unit. He could be an effective soldier but he lacked what Paul Scott has called "the mark of the warrior". Soon after joining the Borderers, he took a church parade in a pretty church down a country lane and read the lesson. The men had never heard anything so beautiful.

When he joined the Borderers, they were stationed in and around Woodbridge, eight miles outside Ipswich on the Lowestoft road. He himself lived in Martlesham, a few miles south, with a family of mild religious mania, "people who seem nice and clean and a bit queer — all sorts of Egyptian tapestries and bric-a-brac, lavender bags and incense burning — or possibly the stuff they burn for asthmatics." His men were billeted in two empty houses across the street. He had to travel to Mess every day at Stratton Lodge, a country house in the centre of Woodbridge which served as battalion H.Q. Gweno visited him at Christmas but her time with him was cut short by a fortnight spent baby-sitting for her sister-in-law in Aberystwyth.

At Martlesham, he made friends with a consultant ophthalmic optician and his wife, Kemble and Greta Williams. Together, they would discuss politics, eighteenth century rabbit snares, poems and paintings. The Williamses lived in a bungalow near camp with their little daughter and he found his refuge with them there. As they talked, they would draw up plans for a future in which everyone would work in "new, equal endeavour" to free the country from "the old ways and old prejudices and old moneybags . . . Churchill could do it tomorrow, but he won't. Tommy Atkins and Dai Jones pay the penalty".

The story which best reflects Alun's experience of this time is 'Private Jones', written during a ten-day leave in February, 1942. It tells of Siencyn (pronounced Shen'kin) Jones, a simple-minded, good-hearted man from Cardiganshire who learns how to survive in the army. The story was designed to celebrate "the ability of the ordinary soldier to resist the depersonalising of the self the army aimed to achieve". The hero is a mask of the author, one described to Brenda Chamberlain and John Petts thus: "I feel very out of it all here, a diffident and nameless subaltern whom nobody notices or at least looks at twice . . . I'm among the enemy — and my soft ways of thought and speech are scorned." The mask was borrowed again for battalion concerts in India in which he would give turns as Shenkin in 'Private Jones'. The point of identification lay in Siencyn's passivity, his ability to feel in "a pernicious fascist system" which no longer requires feeling, his cheerful, accident-prone, endearing goodness. The story is a warmly sentimental farewell to the pastoral world of Alun's imagination, just as 'The Mountain over Aberdare' was his farewell to the valleys. Siencyn can "just imagine himself going abroad"; as for coming back again, "he couldn't see that at all". The army has him in its grip.

"My main task now is to purify and concentrate my writing and thought," Alun told Renée and Bryan Hopkin, "— and it is not easy nor simple to solve, but it leads me down many restless and unprofitable roads. It let me into the Infantry to begin with, and now God knows how I'll get along. It's certainly the Army at its harshest — except in actual battle . . . I've got a lot to learn, and a lot of it consists in knowing how to assert myself against the many obduracies among which I live." The notion that he had joined the infantry in order to "purify and concentrate" his writing is an interesting one. 'Private Jones' gives a deceptively simple demonstration of how, in human terms, he sought to assert himself in a world "where selfish men can bully and manoeuvre to their heart's contents for their *own* purposes", where there were "these continual petty litigations springing from bad temper and jealousy and animosity" and where the "big shots were about as humane as petrified Nazis".

Part of Alun's time was spent guarding the R.A.F. Radar Station at Bawdsey Quay, a promontory just across the river Deben. He found it "a queer isolated life among mists and frost and flat marshes, wrecks and Martello Towers and German raiders and tall radio masts". From it emerged the poem 'Dawn on the East Coast', one of his best since leaving Longmoor. It breathes the atmosphere of the "strange, attractive, lonely place, this flat ending of England".

> From Orford Ness to Shingle Street
> The grey disturbance spreads
> Washing the icy seas on Deben Head.
>
> Cock pheasants scratch the frozen fields,
> Gulls lift thin horny legs and step
> Fastidiously among the rusted mines.
>
> The soldier leaning on the sandbagged wall
> Hears in the combers' curling rush and crash
> His single self-centred monotonous wish;
>
> And time is a froth of such transparency
> His frowning eyes see what they wish to see;
> A girl laying his table with a white cloth.

Verse of considerable beauty, sensitive and shapely, formal but without regularity. The dying soldier sees the life he might have had, the table cloth picturing both the domestic simplicity he yearns for and the cerements being prepared for him by the crone who lurks in the figure of the girl, muse-like.

Throughout the winter, positions were prepared against an invasion and constant night patrolling maintained. Alun acted as battalion Education Officer, Welfare Officer and Entertainments Officer, buying food for the Mess and cookhouse and boots for the men. He had to supervise the digging of trenches and erection of miles of barbed wire obstacles round aerodromes as well as laying mines on the fields along the coast. At night, he read a little (Rilke, again, this time the *Elegies*, which he had asked Gweno to give him at Christmas), and tried to think a bit "in my dreamy way". By now, the third and fourth broadsheets were nearing publication and, though costs had begun to mount alarmingly, they sold reasonably well. Harri Webb remembers seeing one of them, "a tattered, treasured possession in an otherwise very ordinary working class home where it obviously meant something precious outside of daily experience".

Raiders' Dawn was published in March, 1942. To Alun's disappointment, it was in paper covers in a cheap edition of 3/6d, which he feared would deter the reviewers. He needn't have worried; the reception was almost uniformly favourable. The edition went through three impressions before the end of the summer, selling nearly 2,500 copies that year alone. Robert Graves liked it, remarking the "strong poetic thread going through the book", though he had reservations about its "disturbing sensuality". (Alun thanked him at least for not labelling him a "war poet".) *The Listener*'s reviewer said, "Mr Lewis speaks words and they sing. It is not easy to guess the full extent of his resources, but he certainly stands out already as the most assured and direct poet of his generation". (R. N. Curry drew attention many years later to this same quality, remarking the "dignified epigrammatic brevity that shines out from so many of his poems", like the description of soldiers as "little men grown huge with death" or Gweno as a "singing rib within my dreaming side" — "these are phrases that sing themselves into our memories".) *The Dublin Magazine* noted his "deep masculine tenderness, a tenderness which, even when it is evoked by a reckless comrade or by the one beloved woman, has always the quality of universal pity". *The Times Literary Supplement* declared, "Mr Lewis has the tragic vision. It is that which gives to his verse its darkest and deepest notes, and also its preternatural radiance . . . Death haunts his verse, and not always with the hope of resurrection". It is an acute observation. Only Cyril Connolly, of all people, struck a false note when he wrote in his *Observer* review of Alun as "a young Welsh officer" with a "warm heart and a love of humanity" whose poems needed "more thought and discipline, and are too sentimental, but they are poems everyone can enjoy". In *The Poetry Review*, Alan Rook wrote, "Anyone who wishes to know how one poet has felt during this war should read these poems . . . Here is no hero, defending the shores of English against the slavery of barbarians. We see only a young man intent on performing an act which circumstances have rendered necessary, and who, meanwhile, finds waiting dull".

Raiders' Dawn and Other Poems (to give the book its full title) was so named at Philip Unwin's suggestion. The full title appears on the title page but not on the cover and has been abbreviated over the years to *Raiders' Dawn*. Alun tried to chasten the diction of the poems when revising them for publication and provided a note explaining their scope and purpose. In the third poem of 'War Wedding', for example, the second line originally read, "She will not seize the cleft stick of my scream". In his 'Author's Note', he declared:

> Practically all these poems have been written since September, 1939; two-thirds of them have been written on active service; they are not, therefore, a completed statement; but a soldier sees with his own eyes and nobody else's; and they are, therefore, a personal statement. They are not intended to be more than that.

A clear apology: since no "completed statement" was yet possible, a "person statement" might be allowed, hinting at the wider issues. "completed", Alun told Christopher Cheney, "means the fulfilment of 'personal': as 'particular', when multiplied, becomes 'general'. Personal implies ignorance of much that I should know before making any statement upon the world." The reservation was as wise as it was modest, for he knew that the Longmoor poems foreshadowed more than he could presently say.

At the end of the Note came some acknowledgements, including "one to my parents and one to my wife" (originally "one to my mother and one to my wife") and a Prologue, a poem called 'The Grinder'. The book carried on its cover the engraving by John Petts. It was Alun who first suggested using it. "I feel it makes the whole thing rather Rupert Brooke-ish, which may or may not be a good thing from the commercial point of view". Philip Unwin jumped at the idea. "Rupert Brookeish it may be but I wouldn't at all mind your becoming in your own particular way the Rupert Brooke of this war." Alun was obviously inviting a comparison which the engraving emphasises, one that turns on the presence (or promise) of death to the young. The theme is announced at once by the opening poem and deepened by the next, 'All day it has rained . . .', where Edward Thomas replaces Brooke as the type-poet meditating on "Death and Beauty". (We notice how often children appear in these opening poems as innocents while lovers suggest the "holy mystery" of boy and girl together, "Eternity's masters, the slaves of time" ['Raiders' Dawn'].)

The first section of *Raiders' Dawn* is subtitled 'Poems in Khaki' and is followed by 'Poems in Love', all of them save 'War Wedding' dating from before 1940 and marked by acute sexual frustration. The third section, 'Songs', gathers together six occasional poems, mostly prosodically regular, dating from before the war, while the fourth, 'On Old Themes', includes two early poems, 'The Captivity' and 'Poems from the Chinese'. 'The Odyssey', a Longmoor addition, recalls 'From a Play' in the first section (the play in question being Aeschylus' *The Eumenides*) and also deals with soldiers, this time modern ones, meting out death to foreigners, though now there is "no returning". *The Dublin Magazine* reviewer, noting the connection between these two poems, said they expressed the poet's concept of war as "a state of benumbed exile from the goodness and sanity of normal living". The last section, entitled 'And Others', contains three South Wales poems, including 'The Mountain over Aberdare'.

If we analyse the contents of the book carefully, we find that they form an unusually coherent whole exploring various aspects of the theme of Death and Beauty. The pattern remains unobtrusive, the poems which propose it (the best ones) coming first. It is a deceptive achievement and unaccountably overlooked by many critics. A. Alvarez has said that, "with the exception of a few poets like F. T. Prince, Alun Lewis and Henry Reed, what was missing from the poetry of the 'forties was simply a voice, distinct, alive and humanly, reasonably speaking". Alun's was just such a voice, exploring and objectifying the fears of the age.

At the end of February, 1942, he was home on leave. The reverses in Singapore and Libya had intensified his own depression, half-apathetic, half-desperate — "like going down in a lift too long".

> I find it hardest to identify 2/Lt A Lewis with Alun Lewis, but it is a general symptom of the *Now* through which Britain is passing. My great hope is that this sadness and weakness is an adolescent rather than an aged disease, and contains its own remedy. But how *hard* it is, like a black stone.

Not even the news that Unwin was going ahead with a book of his short stories could alleviate his mood. "I feel that I haven't written the stories I want to write — that they are an interim effort — an X-ray of a process." To his parents he declared, ". . . I believe I'm a prose writer rather than a poet, and will write much more than poetry during my span".

In March, 1942, the Borderers moved to Orwell Park, a large eighteenth-century mansion fifteen miles south of Woodbridge on the banks of the river Orwell, halfway between Ipswich and Felixstowe. (Again, by chance, Edward FitzGerald's family had lived at Wherstead Lodge nearby.) The house was said to have the proverbial room for every day of the year and boasted ornamental gardens and grottoed walks on soft grey cliffs. The countryside was more attractive here, especially now that spring had arrived. Great brown sailing barges could be seen going up the "glittering" estuary to Ipswich docks. Even so, Alun could not care very much, trapped in the "botched, where-next improvised work" of the army and feeling less and less of an officer in heart and head. Gweno came up at Easter to stay at Nursery Cottage in Nacton, a small village nearby, in the middle of a wood in lovely pasture land. "Poor Gweno had to put up with a very preoccupied and rather worried Alun," he told his parents. "[I am] in rags and tatters with such friction and fret. Of course I used to fret in Pengam, and Manchester, and it's mostly the nature of the beast, as you know. But this life seems to intensify and isolate each tendency in me, instead of integrating it." To Gweno he confessed:

> . . . I want to know my job, which I don't: as I want my brain to get better, which it won't — it's as it was in 1937 when I'd been crazy with death-love for two years and didn't live in any positive way and my brain was all barbed wire. . . . It's odd having to curse myself day after day for not being able to remember facts or to do things to machine guns with my hands, or conduct range firing in the proper way etc, etc. Lack of experience, deary. And not being "fly" to people in the quick bird-like way of the world. But I was quite wrong when I said I'd become as tough as nails all round. So I suppose there's a long troubled time ahead, through which I must make my way as best as I can.

As at Manchester, his existence had become a death-in- life, haunted by the assailant within who sought to smother him.

> I feel an awful lack of spiritual power, Gweno; a kind of negation of life in me that is like a verminous old blanket bidding me lie and sleep, sleep, sleep; and that is my enemy, my living Mr Death. He carries a hypodermic syringe with him and squeezes into my skull: and I am aware of nothingness. And nothing else.
>
> And you know of this in me, and have always known it: and I am telling you of it again because it might hurt you so much if you thought it was indifference on my part, not suffering. I cast about frantically for an answer, a way forward to the life road, to YOU. It's not Capricorn, darling, it's too quiet and resigned and dumb for him: it's just an inertia in me, a sick animal. And I'm not asking you to fret about it, as once I did, cruelly thrusting it on you also, for I'm growing to think it's a perpetual price on my head, like recurrent illnesses from the Tropics. . . . And it makes you feel so bleak, darling, too, I know. But we have to accept it; this little dose of death in our lives. Forgive me, Gweno.

To his self-contempt as an army man he now added self-contempt for his self-contempt, as though he were "a little subaltern still striving with his own weaknesses" and trying to achieve competence in a world he didn't care for. His sense of inauthenticity was crippling. He feared that, because he did not fit in, he would be siphoned off to the East before he had had any real training. He feared for his very stability, "my inside, my mind and nerve". Here was the atrophy and emptiness he dreaded, an engulfing sense of worthlessness, "morbidity and irritation and ungratefulness, and sometimes a profound despair . . . There are a thousand men here and all they do is a crude anguish to me." Only Gweno's love could save his "chancy nature", the "attenuated spasmodic Alun, a face at a window, coming and going".

Julian Maclaren-Ross, a writer, met him at about this time while serving in a neighbouring battalion. Alun was keen to talk to him because Maclaren-Ross had written some stories with an Indian setting and Alun believed the Borderers were bound for India. (As it happens, Maclaren-Ross had never been to India.) Maclaren-Ross thought him "extraordinarily shy", eyes set deep, the voice quick and with a markedly Welsh intonation. He has left the following record of him:

> . . . Lewis had to rush back in for his Sam Browne: 'I'm always forgetting the damn thing.' He walked along the street beside me buckling on the belt. My R.S.M. was passing on the other side of the parade. He gave Lewis an eyes-right and his stiff jerky salute, imitated behind his back through the battalion. Lewis attempted to return the salute and the belt fell to the ground. He stopped to retrieve it while the R.S.M. passed on stiffly disapproving in his rubber-soled shoes.
>
> 'I made a mess of that,' Lewis said ruefully, getting the Sam Browne round him at last. 'An R.S.M., too.'
>
> 'That's my R.S.M.,' I said. 'Used to be a milkman.'
>
> 'Nothing against him,' Lewis said. 'That's class-distinction.'
>
> I said: 'It's something against him when he uses his war-time authority to work off past grievances and an inferiority complex. He's more class-conscious than either of us. I bet you he votes Conservative.'
>
> Lewis couldn't see my point, although he admitted to having had some pretty bloody sergeant-majors in his time.
>
> Comparing notes about the sergeant-majors brought us to the pub. This was jammed to the doors. It took ages to get a drink and then they'd only mild. We had to shout to make ourselves heard. Soldiers from Lewis's regiment kept on coming up to greet him and to offer him drinks. Eventually they shouted 'Time' and we left. Corporal

Dexter, hanging on the gate chatting with the curious woman who gave us haircuts, turned and saluted. This time Lewis managed to return the compliment without dropping his stick or his service-dress cap falling off. Dexter stared after him open-mouthed. Neither of us had the army knack of surface smartness, and by military standards we must have seemed, officer and private, a pretty scruffy pair.

'Did you ever put in for a commission?' Lewis asked me.

'Failed the W.O.S.B. test,' I told him. 'Returned unsuitable.'

'I'm not certain I shouldn't have stayed in the ranks,' Lewis said. 'I thought that as an officer I'd be able to do something for the men. But one's more helpless than ever.'

The sense of helplessness and the thought of the pamphlets that remained to be swotted-up in the small airless room, while the poems, the stories, stayed unwritten: these were the things that oppressed him. Had it not been for his wife, the idea of India — the jungle, the Japs, something doing at last — would have seemed a welcome opportunity: one that I myself, being without ties, certainly envied him . . .

We arrived at the door of the Mess and Lewis sighed — the pamphlets awaited him inexorably upstairs. He said: 'You must show me your stories too.'

As we were in the street I raised my hand to salute. Lewis said: 'For Christ's sake don't do that,' seized my hand and shook it. Then he doubled inside and I could hear him running up the stairs. But my R.S.M. had observed our parting handshake from the door of B.H.Q. where he was giving the Picquet Commander a dressing-down.

'Ah, Ross,' he said as I came up, showing in a crafty smile his greenish teeth under the clipped white moustache. 'Going up in the world, aren't you?'

'Sir?' I said.

'Consorting with officers. Who was that? Your brother?'

'A brother-writer, sir,' I said.

'Ah, that explains it; I thought something of the sort. I observed him putting on his Sam Browne belt in the street.' The R.S.M. shook his head. 'These civilians — writers and such-like — you can't make soldiers out of 'em.'

'Sir,' I said stiffly — I was standing to attention — 'I didn't know that it came within your province to comment on the dress of commissioned officers belonging to another regiment.'

The R.S.M. opened his mouth. He gasped, and looked round to make sure the Picquet Commander was out of hearing. His eyes narrowed but he knew I had him knackered, as the saying goes. He said: 'One of these fine days you'll go a bit too far, Private Ross, and I'm warning you.'

'Yes, sir,' I said, and went on upstairs to my office. I had meant to write a short story that evening, but I sat down and read Lewis's instead. I started with *Private Jones* and ended with *The Prisoners*.

This is not a work of literary criticism and the stories have now all been published and can speak for themselves. I will say only this: that after reading them, the army stories which I myself was trying to write seemed by contrast a joke in rather bad taste. This feeling had worn off by the next morning, but I went to bed profoundly dissatisfied with myself and my work.

I sent the stories back to Lewis next day by an orderly who happened to be taking a message to the Welsh H.Q. He returned with an odd story. He had accosted a fatigue party who were coal-heaving outside — why, at that time of year, I can't imagine. He asked where Mr. Lewis could be found. One of the fatigue party, in shirt-sleeves and covered with coal dust, had turned and said: "Here I am." This had so shaken the orderly that he'd delivered the packet of MSS without remembering to salute. I don't suppose that Lewis minded . . .

I saw him several times after that. We ate steak and chips together in a café along the sea front, full of snobbish Wrens talking at the tops of their voices about the R.A.F. officers who'd taken them out. I didn't show Lewis any of my stories except one which again dealt with sex, and part of a novel that I was writing. I think that to a great extent he disapproved of what I wrote. I remember him speaking once of the enormous responsibility which a writer should feel towards his characters having once called them into being. He spoke of this almost with awe. [Maclaren-Ross recalls Alun telling him that he would not be mentioning one of his stories in a review he was writing because "it's about sex" and it showed a somewhat sophisticated attitude to it.]

I do not think that in civilian life we could have been friends. We were too different. Where he was genuinely humble and modest, I am arrogant and didactic. Where he felt sympathy and love, I feel anger and contempt. I have only a film-gangster's kindness towards small things — animals, children — Lewis had a deep tenderness towards life itself: a nostalgic yearning for his Welsh village, his wife, whereas I have no roots and regard family life with fascinated horror. That doesn't mean to say I am ascribing all the virtues to Lewis, to myself all the faults. I don't necessarily consider them faults or virtues in either case. We were simply of different temperaments: even our aims as writers were violently opposed. But in the army, where the strangest friendships are struck up, it was natural for us to draw together and to talk of intimate ambitions which in civvy street — in a Soho pub or the Café Royal — we might never have discussed.

The friendship of the two men excited much comment in their respective regiments since they were of different rank. Alun was carpeted by his O.C. but the affair blew over when the Borderers moved to Felixstowe in April. With the passing of the danger of invasion, they reverted to normal training and Alun was sent to one of the new battle schools which had been established at Aldeburgh some thirty miles up the coast. He described the experience in an article published in *The New Statesman* in July, 1942.

> [W]e are crawling along a drain with Bren guns pumping live rounds at any part we expose . . . In the afternoon we do Hate (1). Divided into sub-sections we stalk each other in the scrub. Instructors fire live over our heads and yell their slogans at us. Remember Hong-Kong. Remember Singapore. Get him before he gets you. It might be your sister. Bang. Rat-tat-tat. Woomph. Guts. Guts. On. On. On. Sweat saves blood. Kill. Kill. The little yellow bastard's after you.

Hate (2) was a lecture in the Mess, but it was soon dropped in favour of the newer, more direct infantry tactics, firing tommy guns in a house specially prepared for the purpose with dummy figures and blood from animal entrails. In the thick of things again and having to behave rationally rather than by form, he responded with something like enthusiasm.

Aldeburgh allowed time off for visits to London. He went there without Gweno, who was looking after her sister, Eiluned, recently returned from India not knowing that her husband had been captured by the Japanese in Malaya during her passage. In London, he met some old friends, like Marjorie Walters (now engaged) and some new ones, like Aneurin Bevan, then editor of *Tribune*. Bevan had been recently appointed, with George Strauss, to take control of the paper and had opened its columns to a variety of writers. He published a number of pieces by Alun, including a review of *The Fortune Anthology* in which he complained of "the dead hand of the living Auden, who has educated *and* destroyed so many . . . young writers".

Alun liked Bevan greatly — "a very straight person" — and agreed with his views "most of the way", though he believed he was too isolated politically. "He has no organisation — just his paper and his voice." They talked "just as if we were sitting on the stile over Aberdare, or in a back lane on our bottoms!" At the *Tribune* offices, he met Charles Hamblett, a journalist, through whom he contributed a number of poems to a booklet published by John Bayliss and others called *Call Wind to Witness* (subtitled a 'Quartet of Romantic Poets'). He then returned to Felixstowe to revise his stories, having just signed the contract for them with Philip Unwin. He had completed a number of new ones at Aldeburgh, "a real landslide", written in the front parlour of a postman's house specially hired for the purpose, but he didn't think much of them; the characters weren't objective enough. Maclaren-Ross told him they were the best he had ever done.

1. Cwmaman, looking down valley to the north east

2. Cwmaman, looking up valley to the south west

3. The Lewis family, 1924. From left to right: Mair, Gwladys, Laurie Phelps, Tom, Alun, with Huw and Glyn in the foreground

4. On holiday at Penbryn, 1932. From left to right: Alun, Gwladys, Glyn; Mair and Huw

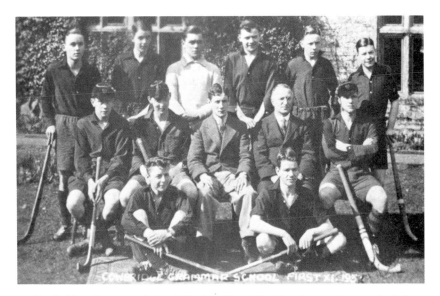

5. Cowbridge Grammar School Hockey First XI. Alun is standing on the left. The team included four Welsh internationals.

6. Aberystwyth Students' Representative Council. Alun is third from the right, back row. Chris Germanacos is on his left. Gweno Ellis is second from the left, third row, Dick Mills, seated fourth from the right.

7. Alun Lewis, 1938.

8. Alun Lewis, 1942.

9. The Lewis family, November 1941. From left to right: Mair, Alun, Huw Tom, Glyn; Gweno, Gwladys, family friend.

10. 158th Regiment, R.A.C., The South Wales Borderers. Alun is second from the left, back row. Those mentioned in the text include, in the back row, Teddy Coles (extreme left), Jack Gush (fifth from left), Dai Martin Morgan (fourth from right). In the middle row: Cliff Vivian (fourth from left), David Drummond (third from right), Alan Gwynne Jones (second from right). In the front row: Major Crewe-Read (third from left), Major Moon (fourth from left), Lt Col Popham (fifth from left), Major Cresswell (fourth from right), Major Evans (third from right), Tony Lewis (second from right).

11. With Jack Gush, Poona Hospital, February 1943. The hospital provides the setting for the story 'Ward 'O' 3(b)'.

12. With Jack Gush, Poona rifle ranges, April 1943.

13. Freda Aykroyd.

Wood Engraving : Debris Searcher.   John Petts.

TWO POEMS *by Alun Lewis*

RAIDERS' DAWN.

Softly the civilised
Centuries fall,
Paper on paper,
Peter on Paul.

And lovers waking
From the night—
Eternity's masters,
Slaves of Time—
Recognise only
The drifting white
Fall of small faces
In pits of lime.

Blue necklace left
On a charred chair
Tells that Beauty
Was startled there.

SONG OF INNOCENCE.

Pyrotechnic shells
From the blackened fair
Break like meteors
In the careless air.

Dancing girls and singing birds,
Poets' and crooners' platitudes
Violently die.

But the simple words
Spoken in shelters, crypts
    and wards
Where the disfigured lie

Are swans in the sky.

Published by the Caseg Press, Llanllechid Caernarvonshire
and printed at the Gomerian Press, Llandyssul, S. Wales.

'Acting-Captain', the longest story he wrote, is an ambitious attempt to present a wide cross-section of soldiers, including the battalion clerk, Curly Norris, a Lewisian alter-ego: "a perpetual student, introspective, individualist, an antinomian with a deep respect for the privacy of others. His gently and slightly neurotic liberalism took the edge off his revolutionary conviction. He lacked the strength to deny what is powerful in men, and he had no heart for extreme action. So he always preferred to be left in peace, to think and observe; his conflicts were within him. He had his own anguish." A better self-portrait it would be difficult to find. His O.C. tells him, "You haven't got enough *push*, Norris. That's what's wrong with you. Too soft-hearted, not enough keenness. You don't go for things as if you wanted them." Norris doesn't disagree; "the conflict smashed itself up inside him like two contrary tides, and he said nothing because the intensity of his feelings made him impotent".

In 'The Children', a soldier on sentry duty dreams of death and love, the familiar Longmoor preoccupations; he recalls "the first ignorant longing when his sex sang unsatisfied in him, and love was a brutal imperative in his blood. And she withheld herself, leaving him sucked-out and vapid". Now his sweetheart is with child: "She had come to him . . . and helped him, begging him to help her. In the darkness of tossed sheets and heated bodies, blind with nakedness and desperate with failure, . . . she guided and loved him out of his hell." A moment later, he is killed by a grenade. The question is once again posed: "What survives?" and back the answer comes, "The spirit".

'Cold Spell' (the title plays on the time of year and the disposition of its heroine) recounts an affair between Gracie, a N.A.A.F.I. girl, and an unnamed R.A.F. flight sergeant.

> Somewhere in the part of a person that melts and flows and overwhelms there was a lump of ice in her that wouldn't melt, you see, just wouldn't; she had to stop, and go back, shamefully, because she never went far enough to realise herself.

In the summer, they lie out of doors; in the winter, they go to a cottage in the pinewoods where the landlady (modelled on Alun and Gweno's landlady at Nacton, Queenie Howard) loans them her parlour. When they make love, the

> pain and panic of that hour broke the dream in her. She had wanted to please him . . . But there was no pleasure in it, no love even; it was the ice in her, that which even then would not melt, a lump of ice blocking the stream.

In time, Gracie reconciles herself to the devil-may-care quality of her lover's existence and he, in turn, decides to settle down and marry her. The fact that Gracie is dressed as Gweno was at the time of their marriage suggests that Alun was offering an explanation of his own impulsive behaviour on that occasion.

In April, the 6th Battalion, the South Wales Borderers was converted to tanks and a team of psychiatrists decended on the men to test their intelligence and aptitudes. Alun was sent to the Driving and Maintenance wing of the Royal Armoured Corps' Fighting Vehicles School at Bovington, in Dorset, to learn engine mechanics and radio telegraphy; the battalion moved to Upminster, a village outside Romford: "oddly, it's another place where Edward Thomas lived and wrote about," he observed. He arrived at Bovington on 4 June and, despite a shaky start, soon settled down. Once more, he was being trained in particular skills and once more he responded to the challenge. There were no parades for him so he had more time to read, including Nehru and Forster's *A Passage to India*. Living conditions were pleasant and the hours regular. Being near South Wales, he could meet Gweno almost every weekend at Bradford-on-Avon or Westbury or Bath (as on the anniversary of their wedding), though she found it defeating having to get into the frame of mind of a "married woman" and endure the miseries of parting. Nevertheless, her visits had an enlivening effect on him and his letters to her show how much his love for her had developed since his early days at Longmoor.

There was another side to his mood, during this summer however and it turns on a further strange coincidence of a literary character. The countryside round Bovington was a little like Penbryn and he moved about it lightheartedly in an open truck, visiting Lulworth Cove, Weymouth and Dorchester (in homage to Hardy) and Clouds Hill (in homage to T. E. Lawrence). The visit to Clouds Hill, Lawrence's home near Bovington, produced one of his finest stories, 'Dusty Hermitage' (added to *The Last Inspection* only after galley-proof stage). He told Lynette Roberts about it: "I'm growing more and more into a mere short story writer, Lynette. I *love* it, just *love* it. I get all the feeling of poetry, with something less miraculous and more credible in the act of writing. I can never believe I write *poetry*. I can draw comfort and power from knowing that I can write short stories." This has been taken to imply that he thought of himself as a prose writer, though it is obviously couched in ambivalent terms and was in any case inspired by the enthusiasm inspired in him by a particular short story. He always valued the sense of achievement story-writing gave him but never confused it with the greater (if less frequent) achievement of poetry. As it happens, the distinction between the two is not a fast one, as 'Dusty Hermitage' itself demonstrates, being closer in spirit to a fable than a tale and with a resonance that is almost entirely personal.

A soldier visits Clouds Hill on the anniversary of Lawrence's death. The cottage is kept by woman who treats it as a shrine. The only other visitors are a philistine middle-aged couple (rather too patly done) who fail to understand how unhappy Lawrence had been in the Tank Corps, where he served for two years, threatening to commit suicide unless he were allowed to return to the R.A.F.. Clouds Hill, set amidst twenty-nine miles of broken heath in a river valley filled with rhododendrons, was his sanctuary, "a kind of boy's hide-out with makeshift sleeping and cooking arrangements; a cottage imitating a tent" — a perfect nomad's place, just the sort of habitation the soldier of 'Lance-Jack' could appreciate, "casual, rough, hazardous and incomplete". There were no beds, just two sleeping bags labelled "Meum" and "Tuum" ("mine" and "yours", reminiscent of the fishing lugger Edward FitzGerald and Joseph Fletcher kept at Lowestoft, the *Meum and Tuum*). What Edward Thomas's poems signified at Longmoor, Lawrence's cottage signified here, "a *private* atmosphere . . . not happy, but private and silent", what E. M. Forster called "a happy casualness, . . . the feeling that no one particularly owned" the house. Over the front door were carved two words by Lawrence: "ou phrontis", "I don't care", in the sense of carefree, relaxed. It was a resting place. "Clouds Hill isn't so much a house as a point where T.E.'s feet tarried for a little on their all too swift passage through this world," Forster wrote. When the housekeeper turns to meet the soldier, "she knew she had seen his face before".

They go up to the music room and discuss Lawrence's work. She says Lawrence always disliked it because it was "never innocent":

> 'He was an artist,' the soldier said slowly, looking through the window into the dusty thicket of rhododendrons. 'But an artist who couldn't commit himself to his choice.'
> 'How do you mean?' she asked, swinging the door to again soundlessly.
> 'Well, the artist has the best chance of pursuing the good,' he said, 'because as an artist he has no vested interests in the warring elements. He is just so much an artist as he is disinterested. But that is

only his potential. His actual power depends on the vigour with which he pursues his choice once he has made it. He couldn't make a positive choice. That's why he was unfulfilled.'

'You have chosen?' she said, smiling a trifle ironically.

'In so far as one can,' he said, laughing a little and standing up. 'My trouble is —' and he laughed again, evading her without being evasive. That was a habit she had met before also. 'Oh well, we grow up by the time we die. One learns self-respect after learning to respect other things. It's just the order in which things happen that puts you all wrong.'

The argument comes to an abrupt end when the soldier realises he has only five minutes to get back to camp at four o'clock — the very moment of Lawrence's death (adjusted for the purposes of the story). Every year at this hour, the woman closes the windows of the cottage in tribute to him. The soldier hurries down the steps and makes for his motorbike. ("Something jumped inside her, like a dark fist"). He promises not to intrude again.

'Good-bye,' he said, waving his beret and smiling.

'Good-bye,' she waved back.

She followed him downstairs and watched him set the controls of his motor-bike.

Before the engine made speech impossible with its roar, she called out to him.

He turned his head towards her.

'Be careful on that motor-bike,' she said. 'The road is still oily where he was killed. The tanks cross it there. *Be Careful.*'

'Yes,' he said, laughing back, fresh and suddenly care-free. 'Good-bye.'

The engine roared at his kick. He revved her up, put her in gear, let the clutch out. He was gone with a whirl of dust.

She looked at her watch. It was 4 o'clock.

She knew she wouldn't see him again.

A sense of tension intermixed with happiness is wonderfully caught by these haunting, brief paragraphs. The details — one man's path crossing another's, a lurking death — suddenly set the direction yet there is an odd sense of exhilaration in the air. The housekeeper's loyalty has grown to embrace a man who is, to all intents and purposes, another version of her hero. She is

inexplicably happy despite her unreasoning agitation as the sound of the motor-bike died away. And quietly she turned back to the empty cottage to close the windows. Another such as he had come and gone.

She was remembering his last letters. 'I find myself wishing all the time my own curtain would fall . . . There is something broken . . . my

will, I think . . . As for fame after death, it's a thing to spit at; the only
minds worth winning are the warm ones about us. If we miss those
we are failures.' And how some evenings he watered the flowers.

[ellipses in the text]

And there the story ends.

The queer sense of laughter which pervades 'Dusty Hermitage'
arises from the identification between soldier and Lawrence, a sense
of destiny confirmed. Once more the question is asked, "What
survives?" and this time the answer is, "The warm ones about us",
those whom we work for with "the imagination alive with goodness".
Yet the commitment to them vies with the different obligations of the
artist. In 'Last Pages of a Long Journal', Alun had warned that writers
who climb the Jacob's ladder from the people into loneliness and
introspection have gone wrong; they must "come back to Tolstoi, to
the art which works through vast human sympathy, through the
community of human beings": "T.E. Lawrence would have gone into
[the wider] universe if he could have found the way in himself. He
could only do it negatively, unfortunately, by making his frustration
always the most significant experience of his life". Only by going into
life do we find self-perfection. That is why learning self-respect comes
after we have learnt to respect other things.

Alun's identification with Lawrence grew early, as we have seen,
and centres on the idea of a challenge to the spirit — out East, with
haversack, in trench, journeying far away on the soldier's dangerous
mission. One fights not as the army fights but as leader and
companion, one who "ate the rank's food, wore their clothes, lived
level with them, and yet appeared better in himself". From that grew
the dilemma both men faced as sensitive beings trained to kill.
Continually, Lawrence had to put aside his own problems to meet this
or that contingency and in the process so damaged himself (as Andrew
Rutherford contends) that he never recovered. He was torn between
will and instinct and sacrificed himself eventually to action.

There are other points of similarity between the two men.
Lawrence was born in Wales (in Tremadoc, in Caernarvonshire) and
showed an early interest in medieval cathedrals. He joined military
intelligence, despite his preference for the ranks both as man and
writer: "the best place to see a thing is from the ground. It wouldn't
'write' from the officer level." Like Alun, he saw in the army a
"stunted version" of a way of life opposed to bourgeois capitalism, an
idea of "comradeship and common effort", and, like him, trained at

Bovington for a while. Both had Robert Graves as a friend and both served in British India. Above all, both understood that, while it is not death so much as the affirmation of the self in the face of death that the soldier repeatedly has to make, it was an affirmation that neither knew how to make, being divided artist-soldiers. Ian Hamilton has written of the problem facing Alun:

> Commitment to one's art, to the solitary routes of the imagination, to the steady personal quest for a fulfilment that will transcend, although it may be occasioned by, 'the warring elements', or commitment of a practical, energetically loving kind to 'the warm ones about us'? It is the crucial conflict, and it is there in Lawrence's statement; the death-wish colliding oddly with the belief in 'minds worth winning'. Lewis could never finally accept that these pursuits need be distinct, or that a choice must be made between them, but he was often consumed by the failure of energy which can arise from their antagonism — and often enticed by thoughts of a death in which they might be absolutely reconciled.

It is this affirmation before death that 'Dusty Hermitage' makes, now more secure in possession of the knowledge first gleaned in the Longmoor poems.

At the end of July Alun travelled to Mountain Ash after his course had finished. Thinking about himself and Gweno, he told Lynette Roberts:

> I don't know whether we will create anything as real as children now. I'm due to sail in September and I don't feel keen on saddling Gweno with a child. If she decides finally she wants a baby I shall be very glad. But it's entirely her decision. I shan't even see her lose her slim waist myself.

That he did anticipate children is witnessed by the repeated imagery of unborn children and pregnancy in his work from at least the time of 'War Wedding'. It was to cause Gweno some embarrassment. Hollow and frozen himself, he had repeatedly been rescued from isolation and nothingness by her. It was what he valued her for most, her ability to free him from "the places of pain and sweat". "I was fast becoming something out of a Russian novel when you decided with some misgivings to try and make a man out of me," he told her later and recalled "that sad afternoon when the heavy warning of a breathless impending trial made everything so dark and confined".

> And you said just two words that I take with me now wherever I go and whatever tedium or agony or despair I find myself. And you have

> the power of love and of the beloved over me. You can make me
> believe in the words your thoughts put forth and make them an action
> and an experience in me, a motive and a faith . . . You saved me twice
> in the deepest and loneliest pitch of night. And brought me back and
> sustained me — and this is the most wonderful of all perhaps, you
> made me return that way again and so destroyed the failure that had
> so nearly destroyed us.

Nevertheless, he told Leslie Sykes that they hadn't succeeded in
creating a child; to Andrew Davies he confessed that they lacked "the
courage to beget". Repeatedly, however, he expected to receive good
news, but none came. Describing his embarkation leave with Gweno
soon afterwards to Dick Mills, he wrote, "Gweno hopes to have a
baby, but it went wrong, and we were very very sad about it, very very
very — ".

By this time, *The Last Inspection and Other Stories* was ready for
publication. It was named after the story Philip Unwin so admired,
though on this occasion the full title appears only on the dust jacket,
not the title page, and has been abbreviated to *The Last Inspection*. In
his author's note, Alun emphasised that the stories dealt with the "two
years' attente" since June, 1940:

> Death in battle, death on a large scale, and all the attendant finalities
> and terrors — these are outside. They are the bread and water of our
> comrades overseas; we have the cakes and ale . . . the main motif is the
> rootless life of soldiers having no enemy, and always, somehow,
> under a shadow.
> Written out of immediate experience, typed up on leave, impelled
> by a perpetual sense of urgency, they are rather personal
> observations than detached compositions . . .

The stories are personal in that they do not cover the full range of the
soldier's experience nor even the most important part of it yet they are
less personal than the poems in that they concern themselves with the
factual issues of the soldier's life. To Robert Graves he confided that
he was a "bit dubious" about them:

> but I think you'll not find the disturbingly sensual vein there that
> interfered with the poetry of the poems. They're all very objective,
> the stories; and I imagine you'll lay them aside for pointing too
> regularly the social moral. I'm becoming very left; and my prose is
> tinged.

The first part of the book contains studies of army life, the second
non-army wartime stories and the third army stories with a strong
civilian element, all playing on the theme of love. Some of the details

in the first section of 'It's a Long Way to Go' caused offence, being too near the real-life models, and were altered, as were some passages in 'Private Jones'. The book was eventually published in February, 1943 (despite the 1942 given on the reverse of the title-page) and received an even warmer welcome than *Raiders' Dawn*. It sold out within a month; by the end of the year it had sold 3,500 copies.

Of the reviews, two are worth mentioning, the first by C.F.S. in *Punch*:

> Mr Lewis is a poet . . . and it is therefore not surprising to find in his prose a paradoxical blending of the sensitive mind's revolt against the ugly, the sordid and the brutal side of war with a consciousness of the beauty and dignity of sacrifice . . . at his best (as in 'Private Jones' and 'They Came') he is very good indeed, his prose — a poet's prose — nervous, controlled and sincere.

The Tatler and Bystander offered a fuller, sensitive account of the contents. The reviewer was Elizabeth Bowen.

> The stories deal, mostly, with Army life during those months of tension, violent air raids and inactive alertness that, in 1940 England, followed the fall of France. In the camps, the soldiers chafe and wait, while, left behind in the cities, their women are being threatened and killed by bombs. Can one wonder that exasperation is the governing mood, and that homesickness and anxiety rack the men? In such a mood, ineptitudes on the part of their officers are not easily pardoned or lightly seen. Also, the soldiers are Welsh — without the Cockney philosophy, without the placidity of the rural Englishman. When the Welsh feel, it is not in a small way. Criticism of what war does to human life — and, worst of all, war before there has been fighting — is implicit in every line of *The Last Inspection*. Only two bright things stand out: the support the men give each other, and the inarticulate love between man and woman.

And it is these two themes that give the book its universality.

In August, Alun rejoined the Borderers — now renamed the 158th Regiment, Royal Armoured Corps (The South Wales Borderers) — in Southend. "When the tide is in, [it is] magnificent," he told Gweno, "all massed convoys and trawlers and coal barges lined across the huge flow and sweep of the estuary, and very pleasant little fishing villages, with queer beached craft and trees and an old grey church tower, along the line from London." He was in command of a reconnaissance squadron under his friend, Tony Lewis, instructing the men in wireless communications. Gweno came up for three weeks at the end of the month and stayed with him at Thorpe Bay. This was the period of their greatest contentment together, as he told her:

> . . . I love you utterly, You know it of course. Even in that most secret of places, your heart of hearts, you know that every scrap and drain and dreg of love there is in me, and every rag and tatter of good, is inextricably now bound into your love and your good, breathing the same air, with the same pulse, the same lungs. You've made me, Gweno, that's the simple truth. You've just made me. I've realised myself in you — not wholly yet, but you have begun the process and there is only the continuance through you. I will go into all the world, into other places and other people. While the world is imperfect, I will wander among its imperfections; but it is you who have fortified the ache in me to take goodness into the darkness. And it is never dark now, for you are there.

He repeated the idea when they went on embarkation leave to Cardiganshire shortly afterwards.

> But darling, we are not creatures of darkness. We have moved through our particular darkness two years ago. We are a real man and wife and have no fear of each other, no darkness . . . No one has ever spoken with such authentic faith to me or so convinced me by simplicity as you did, you know when.

They stayed in a boarding house near Llangranog, a mile or two from Penbryn. It rained most of the time. Together, they journeyed back to Yr Hendre, the farm they had visited in the summer of 1939, walking all the way from Cardigan. There, like Siencyn Jones, Alun said his farewells. In a poem written during his leave, 'On Embarkation', he described a child growing "shapely in the loins I love".

After Llangranog, he and Gweno travelled to Aberystwyth and then on to Aberdare. They parted at Cardiff station.

> [W]hen he laughs and bends to make
> Her laugh with him she sees that he must die
> Because his eyes declare it plain as day.
> And it is here, if anywhere, that words . . .
> Cast off the habitual cliches of fatigue
> — The woman hoping it will soon be over,
> The fat men saying it depends on Russia —
> And all are poets when they say Goodbye
> And what they say will live and fructify . . .
> And I — I pray my unborn tiny child
> Has five good senses and an earth as kind
> As the sweet breast of her who gives him milk
> And waves me down this first clandestine mile.
>
> ('On Embarkation')

Tender, truthful, poignant lines.

In his poem of farewell to Gweno, 'Goodbye', Alun wrote:

> So we must say Goodbye, my darling,
> And go, as lovers go, for ever;
> To-night remains, to pack and fix on labels
> And make an end of lying down together . . .
>
> Everything we renounce except our selves;
> Selfishness is the last to go;
> Our sights are exhalations of the earth,
> Our footprints leave a track across the snow . . .
>
> Yet when all's done you'll keep the emerald
> I placed upon your finger in the street;
> And I will keep the patches that you sewed
> On my old battledress tonight, my sweet.

A threadbare simplicity in the service of true feeling.

To his parents, he wrote:

> Also be *ye* tranquil, specially Gwladys Elizabeth. I know I will get
> through the next and worst years of my life if I keep a cool head and a
> disciplined body and mind. And I am determined to do so. I am
> helped by being with so many other men who are going through the
> same crisis. And I won't falter or fail. That is why I could say
> goodbye to you with such lightness. For however long and arduous
> this passage, there is nothing final in my goings. I have always known
> I had some such journey and separation ahead of me, *always*. So let's
> all take it in our sweet stride.

The theme of the journey is here fulfilled.

"Everything is running zerowards," he told Gweno on his return to
Southend. Embarkation was delayed several times, so she was able to
punctuate the "miserable interim" by visiting him in Southend or
London. There was even a mad dash by him to Cardiff after she had
had to cancel a weekend in London through illness. He arranged that
they should meet in a hotel but she felt unwell and had to cry off,
heartbroken. Unaware of this, he arrived at 3.30 in the morning and
toured all the hotels in the city knocking up the porters in his search
for her. Eventually, he caught the 5.45 a.m. bus to Mountain Ash and
arrived whistling 'Cherry Ripe' (their signature tune) through the
letter box. A quick bath and breakfast and he was gone. He left behind
a secret code to keep her informed of his movements.

As Regimental Baggage Officer, he was thrown into a final flurry of
activity fitting six hundred men with shirts, studs and topees. The

battalion prepared to leave for Liverpool and there was a grand parade and march past. General Morgan Owen, Colonel of the Borderers, took the salute and surprised everyone by disclosing the battalion's eventual destination to the assembled viewers. It was a wet October dusk when they left and a wet dawn when they arrived. Alun sent Gweno a coded message at the Control Room at school where she was helping with air-raid precautions — "How's your liver?" — and she hurried home to pack a suitcase and catch the first train to Liverpool. The trams were so noisy that night they had little sleep. The next day they attended a concert and walked around the city.

Remarkably, on this, their last meeting, Gweno was revisited by the doubts she had felt about his love on Hengoed station three years before. Alun recalled the moment later:

> And I remember what you said that night in Liverpool — and I wasn't angry because it was like meeting an old friend, your *doubt*, that I used to meet so often once upon a time, but who ceased to live in our house till he suddenly on the last night poked his nose in at the door and grinned all over his face and went away.

The last morning, they rose to say goodbye at five o'clock; it was bitterly cold. Gweno felt like yelling her head off. Alun stood at the door of the dark bedroom and said, "Goodbye darling". She reached for a handkerchief only to discover it was covered in Alun's blood from a head cold. Later that day, the *Athlone Castle* set sail in convoy, destination India.

> Well, Gweno Mererid Lewis, this is the last of my daily letters, my dear. The distance will widen now between the solid and the fluid, and the magnetic attraction of the unknown will alter the position of the stars and the continents as we plod softly through the spaces of the globe. And all the time, because the world is round, I am coming back to you — and what seems a long way, Gweno, is not far to go.
> Wait for me. I'm coming.

XIII

Passage to India

One moment in Annihilation's Waste,
One moment, of the Well of Life to taste —
  The Stars are setting and the Caravan
Starts for the Dawn of Nothing — Oh, make haste.

Five thousand Borderers and men from the 9th Royal Sussex Regiment, together with six nurses, filled *The Athlone Castle* but though they were all in the same boat, they were by no means in the same cabin: "a svelte luxury liner, it reflected precisely the social system that constructed it," Alun observed. The officers shared the first-class accommodation, four to a cabin, with bathroom and spacious lounge; the sergeants were in the top deck, the other ranks in the lower ones, "the most incredible coal cwtches" (houses), the Borderers right at the bottom. The air was stale and there was hardly any room to stand; the hold had been hastily converted to hold bunks in layers of three with scarce a yard between the rows. Everything was soaked in condensation. The ventilation was by a single hatchway on the top deck via a canvas funnel. "Yet one man was court-martialled for saying that the officers had a bloody sight better time than the men."

Alun was Entertainments Officer and had his work cut out keeping the men amused with all manner of concerts, quizzes, parlour games, competitions and ship's broadcasts. "[H]ere on this ship in the middle of the ocean," he wrote, "thousands of men are being made to *think*." It was "a sort of incessant end-of-term concert" and his skill and energy won the admiration of even the most senior officers. Night after

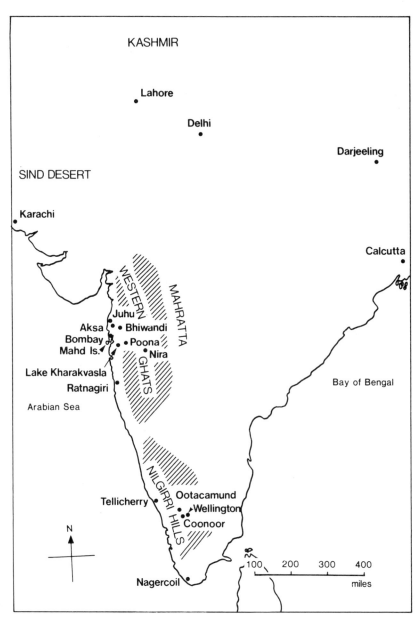

2. India, showing locations named in the text.

night, a small stage was rigged beneath the low ceiling among the tables and concerts were held, each show running until all the men had seen it. Alun himself played Thisbe in a performance of an extract from *A Midsummer Night's Dream* and addressed the Social Reconstruction Group on postwar education. He attended Hyde Park Corner weeklies, where men talked on subjects like "I accuse" or "I want to change this". One speaker made a particular impression on him, "little George", who had joined the army at sixteen after failing to emigrate to the colonies. He gave

> the loveliest talk I've ever heard, in his sing-song illiterate unaspirated Welsh voice, about the Jewish collective farms of Palestine which he'd seen when he was shooting Arabs out there. 'No one grows for money, they breeds beautiful 'orses and they got lovely orange groves an' the doctor don't ask for money for 'is services but you pays 'im with food or clothin' or whatever you do make. An' I never seen a 'appier people in my life and by God I wish I could a' stayed with them.' I felt the loveliest feelings while he spoke as if a little child were telling me some quaint and innocent story rich in human goodness and all the richer because it was so artless and unconscious.

Aboard ship, he told Gweno, he felt "none of that old nervous strain. Remember it in Hengoed?"

The *Athlone Castle* sailed around the north of Ireland and out into the Atlantic accompanied by a couple of destroyers. The men took to sleeping on deck at night, bringing their mattresses with them. Alun joined them though, as an officer, he was forbidden from doing so. The sound of a bingo game or hand of poker merged with the snores of early sleepers and the subdued rhythmic pounding of the engines and the swish of the sea. One night, they were disturbed by a siren; a dozen or so survivors from a torpedoed Norwegian merchant vessel had been sighted and were taken aboard by an escorting destroyer. The snores resumed.

During the day, there were boxing tournaments, Hindustani language classes and a Welsh choir, which Alun called "the 'success fou' of the trip". Some training continued in the limited space available — indeed, was so strictly maintained that there was talk of pushing Colonel Popham overboard. Once discipline was relaxed, however, there was always the difficulty of recovering it and the example of the somewhat more light-hearted Royal Sussex did not help. Yet there was a question of degree and Popham probably overdid it.

The *Athlone Castle* was bound for Freetown, in Sierra Leone, but because of the submarine threat from neighbouring Vichy French forces in Guinea it was diverted to Bahia, in Brazil, where it arrived on 15 November.

> [A]s we went in through a blue lagoon with a soft brown fortress at the harbour mouth, my glasses picked out people on the verandahs of windows, wakened from bed by our stentorian hoot, men, women, little children, all the intimacy and safety of family and bed and ordinariness. The ship slowly pulled and pushed herself into position and while the black dockers and green uniformed police and blue clothed customs officials and yellow fire brigade men fought each other for pennies and cigarettes and sold bananas and green oranges by putting them in berets lowered on lines, on the sea side men in bathing trunks rowed past in swift outrigger canoes and white square rigged yachts.

A stand-pipe and fire hydrant were all that could be mustered to fill the tanks of the ten ships with water and it took them all of four days to do so. The men tried out their tropical kit — Wolsey helmets, long shorts, voluminous drill — and marched through the town. The Bahians were wary at first but soon broke out into cheering and dancing. Brazil had only recently joined the war against Germany, though not Japan (Japanese ships were moored alongside the *Athlone Castle*), and the Borderers were the first Allied troops to land there.

To men inured to weeks of monotony and discomfort aboard ship, not to mention years of blackout at home, the colour of Bahia made the greatest impression. Houses and roofs were painted in brilliant clashing tones. The spectacle was all the greater for being viewed from aboard ship. Bahia is built above a port on the slopes of a hill which falls down steeply to cliffs, the two levels being joined by a funicular; it forms a natural theatre. Closer inspection might reveal a grimmer reality — the doors of the hovels crowded with naked babies with huge bellies and "navels like eyes" — but that was soon forgotten as various ages jostled in the streets, the men in white slacks, the women in coloured frocks. The churches, topped with onion-domes, flashed their silver and white livery; soldiers marched by in chocolate-brown uniforms, gold-braid glinting in the sun; purple bougainvillaea grew everywhere. "It's marvellous to see such a mixture of race and colour as in this melting-pot," Alun observed.

The next port of call, Durban, in South Africa, made a different impression. It was reached on 4 December after a diversion four hundred miles south of Cape Town to pick up survivors from a British freighter sunk within sight of Table Mountain. The water taken on in Bahia plagued them with diarrhoea and the toilets were besieged, barely withstanding the strain; the flushing system failed, basins overflowed, the floors were covered with water. Up above, though, there was "still tea at four, gin and bitters, before dinner, bridge and deck tennis at all hours, tittle tattle sans cesse". Leaning over the rails with his new moustache recently removed, Alun found two lines forming in his head: "The moon in her gentleness/ Meekly companions us . . ." He sent the rough draft of the poem to Gweno. "Do you see how a poem is made — or fails? By perpetually trying, by closer and closer failing, by seeking and not finding, *and still seeking*, by a robustness in the core of sadness. What else is there by which we can live now . . . ?" He meant the determination to fight in tragic times, but the tone is somewhat different from his usual pronouncements on the subject. It is as if the moon (with its intimations of the goddess) had become the only thing to live by.

In 'Song' ("The first month of his absence"), a poem inspired by the sight of dead bodies floating off the Cape, the beloved declares herself barren (". . . where he'd left his promise/ Life did not turn or kick/ The seed, the seed of love was sick.") She surrenders to her worst fears:

> All this slowness, all this hardness,
> The nearness that is waiting in my bed,
> The gradual self-effacement of the dead.

Gweno's anxieties about Alun were indeed intense and he repeatedly sought to comfort her. The poems written on board ship have a greater formality as they warn her "NOT to withdraw into the hard core of waiting and lacking, but to project herself — to all waking and surprising sights, all sadness and relaxities, all cruelties . . . I want her to accept death as one of the implications of the projection and profusion of Self, a knot in the series of casualties". He felt confident in his mission and confident at last, thanks to the seclusion of the ship, "that I'm going to be a poet after all". He had always believed, as Ian Hamilton has said, that the suffering world "could be altered into harmony if 'you put it to them decently' " and was sustained by "his continuous sense of a hidden mysterious outcome to what has all along been a destined voyage".

Durban struck him as a large city of "skyscraper flats and pseudo-American stores, degraded knick-knack shops, plenty of cinemas and hotels, and integral with this conscious Western mode a bastard kind of native life". Black schoolchildren spent all night cleaning the ships' oil-tanks for nine shillings a time. Out on a drive in the countryside, he was convinced that what he saw spelled trouble.

> I don't agree with those of my friends who say they'd like to settle in South Africa after the war. I think it's got savager problems to settle than Europe has, and I doubt whether they're heading towards a solution. You can't educate and suppress a people at the same time — if you do you repeat the battle for India.

The five days they had planned to spend in Durban became two when the *Athlone Castle* and *Stirling Castle* detached themselves from the convoy and sailed full steam for Bombay. They arrived there on December 17th. On board ship, Alun wrote:

> I don't know whether to dive in or stay on the bank and concern myself with tanks only. At least I considered both courses, but the insatiable humanist and the restless writer in me will probably impel me to abandon neutrality and seek in India as in England the true story and the proper ending . . . my final task is to forget all I've talked and thought, to forget all the opinions of others . . . and just observe lucidly with my two simple eyes what I see happening there then. Of course it's almost impossible — but I shall do my best. I'm not going to land there full of violent opinions and passionate beliefs about the destinies of nations. Why should I? I'm only a subaltern, for one thing. And I'm a poet for another thing. Both demand a certain humility and a willingness to start anew.

Just before disembarkation, he fell ill with food poisoning and in a dream saw himself with Gweno in Wales. He had just died and she had become a blonde, lavishly dressed, be-jewelled and unobtainable.

> I realised the significance of that dream before I got out of bed. It came seeping uncomfortably into my understanding, *that I had gone back there in the only way possible, the spiritual way*, having passed first through the spiritual experience of death.

Turning to his familiar Rilke, "I asked him about *silence*, and what price one paid for going my way — through the panzer divisions of the century — and whether he would have found his silence there". The "silence" is the serenity of achieved being, with hints of an eternal rest, like the peace he and Gweno had achieved "but in Oh a distant land". He now started to write a poem called 'To Rilke' in which he recorded his belief that "unknown lands" were near "like an act of birth". Rilke — the "Santa Claus of loneliness", as Auden called him

— had taught him that the way to oneness in life lies in the acceptance of death or, rather, the "spiritual experience of death". In a review in *Poetry (London)* (which Alun may have read), Lawrence Durrell wrote:

> Poetry is a man's death coming alive in him. The poem is an incubator in which the spirit can kill itself off in order to gain a kind of eternity in time, in the rhythm of duration. They say that when Rilke was dying, and the doctors wanted to give him morphia to help him away, he would not let them do so. '*Because*,' he said, "I want to feel my death *ripening inside me.*' He had already conquered Death by making it personal, by expropriating it while he lived.
>
> '*In the Elegies*,' he had written to his Polish translator, '*affirmation of life AND affirmation of death reveal themselves as one. To concede the one without the other is, as is here celebrated and experienced, a restriction that excludes all infinity. Death is our reverted, our unilluminated, side of life: we must try to achieve the greatest possible consciousness of our existence, which is . . . inexhaustibly nourished out of both . . .*'
>
> (ellipses in text)

The notion of death as an integral part of life, something that enhances the value of life, came more easily to one who was not a Christian. Without it, Alun would always have been beset by fear. It was a steadying thought — and an act of preparation.

The battalion travelled by train from Bombay to Poona and then by truck to Nira, a small village some fifty miles away up in the great ghat of western India. A freak storm broke out and the transfer of baggage from one gauge railway to another and on to trucks had to take place in torrential rain and pitch darkness. Alun lived at the station for two days and was drenched and shivering. The road to camp became hopelessly flooded, the trucks bogged down in the mud, bullocks were swept away, squadron lines washed out and tents felled.

The next day, a different Nira presented itself, hot, dry and dirty. A few low trees dotted the hillocks around. It was like being put down in a vast bowl of desert. The sun fell hard as iron on the purple blue mountains, on the ramshackle villages with deep circular wells and on the green fields around the camp.

> A few grasshoppers intermittently chirping, three mules and a white turbanned villager drawing water from the nullah across the fields to irrigate the green sugar and millet crops that enclose the pauper native village in a green girdle, great heavy kites wheeling around in search of food, and I, sitting in the shade of my tent . . .

During the day, the heat was so intense that the men could scarcely touch the tanks to carry out maintenance work. Centipedes, snakes and scorpions abounded. A whole regiment of women and children had to be employed to keep the dust down. For recreation, Alun walked about the hills and dry, sandy river beds and along the canal, where he went swimming. He watched goatherds and children with "eyes like paraffin" begging and secretive women carrying their pitchers from the wells. Vultures kept guard over thatched huts, unmoved by the approach of intruders. At night campfire songs mixed with the cry of hyenas rooting for dead sheep and bullocks that lay rotting among the black and grey beds of silt.

> It's an amazing country, that's all there is to it, it takes the film off the white man's eyes and he sees the most elemental and primitive existence going on about him as it did in the Old Testament — the peasants in their villages of mud with their tinkling bullocks and naked children and red turbans, the deep stone wells which the oxen draw water from all day on the treadmill, back and fore, up and down, spilling the water by stone gutters, into the fields. And the houses without doors or windows or chimneys, no shops, or coal, or roads, or *anything at all*. You can scarcely believe it. I've found an eternal fascination in it. And I hope to learn more about the dark shy people who cluster into the little kraals that dot the occasional green valleys among our dusty mountains.

He was reading the Hindu scriptures now and waiting for "a big poem". His hot forehead lay on his bony wrists, "tired of the love and the words that do not come to me. But they will. And what then but a renewal of waiting, again and again a renewal of waiting, world without end. Such is my life. Nor would I change it."

On one of his walks, accompanied by Tony Lewis and Jack Gush, he had a signal experience when they came across a shrine by the edge of the track,

> a little granite Buddha, carved in relief from a block about ten inches by six inches, the stones loosely protecting him like a hood. I didn't detect an 'experience'; I don't even know whether I had one. I did ask a question, and know a primary failure though. You can't pray the first time you try; nor can a fussy officer sahib expect to 'understand the East' at the point of a pistol, as it were. But standing by the small shrine, in the desolation of hill and plain, by the loose stones and the small granite relief, the sun beating on my neck round which I'd slung my bathing trunks, *I felt the refusal*. A wall of darkness, hard, resistant, smooth-surfaced. In reaction to this utter failure I became several more degrees aware of myself, my physical self, as though the stone figure had indicated the cause of my rebuff. I wanted to scratch

inside my nostril, and did so. My stomach rumbled and slid a little; I tasted my egg for breakfast; I wanted to fart and did so. For about half a minute and the only time during the week I've been here, I was aware of physical desire; a local itch, entirely local and thereby quite definite, in the sensitive inch or two of flesh that always has represented the simple physics of love. I went and *I forgot all those intimations of being a human being* once they had stated themselves. What happened then? It's hard to say, now especially when it has already veiled itself in time and recollection and the pre-occupations of this life. But I can guess it was nothing to do with anything that belongs to my rank or to any job or responsibility I have ever held. Certainly to no ambition I have ever entertained. Yet it was not a renunciation. That is not surprising, for the material and spiritual are never separate in me . . . And the whole mood was one of humility without submission, of being accepted without any conscious offer, without any of the vows which priests are asked to take and princes of old swear solemnly in story. It was a service of perfect freedom, a sense of infinite space to *be* in, just to be in. Also a sense of a journey I have long wished to make, but never had the time or money or understanding either to envisage or plan. A journey through lands whose existence I did not know but whose location I had been ignorant of till then. The map of the spirit's geography.

> Oft of one vast expanse have I been told
> Yet never did I breathe its pure serene

Here is the beginning of the "tremendous experience" he had told Dick Mills he was going to have, the discovery promised in the prologue of *Raiders' Dawn*: "Existence in its native nakedness". It is the "spirit world" of 'Peace', an upland landscape filled by Rilke's "silence". The physical self asserts itself and then disappears, leaving the spirit space in which "to *be*". It "IS" (as the poem to Rilke puts it) because it is no longer. The Buddha can be attained only when the senses have been shed, though not in any spirit of renunciation. Pure being is a cessation of life. Mules stamp and graze, grey monkeys hang from the trees, long-nosed swine grope for carrion in the dust:

> alone by a heap of stones in the lonely salt plain
> A little Vishnu of stone,
> Silently and eternally simple Being,
> Bidding me to come alone,
>
> And never entirely turning me away,
> But warning me still of the flesh
> That catches and limes the singing birds of the soul
> And holds their wings in mesh.
>
> ('Karanje Village')

A Yeatsian note. (Vishnu, one of the principal Hindu deities, is the supreme god and preserver of the world, though it might also be Siva, the Supreme Self who is pure consciousness, free of all save "being, consciousness and bliss".) The experience may, too, owe something to D.H. Lawrence's *The Rainbow* when Ursula Brangwen, gazing through a microscope, attains a consummation with "a being infinite": "To be oneself was a supreme, gleaming triumph of infinity."

There was another development a few weeks later on 13 January when Alun took part in a regimental soccer match. Fifteen minutes into the second half, Gwynne Jones kicked the ball up to the goalmouth and he ran to tackle a defender, L/Cpl Austin. The two collided and he fell to the ground; Austin's boot had met his jaw. In great pain, he was helped off the field and put to bed. The next day, he was taken to Poona in a truck, his mouth stinking. He couldn't swallow anything. The truck broke down and he had to drive the last part of the journey himself. The doctors discovered that his jaw had been fractured and reset it. All his teeth had to be wired back into place. He spent the next six weeks recovering in the Junior Officers' ward.

The hospital in Poona stood on slightly-elevated land with an extensive view of a maidan (or open space), part of which was used as a rifle range. Beyond rose a gaunt range of hills some three miles away showing in sharp relief a circular white building, the Tower of Silence, on which the Parsees (non-Mohammedan Indians of Persian descent) left their dead to the vultures ("like a rubbish destructor", Alun called it). He tried to slip up to the hills every evening and dawn. "It is so piercingly fresh in the morning and . . . I look out at the misty tree-girt plain where Poona is scattered, and the bare rose peaks beyond and the brilliant annunciation of colour where the sun is coming". He sat watching the view from his first-floor verandah, his jaws wired and fastened together; "the beat of the sun on dry walls and slopes takes all the greenness out of youth somehow," he told Gweno.

> I've been just a little estranged and indifferent to everything, everything in the world, from you downwards! . . . It's the first spasm of 'cellos' I've had since leaving home. I still hate it as much as ever.

Unusedness had once again thrown him into despair. "The only futile and dangerous thing is to lie and do nothing as I've been doing during the last fortnight," he confessed. Eating was laborious, exercise tiring, sleep continually broken by gum ache. He read a little (Ghandi's *Life*), dozed in the afternoon, walked in the maidan and watched the women outside making fuel out of straw and dung for use in their cage-like tenements, so different from the cool, scented bungalows of the English doctors. He listened to a green woodpecker with bright crimson head hammer at a jacquaranda tree. Buffaloes so skinny all their ribs, haunch bones and vertebrae showed outside came passing by. Slowly, the world spun round on its axis.

> My mind has gone into such frozen, desolate wastes that I've been appalled; and the pain has been the taut enduring pain of being frozen by the whiteness and blankness of the scene and the failure to find any relief or hope or any familiar sign.

It was evidently a mental as much as a physical distress, though the latter increased when he caught dysentery and had to be moved to a separate ward for a fortnight. After that, a second operation was performed on the jaw. The teeth over the fracture were suppurating and had to be removed. The wires holding the jaw together were cut since they were screwed round the teeth. He told Gweno about it.

> When they wheeled me into the theatre for my second operation, I remember lying on the table looking up at the brilliant white glitter of the blue sky in the window — off the white walls and ceiling and the glittering lamps — and my spirit tried to call you through the great gap there seemed to be in space: and then I was swallowed up in the engulfing darkness of the injection they had jabbed into my arm; and I had entered the unknown place that Edward Thomas wrote of in his poem
>
> >   that has not any book
> >   Nor face of dearest look —
>
> And when I came round I was just sick and parched and blind with dope and thoroughly miserably ALIVE!! So I don't think I need any further experience of leaving this life, although it was all planned and safe, it was the very like I believe, of what does happen.

Most extraordinarily, he had experienced his own death. Even more extraordinarily, he had come back to tell of it.

Following this, there was more pain and resting and reading and watching the woodpeckers nesting and the flowers being watered. "Thought is like a razor or a cupboard of poison drugs," he told Dick Mills, whom he had met again a few weeks before in Poona; "— must be used by one who knows how. I'm afraid my knowledge is inadequate to control my mind and I kicked against the pricks a devil of a lot. The world seemed to have been frozen — a vast ice-cap lay on it [language reminiscent of the frozen compression he experienced at Longmoor] — and life was an isolation of the spirit, seeking through impossible lengths of time, attempting to define and chart and measure. And it got me down, this coldness and cheerlessness and inhumanity of mind. I got frightened. But why write about it? . . . I've thought most of the romance off things; they look more naked now, and the ugly things are not disguised in pretty paint." Not having heard from Gweno recently (none of her letters had arrived since he had sailed) and lacking his army friends, he was left alone in the spirit's geography.

Out of this experience came a number of poems. "I feel they are *wicked* poems," he told Dick. "They've distressed me a lot in writing them and I shall be glad to reestablish my contact with solid things by leaving the dream world of hospitals and reentering the rough and warm material Earth world of every day". It is a familiar contrast, the "dream world" of reflection (as in 'All day it has rained . . .') opposed to "the warm ones about us", a conflict sharpened by his spiritual exploration of the idea of death. In explaining the poems to Gweno, he said that they were "more morbid than usual. I was reading my Rilke this morning — he says a poet cannot write of joy until he has lamented; and that he has no right to lament unless he has the power of joy. I know I've the power of joy in me: you know it, too: so Rilke *will* authorize my black tone-poems". In this apologetic fashion, he sought to link his depressions to poetic necessity and soothe her anxieties.

> I'm deliberately trying to explore the spirit world — I don't mean spooks, but the soul world, space, life, eternity, because I think all the answers to the things that grieve and afflict us today lie there. And my normal life is so absorbingly material, there are so many practical jobs to do, and the future seems to be only a series of campaigns with problems of supply and ammunition and keeping the engines and the wireless sets running and the batteries charged, that I'm glad of this sick month to try and explore the other world. But it's a huge unfamiliar world and it gives you a feeling of being lost in space, there are no landmarks, signposts, familiar faces or ideas, nothing solid: you suddenly want to get back again and are relieved when you do feel the warmth of being back again . . . I feel guilty sometimes, as though I'd deserted you, coming so far away from you and not being able to say when I'll return. And then suddenly a great gust of triumph rises in me, and sweeps all the niggardly fears and scruples of day to day away, and I know I'll come raging back like a young lion, laughing and glad and unscathed.

There would, after all, be "some returning".

'In Hospital: Poona (1)' confirms that "love survives the venom of the snake" and reunites Alun with Gweno. 'In Hospital: Poona (2)' focusses on the poverty outside the hospital and Alun's anaesthetic experience and brings human love and the corrosive power of the universe into balance — just. 'Burma Casualty' goes further. Like the short story 'The Earth is a Syllable', it was inspired by the experiences of Captain G.T. Morris, whom Alun met in hospital. Morris had been wounded in the retreat from Burma and was left nursing a gangrenous leg. 'Burma Casualty' describes how death might appear seductive to such a man and shows once again the soldier penetrating the "darkness" without actually committing himself to it.

> The dark is a beautiful singing sexless angel
> Her hands so soft you scarcely feel her touch
> Gentle, eternally gentle, round your heart.
> She flatters and unsexes every man.
>
> And Life is only a crude, pigheaded churl
> Frowsy and starving, daring to suffer alone.

One does not know whether to applaud the soldier's commitment to life or to disapprove of it as being merely stubborn in the face of such blandishments.

In his journal, Alun elaborated on his anaesthetic vision.

> Long cold fields, uncharted, difficult to navigate — *a very brilliant and uniform white light.* This light has its counter in *an enveloping darkness* that surged up softly and irresistibly like a sweet oil from the interstices underneath me as I lay on the operating table. It was about two seconds in completely annihilating me — I surrendered to what Edward Thomas foresaw — the land he must enter and leave alone. The light, though — the sun and blue over it, the spiritual light that was very profound; somewhere there was a massive line of poetry, one for the dark, jagged and bleeding, all nervous and muscular . . . and I was very tranquil and I pretended that Gweno might travel spiritually towards me through the light.

The wife and the "beautiful singing sexless angel" stand opposed but they are also different aspects of the same figure, as the imagery of light suggests, related masks of the Goddess who gives and denies.

'The Earth is a Syllable' plays on the Hindu belief that the earth is a syllable which the mortal self "breathes" in pursuit of true selfhood; at the moment of perfection, it gathers its senses and withdraws in preparation for its journey to a new life. In the story, a soldier who has "always known he'd die if he caught up with" the war in Burma lies wounded near to death. He thinks of the scruples he sank on enlisting and "the little meetings he's tried to run, debates round a hurricane lamp on the FUTURE, talks he'd carefully put together on RECONSTRUCTION, gramophone records he'd borrowed and played for the lads, the choir he'd tried to make something good of". All these now fade, as does his wife, who had wanted a child but "it hadn't turned out that way". Her influence cannot prevent him meeting his death, which he does as he tries to reach out for her in his delirium. For the first time, a limit is placed on love's beneficence.

When the story was printed in *In the Green Tree* (1948), John Petts provided an illustration that, without trying to, turned the soldier's head into Alun's. Gweno asked him to change it and he did so, though the resemblance still shows through, as he felt it should. (The marks on the soldier's forehead — M 100 (hours) — refer to the time he received his morphia injection; they were made in the field for the benefit of the main dressing station.) Alun told Gweno: "[D]on't think it's about 'me'. It's a way of averting ill fortune, rather than inviting it".

These hospital poems and stories have a peculiar quality which Alun defined in a different context thus: "The sick have their own slightly different world, their jokes are as necessary and peculiar to them as their medicines; they can't afford to be morbid like the healthy, nor to be indifferent to their environment like the Arab. The outside world has been washed out; between them and the encircling mysteries there is only the spotlight of their obsessions holding the small backcloth of ward and garden before them." This description comes from 'Ward "O" 3(b)', one of his finest stories and one that was to establish his reputation as a short-story writer, though he himself thought it "too 'all of one breath' somehow" and kept it for a while before revising it. The story's protagonist, Lt. Weston, suffers from a "death trauma" which is occasioned by the extraordinary injuries he has received: his jaw and shoulder-bone have been shattered and a great clod torn out of his neck and thigh, baring windpipe, epiglottis, lung and femoral artery. "There had been an annihilation, a complete obscuring; into which light had gradually dawned". (This recalls the "salt pillar" and "Arctic silence" of 'In Hospital: Poona (2)'). Some "mutation" has occurred and it leaves Weston to endure a pain in which he "desired wildly to return to the timeless void where the act of being was no more than a fall of snow or the throw of a rainbow; and these regions became a nostalgia to his pain and soothed his hurt and parched spirit". To one suffering all the tribulations of wartime life, the calm of the dark is a light that is deeply attractive. It is an enthralling progression: where once hope had been identified with the beloved or the soldier's own determination to fight for life, now it comes with an annihilation of self which occurs in the brightest agony of pain. The void is Vishnu's "being", Rilke's "IS", and Weston resolutely declares: "I want to have a look at Burma. *And I don't want to see England"*.

The question of what is going to happen to him and his colleagues after the medical inspection board provides the main narrative interest and is developed by means of a beautifully delayed dramatic mechanism, one wrapped in symbolic subterfuge of the subtlest kind. Weston, we discover, is the son of a collier who got rheumatism and nystagmus and went on the dole. (It is a fascinating feature of Alun's autobiographical projections that he always provides himself with a father who is a miner, rough and energetic, and a mother who is a "mam", weak and sickly, the very antithesis of his own parents.) Weston remembers:

> I used to watch the wheel of the pit spin round year after year, after school and Saturdays and Sundays; and then from 1926 on I watched it not turning round at all, and I can't ever get that wheel out of my mind. It still spins and idles, and there's money and nystagmus coming into the house or no work and worse than nystagmus. I just missed the wheel sucking me down the shaft. I got a scholarship to the county school. I don't know when I started rebelling. Against the wheel in my head . . .

1926 recalls the economic deprivation that followed the General Strike and miners' lockout (the wheel stopped spinning) but also his own deprivation as a scholarship boy (the wheel turning in his head). These, brought up sharp against India's "old shrunken tribes" ('In Hospital: Poona (2)'), its ineradicable sense of suffering, goes a long way to explain his preoccupied state.

The medical board pronounces, but we learn nothing about its decision concerning Weston for the simple reason that his is an inner destiny. We learn of it when we last see him sitting with a friend on the ledge of the hospital garden pool:

> Weston put his hand in the water; minnows rose in small flocks and nibbled at his fingers. Circles of water lapped softly outwards, outwards, till they touched the edge of the pool, and cast a gentle

wetness on the stone, and lapped again inwards, inwards. And as they lapped inwards he felt the ripples surging against the most withdrawn and inmost ledges of his being, like a series of temptations in the wilderness. And he felt glad to-night, feeling some small salient gained when for many reasons the men whom he was with were losing ground along the whole front to the darkness that is.

He has his light against the darkness. The meaning of the contrast derives from the pose of Narcissus he adopts here. The tone sounds optimistic: Weston is apparently heading back to the war, his "temptations" acknowledged. But what are the watery circles he watches? The eddies moving in and out have a gentle harmonic quality in keeping with the timelessness of the pool; they are simultaneously soothing and disturbing. They recall the deliquescent trance of 'All day it has rained . . .'.

'Ward "O" 3(b)' was written during Alun's last fortnight in hospital. "It's been an enriching experience, these five weeks in hospital," he told Gweno, writing in the garden by Weston's pool and listening to the water's "lovely cool sound", "and I shall never regret them". The poems he had written there, he said, had both hurt and exhausted him, but he felt the wiser for them. He left with a silver splint cemented in his jaw (to be removed a month later) and returned to Nira to take up his new duties as battalion Intelligence Officer. As I.O., he was drawn even further away from the men and had to drive hundreds of miles on reconnaissance trips. During these, he feasted his poet's eye. And what he saw was the sun, "brilliant and violent, like an ancient god". In India, the cold, such as it is, departs in mid-March, to be followed by the pre-monsoon heat and Alun moved about his "eerie dirty halfworld" ('The River Temple: Wai') in heavy mood, "wreathed in a reflective sadness now that cannot really grip a living hope. I often feel that I am trying to make my final peace with the world. And all that means is that I am trying to assure Gweno that there is nothing in my power to give her which I did not give. I have withheld nothing. Therefore do not mourn me."

In 'The Mahratta Ghats', an excellent poem, the Indian scene glows with a primary heat. It is a pitiless world, utterly beyond man's powers to correct: "Dark peasants drag the sun upon their back". Life for them is a burden that denies nourishment even as it sustains. Like Ixion at the wheel, they struggle on. For one of Alun's temper, the refusal was final. Even so, his compassion for the lean folk made him feel for the first time that he was coming to terms with India, its arid, irresistible, beaten quality.

> Who is it climbs the summit of the road?
> Only the beggar bumming his dark load.
> Who was it cried to see the falling star?
> Only the landless soldier lost in war.

"Landless" is interesting: the soldier of 'Lance-Jack' has become a tramp of the road, no longer related either to country or cause. When Alun read Philip Toynbee's review of *The Last Inspection* in *The New Statesman* which referred to his "guilt complex" and "isolation" and described him as a "left-wing intellectual", he told Gweno: "Well — maybe I used to be. I'm not so now and never will be. I seem to have stepped outside all that. That's just a bit of froth on England's whirlpool. There's all the patient suffering world beside, and I'm in that now for better or for worse".

In an article for the *New Statesman*, published in May, 1943, 'Bread for Stones', he wrote that what he had found in India was "like acid in the brain", the "universal evil eye": emaciated beggars, destitute villages, camp followers swilling from the soldiers' bins, every child a pauper, the "tumbling ordure" of the villages, the shrivelled women and verminous old men — "that is what broke Nehru's heart". This, added to his hospital experience, induced in him a terrible sense of waste. "An awful lot of people are asking for bread," he wrote, "and all they seem to be handing out these days is stones". These days? It was ever thus.

At the same time, he began to feel the burden of his separation from Gweno and expressed it in a number of poems: "Life is dangerous, indifferent, ignorant" he wrote in a letter: "whither are we going, sweet lovers?" In 'Karanje Village', he asks love to wait.

> And when my sweetheart calls me shall I tell her
> That I am seeking less and less of world?
> And will she understand?

In 'Motifs', he cries, "I bid Love ask no further proof of me", unable to cling any longer and wanting no clinging in return. When all peasant life was subject to the law of "Not being and then being" ('Village Funeral: Maharashtra'), going from one birth to another birth, life and death, how could they hold out?

> The close and sentient mind is helpless here,
> And I who do not fully understand,

> But half forgetting, half expecting lie
> And let the world fall softly from my hand,
> Conceal my heart's great love and love's great fear,
> And would forget you if I could, my dear.
>
> ('Motifs')

Frightened and hurt, he was drifting away, aware only

> Of the withering obsession
> That lovers grow to fear
> When the last note is written
> And at last and alone
> One of them wakes in terror
> And the other is gone.
>
> ('Bivouac')

Alun was back in Nira for only three weeks when the Borderers were reconverted to infantry as part of the 72nd Indian Infantry Brigade, the 36th Indian Infantry Division. They moved from Nira to Lake Kharakvasla, one of the dams conserving Poona and Bombay's water supply some fifteen miles the other side of Poona. The change, on 20 March, was unpopular, mainly because of the uncertainty it created, though there was also resentment at the prospect of route marches again, but there was nothing for it. Russian successes in the Caucasus had removed the threat of a German invasion of Iraq and Iran and, together with the British victories in North Africa and Japanese reverses in the Pacific, had lessened the threat to India. The Borderers now trained for combined operations, which involved amphibious exercises in naval whalers fitted with levers, flat-bottomed boats converted for the purpose. The men had to swim in the lake with full equipment and scramble up seemingly unclimbable cliffs day and night. After the fall of Singapore in February, 1942, the Japanese had overrun Burma with extraordinary ferocity, creating an atmosphere well-captured by the reference to "lynx-eyed Japs" in 'Burma Casualty'. Just as the Borderers landed in India in December, 1942, an attempt was made to retake the Mayu peninsula and Akyab on the Western coast of Burma (it was this that precipitated the *Athlone Castle*'s early departure from South Africa) but it failed and by the spring of 1943, the British had withdrawn to Cox's Bazar, holding Bawli Bazar as an outpost. With the arrival of the monsoon, operations were effectively halted for the next six months. At the Casablanca conference in January, 1943, the combined Chiefs of Staff recommended that another general offensive against Burma be mounted in November and it was for this that the Borderers now prepared.

Like most of the men, Alun enjoyed Lake Kharakvasla. His tent was on the shore and he could see the glimmering stretch of water before him redden in the sun every morning as he shaved. He told his parents that he thought it was "a fair substitute for Penbryn" — than which there could be no higher praise. To John Petts and Brenda Chamberlain, he expressed his delight in

> The arid resistancy of these mountains to the human request for softness, response, peace, hospitality. And there is always the wonderful elation of newness, difference and the heightened vision of the pellucid blue climate. I'd fail if I tried to describe the hills. They're grassless, burned to dust, surfaces of shale and crumbled rock, and they rise in fine concave ravines and courses to sharp skulls of rock on which there is nearly always either a temple or an old Mahratta fort. I've spent long days amongst them, and while I prefer our blissful lake with its enormous dam, I shan't forget some excursions I've made . . ., guided by a homing villager or asking my way of the goatherd to check up on my compass. One morning I woke up in a green valley among the foothills. There was a hamlet nearby, and in that part they keep the harvest sheaves in the trees, on platforms cupped in the branches. A group of villagers filed past me in complete silence, with turbans and white dotis, the women silently carrying their gleaming brass pitchers on their heads, barefooted and in red and blue saris. And the sky grey and translucent with the first clarity of morning. Utter silence, and me lying there seeing these silent people going about their pastoral and eternal work, accepting me as a newcomer lying there waking. And I really felt that I had wakened up in Heaven. And I think that's how Heaven would be, most nice.

He had gone native with the peasant, "pastoral and eternal". He told Robert Graves about it, too:

> There was a zareba of dead thorns filled with lambs, a tree like a gibbet with hay drying in the branches, a party of silent peasants walking barefooted across the valley . . . and the dawn grey on a precipitous steep, and over all a most innocent and empty sky. I had the queer certitude that I was waking in heaven. Not the Heaven that doesn't exist, but the heaven of the peasant's mind, where all is silent and normal and tranquil, and the newcomer wakes and stretches his limbs and is neither questioned nor shunned, but tacitly allowed to become familiar with the simple continuity that exists.

It was the silent spirit world he had been searching for.

Travelling about in his truck or leading the company on route marches through the jungle, he picked up enough of the language to talk to the villagers but found himself either "all keyed up and busy, or flat and bored by reaction". As ever, he had to be busy to be normal, and that meant being productive as a writer, too: "when I've been busiest I've written best", he told Gweno. The experience of the past four months had brought him up sharp against the question "What is life worth?" and it pushed him to the brink. The vitality he was expending was not being replenished; there was nothing coming in to counter the stark futility of the baked Indian scene and it rendered his joy in renewal circular, depleting him to the core. He was invited only to further and further simplification. In a letter to Gweno, he wrote:

> All the poems that have any personal feeling in them are variations on one majestic and absorbing theme nowadays, and I fear I may be doing little except distress you and bore others. But I will still go on writing and sending them, because it's the only possible way I have of gathering the fruit of the wayside or seeing what is happening to me. And I'm glad I have this absorbing thought, for I wouldn't experience war, and so comprehend life, if I didn't realise the implications of the death it entails for so many wonderfully fit and healthy strong young men. Nor what that semi-religious preparation for death means to the others whose part is to love and to love and to hope and to fear. It's the texture of that experience which moves me more deeply than our great steel victories and the trial and incredible endurance of the jungle fighters.

This "semi-religious preparation for death" was explored further at Lake Kharakvasla that Easter, where he wrote six poems which he believed contained "more simple poetry" than any he had written before. He was feeling disconsolate, with the familiar sensation of a weight pressing on him, and he turned to the poems as to a revelation:

> they aren't as pointed and severe as the hospital ones and they're simpler in their melody and wording . . . It's interesting (to me) the way they've evolved. I've had a few pages of jottings for the last fortnight but couldn't get anything out of them at all. Then, last week-end, I had a sort of mood. My head seemed to develop a spasm of music and lovely phrases appeared in the water. It didn't recur, but each night this week from ten to midnight I've sat down in my quiet tent and disciplined my thoughts successfully enough to hammer out these six poems from the raw material. There've been several versions of some. Each version I worked to simplify and abbreviate. I've cut out nearly every 'rich' adjective and high metaphor . . . and in as casual sort of way reduced them to their minima.

The six poems were 'Village Funeral', 'Home Thoughts from Abroad', 'Bequest', 'River Temple: Wai', 'Shadows' and 'Water Music'. In 'Shadows', the optimistic message of 'In Hospital: Poona (1)', that "love and beauty" will survive the "grey malignant hours", is repeated only to be ignored:

> He chooses best who does not choose
> Time and all its lies;
> Who makes the end and the beginning One
> Within himself, grows wise.
>
> The cold winds of indifference
> Disturb the scarves of night,
> As earth and moon go voyaging
> Through dark, through light.

From his earliest days, Alun had used elemental imagery to describe the human condition; it was eternal, detached but capable of expressing human potentiality at its highest (especially in love). Indeed, the Yeatsian mode of art he valued most highly he defined in 'Last Pages of a Long Journal' as being "wonderful and lost . . . among the galaxies". Of late, however, he had been struck by the "alternation of sad human ineffectiveness with vast inhuman cycles of activity" described by James Joyce in *Portrait of the Artist as a Young Man* (which Alun had recently been reading) when he has Stephen Dedalus contemplate Shelley's moon:

> Art though pale for weariness
> Of climbing heaven and gazing on the earth,
> Wandering companionless?

It is this mood 'Shadows' expresses. It is suffused with great heat as reflected in the cool of night (Alun usually wrote late at night after completing his duties and attending to a voluminous correspondence); it urges the release of the soul from the flesh that limes it and holds its wings in mesh.

Both 'Bequest' and 'Home Thoughts from Abroad' relate his Indian experience to Wales, the former by tracing the poet's family inheritance. It ends by addressing Gweno:

> I leave you in their company,
> The winter snow heaped on your door,
> In the dark house in the mountains
> With a robin on the floor.

> And yours are the mysteries
> Of Love and Life and Death.
> But I, in what remains, only recall
> Your beauty quickening my breath.

Love is again recalled but, for the first time, it is limited to "what remains".

> 'Bequest' — well, if you don't like it, Gweno, throw it away. I told you I was sending you something not happy at all. And although I'm more and more engrossed with the *single* poetic theme of Life and Death, for there doesn't seem to be any question more directly relevant than this one of what survives of all the beloved, I find myself quite unable to express at once the passion of Love, the coldness of death (Death is cold) and the fire that beats against resignation, acceptance. Acceptance seems so spiritless, protest so vain. In between the two I live . . . but your old husband is so terribly anxious to get back to you that he hits out violently at any suggestion the poet might make to the contrary.

Suddenly, the poet is differentiated from the man. In his journal, Alun observed that his letters were "coloured more than is legitimate with the warmth of the ego", being addressed to his loved ones; "the poems are even more biased and bigoted. The poet in one sees only a little of it. Sees what I do not see in daily ways, what I do not talk about when I discuss the future, what I exclude from my hopes for a better world". India is the story of the emergence of this poet and the difficulty Alun had in recognising and acknowledging him.

'Water Music', the greatest of the lake poems, develops the snow images of the hospital poems, and shows this new kind of knowledge emerging. It came to him as a gift, without much revision. These are truly lovely phrases that "appeared in the water" and they issue their invitation with the most sinister encouragement. I quote from the original draft:

> Deep in the heart of the lake
> A stranger is singing
> A song empty as death . . .
> Do not fear to venture
> Where the last light trembles
> Because you were in love.

The great religions are over; great battles leave but dust on earth.

> Cold is the lake water
> And dark as history.

Hurry not and fear not
This oldest mystery.

This strange voice singing,
This slow deep drag of the lake,
This yearning, yearning, this ending
Of the heart and its ache.

The siren muse calls the poet from love and life; as she does so, we
reach the climax of Alun's spiritual acceptance of death. Gweno still
remained a powerful influence, as he reminded her when he told her
that he never lost her "in the jungle of my mind", but the fact that his
mind *had* become a jungle seems the more pressing admission.

Regularly, the letter-writer sought to reassure her:

> [D]eath doesn't fascinate me half as powerfully as life: . . . but you
> know really, darling, how I turn insatiably to more and more life,
> don't you? Death is a great mystery, who can ignore him? But I don't
> *seek* him, oh no — only I would like to 'place' him.

He recalled the "atrophy" in him which she battled to dispel at
Llangranog and Aberystwyth in the spring of 1940 and told her that
he thought death was "another instance of the contrary twist we
always meet sooner or later in our fascinations". He hoped, in the end,
he might, with D. H. Lawrence, say, "Look, I Have Won Through!",
but the pain was great.

> Yesterday and the night before, I was enticed, seduced and destroyed
> by the long octopus arms and hungry hard mouth of a shapeless poem
> that will never be written. It seized me with soft little thrills as I
> entered the tent, and each night till long after midnight, I've wrestled
> vainly with it in the long battle of thoughts and words. When I did at
> last go to bed I felt spiritually bewildered and unnerved, as though
> the thoughts had battered and exhausted me. And I knew last night,
> that I couldn't *live* with the thoughts that encircled this particular
> poem and I was afraid of being alone with them after I had put the
> lamp out.

Repeatedly, the "beautiful singing sexless angel" tempted him with
revelations he could scarcely bear with equanimity. Where earlier the
question had been what survives of self, the question now was what
survived of the *beloved*, the living forces beating against resignation.
Poetry, love and the army all contended for his allegiance.

> [T]here is constantly a darker reserve of judgement, a sort of refusal
> to believe that there is a future left for the taking. It's at night that this

sort of disbelief grows to the plane of a sensation as physical as gooseflesh, and I've wrestled with some bitter shapeless embryos of poetry between 11 p.m. and 2 a.m. in an attempt to word my statement to the inscrutable.

By the beginning of May, he was in a "simple restlessness that is a permanent state of mind", "stoical and rather grimly untrusting ... I don't ask, expect or believe in help from any other quarter than myself". The battalion was training on the beaches round Bombay and it was abominably hot. At first, their tents were pitched in the baked mud plains bordering the coastal forest at Bhiwandi, which the Borderers reached on 30 April, and then at Juhu, a few miles north of the city in the sand dunes among date and coconut palms, where they arrived on 21 May. The beach at Bhiwandi was connected to the mainland by a causeway over an estuary which separated it from the cliffs beyond. On returning from training, the men had to wade through the mud avoiding the causeway. If the stream were in, they had to swim across with toggle ropes held together, each hauling the other over. They practised mock invasions on the beaches with long marches inland followed by the reboarding of their vessels in the correct order of priority — infantry, artillery, tanks, lorries and so on. Though the training was difficult, however, they appreciated the benefits of living beside the warm sea, the sand silvery, tiny crabs swarming in the sand, white-sailed dhows in the offing.

The monsoon was presaged by powerful, rushing winds, a novel coolness, violent silent lightning and the first scurries of rain. When it arrived, there was continuous blue lightning in sheets, thunder and torrential rain which flooded the tent lines and brought palm trees crashing to the ground. There was little time for writing now save for a few poems like 'Assault Convoy', 'The Patrol' and 'The Run-In' and short stories like 'The Raid', an excellent account of the capture of an Indian responsible for a bomb outrage in a cinema. (Another story, 'Manuel', reflects Alun's fascination with Portuguese India.

The soldier's regiment had been training on this strip of torrid coast all through the hot season, training strenuously in the mud flats and black, oily creeks thick with cactus and sea holly, black reptiles and sea snakes. The aridity and heat of the baked crumbling earth and the limp palms with their clusters of unripe gourds had induced a torpor in the men. They seemed to be pinned eternally among these bankrupt villages with their bamboo and reed hovels, the harbours with drying platforms for the nets, stinking of putrefying fish they

had failed to sell; the dark Hindu temples with their erotic statuary,
and the sallow Portuguese who could not afford to go home, but must
be dragged down to the hunger level of the native Mahrattis.

It is as if the decline of the Portuguese into villagers as squalid and
malodorous as the natives carried a secret message, one akin to
Conrad's *Heart of Darkness*. Something had gone wrong at the root
and he recoiled with fascination at the thought. "Perhaps it's just the
climate," he told to his parents,

everybody must be dysenteric subjects for they relieve themselves
anywhere and everywhere and the whole place was filthy with human
dirt. Again and again I realise that we just can't cope with things out
here. It's alright if the white man can afford to live in Darjeeling or
Simla or the Taj Mahal in Bombay [a hotel on the waterfront
opposite the Gateway to India]. But he's only got to potter into the
villages to realise what an unknown world he has put his crown upon.

It is a central observation. A padre posted to the battalion repeated the
message in a different way: "He's been a missionary for five years up in
the wilds . . . — and he says that eighty per cent of the missions out
here are sham. He came out to join a mission that claimed 35,000
converts and found that all they did was sprinkle water on peasants'
heads during the famine when they came to the 'mission' for free
grain. No churches, no schools, no nothing except a warehouse of
grain and a bucket of water. Isn't it awful?" He himself thought he
could be happy in India "but only if Britain and India were good
friends." He wished he had arrived as a doctor, teacher, social worker,
"anything but a soldier. It's not nice being a soldier in India". When
The Times refused to print two of his poems for publication, he
remarked, "They want Virgil's imperial gaze these days, but not for
me, because I don't see the splendour at close quarters, I see
something much more bitingly real and distressing and inescapable"
— slithery chameleons, decaying houses, dirty garbage humps and
black crows cawing on them. He told Robert Graves:

It is easy to write prose in India, there is so much to satirise or hate or
shrug one's shoulders at. But poetry is harder to command, mainly I
think because everything is somehow remorseless here, arid, pellucid
and incurable. Politics at home is an inviting dance because things are
more plastic and organic. Here I eschew them entirely, and have no
sympathies with either side. The peasant remains, and it's in the
villages that I've found what I'm always seeking.

The villages, so politically disillusioning, so humanly distressing,
were what he wanted to feast his poet's eyes on. "In many ways," he

told John Lehmann, "I'm glad I'm not in England. I'm sure I can see straighter here. Human behaviour is as clear as the lucid climate, and as hard and immutable. Change seems less simple than it did at home. Everything was possible then". He told Gweno he was glad to be free of "the sort of microscopic examination that makes the English literary boys so short-sighted. And I don't intend to lose the *chance* that I may develop a greater lucidity than I could ever obtain in the close-fighting factions of left and right at home".

The publication of the article 'Stones for Bread' in the *New Statesman* caused some offence and Colonel Popham ordered him to show his work to the authorities in future. Alun refused, saying he would not be gagged, but all his stories from this time bear the military censor's stamp, including 'Ward "O" 3(b)', rewritten at Juhu in May. As it happens, Popham's time with the Borderers was nearing an end. On 3 June, he was transferred to G.H.Q. and handed over command to his 2nd i/c, Robin Cresswell. The next day, the battalion swapped camps with the 9th Royal Sussex at Aksa and a week later moved to Bhiwandi for further training. Alun led the way through straggling miles of bullock carts, cyclists, peasants, gypsies and stray cattle.

Bhiwandi is on a flat plain. The men lived in European pattern/ Indian pattern tents, double-skinned to protect them from the rain and pitched on square platforms 2'6" above flood level. The discomfort was intense. It was now the height of the monsoon and everything was hot and sticky. The rain lashed down; the men's skins got so waterlogged they ripped easily. Russell's vipers, mosquitoes and huge flying beetles abounded. Dysentry was rife, as were footrot and jungle sores. The humidity was defeating. At night, the air filled with the sound of frogs and crickets, fireflies "like floating embers". Colonel Cresswell insisted on the mess dressing in starched jackets but no-one minded, least of all Alun. ". . . I find more and more and more," he wrote, "that we are all living through an identical experience in the same way — all of us cherishing the same simplicities, afraid to lose the same things, and willing to share the same tasks and the same anxieties". It was a feeling of comradeship that was to sustain the men as the possibility of action loomed nearer. There was a greater sense of tension in the air, caused partly by exhaustion now that "the long crisis and the perpetual rough work" seemed to be coming to a head ("There are charcoal fires burning in

tins this morning for the men to dry their clothes, yet in an hour's time
we have to swim in full equipment, so what's the use?"), partly by the
feeling that the training was at last in earnest after the mixture of
frustration, boredom and arduousness of the past three years. The
Borderers had seen no battles in that time but as the reality of their
position dawned on them, their awareness of danger increased. Battle
has an energy of its own which training lacks, the latter being more
continuous and, in a way, more tiring. "Toil, tears and sweat," one
man wrote home, "— blood to follow." Alun told Gweno:

> I tried to read last night, the Hindu scriptures; but I'm in no mood
> for reading. There's something smouldering in me all the time and a
> sentence or two or a poem or two are like petrol — there's a flare-up
> and I cast the book away and plunge into the moody half-tones of
> thought and longing and impatience and try to get some relief from
> scribbling, and fail, and return to the book, and so on and so on. I'm
> very selfish, indulging in personal emotions like this. The historians
> of the last war called it attrition — anyway we'd go into action like a
> lot of hungry wolves after our dragging vigil in this nobody's land.

The battalion frequently moved from camp to camp (a month is the
longest they stopped anywhere) avoiding roads and making
alternative paths through the countryside. The burden of this fell on
Alun more than most since, as I.O., he had to help plan and execute
the Borderer's movements. He enjoyed it, revelling in "the freedom,
the new sights, the utter disconnectedness of each day . . . It satisfies
the nomad in me". His friends thought him very abstracted by now.
He was thinner, with a bronzed, almost gaunt, appearance, the eyes
sunken, restless. There was a quality of foreboding in him,
exaggerated by his high forehead and noble head. To those meeting
him for the first time, he could exercise a disconcerting power. There
was a mixture of the intellectual and fey in him, mysterious, quiet,
concentrated.

Alun got off to a bad start with Cresswell, who refused him
permission to broadcast his poems when invited to do so by All-India
Radio, but he appealed to Divisional H.Q. and won his case. He made
two recordings in June and July and was surprised to find that he had
avoided the "natural indolence" of his voice. On the first occasion, he
read 'Raiders' Dawn', 'The Sentry', 'All day it has rained . . .', 'Post-
script: for Gweno' 'A Troopship in the Tropics', 'Village Funeral',
'Mahratta Ghats' and 'Water Music'. He thought the selection was "a
bit sombre, but it says most of what I've tried to say in the last two
years" — an interesting piece of self-criticism.

One of his trips, a ten-day affair between Aksa and Bhiwandi some two hundred miles from Bombay, made a particular impression on him. He and his driver stopped from time to time at dak bungalows (government buildings erected for the use of officials travelling long distances across the country and available to travellers, "like a Youth Hostel, for a rupee a night"). He told his parents:

> We saw tribes of gypsies with little mousey grey donkeys and a couple of enormous camels to carry their few belongings . . . And rivers in flood that somehow we managed to drive our little jeeps through, and jungle tribesmen slipping through the trees with bows and arrows, thin brown soft eyed men like antelope, and beautiful peasant girls beating their saris clean at wayside pools and running away if we stopped to examine the road or bridge. It was a colossal experience and I feel I could go on travelling like that for years, yes literally for years. My mind stayed in its proper place, my imagination was content to watch the marco polo wonders of ordinary life, and my body was just part of the car and the speed.

"I haven't got an address now," he told Gweno, "I'm just a gypsy — nobody knows where I am except myself — and I don't bother to find out". Having left the familiar world, he was content to live moment by moment, expecting at each turn some new surprise. He wanted to see more of this India, a cleaner, more beautiful India, "camels, flamingoes, monkeys, hillmen with bows and arrows, wild and beautiful as black grapes". The camels, splendid as bishops, mixed with the donkeys led by tall girls with great eyes and greasy black hair.

> [W]e'd come to a swollen river and crawl in bottom gear across the sand to the channel, and I'd wade in to see how deep it was and there'd be bullocks and donkeys and peasants crossing, and perhaps a bus drawn up there and the passengers all rucking up their skirts and saris and dhotis and wading across with bags and sandals above their heads. Then we drove one nerve-wracking day through interminable twisting lanes all flooded by incessant rain, and the only way we could choose one lane from another was by keeping steadily to our compass bearing . . . And through it all, the infinite feeling of a star in endless motion, a sort of lack of connection, as though no yesterday and no tomorrow could affect this steady Now. And my mind and body were content to accept just the road and the motion of the car and the silence of the man beside me and the casual talk at night at our hastily cooked meal of tinned sausages and jam.

One could get lost there. Increasingly, the writer was moving in a different direction from the man and lover. To Gweno, he wrote, "I take all that comes with the eagerness of a writer and the open arms of poetry. But I myself only miss you and miss you, and grow less and less detached because I can so rarely forget just what has happened". Once again, the poet is distinguished from the man and once again turns to the muse as the human self falters.

By the middle of July, he was typing "oblivious" a story that defined his "colossal experience", 'The Orange Grove'. It was composed "in a kind of drunkenness of composition, completely gripped and convinced and compelled". For the first time, he felt he was writing from "inside India" and the result is his masterpiece in prose. It tells of a ten-day reconnaissance trip taken by Staff-Captain Beale and his driver in a remote part of central India. They stop for the night at a dak bungalow, the atmosphere tense with the pre-monsoon heat and the aftermath of Ghandi and Nehru's arrest the previous week for their anti-British "Quit India" campaign. Beale questions his driver about the collective farms of Palestine (an echo of little George's speech aboard the *Athlone Castle*) and he waxes lyrical about the one happy event of his life: "They didn't have any money, they didn't buy and sell. They shared what they had and the doctor and the schoolteacher the same as the labourer or the children, all the same, all living together. Orange groves they lived in, and I would like to go back there". But he doesn't; shortly afterwards, he is stabbed in the back by an unknown assailant.

Beale, ignorant of his death, ponders an orange grove in Palestine:

> He was experiencing one of those enlargements of the imagination that come once or perhaps twice to a man, and recreate him, subtly and profoundly. And he was thinking simply this — that some things are possible and other things impossible to us. Beyond the mass of vivid and sensuous impressions which he had allowed the war to impose upon him were the quiet categories of the possible and the quieter frozen infinities of the impossible. And he must get back to those certainties . . .

The imagery of cold, silent wastes alerts us to the drift: lost in the universal cycle, Beale has forgotten the ideal of collective effort. Just then, he discovers the body of his driver. The nearest cantonment is four hundred miles away. The roads are flooded, the lines are down; he cannot stay in the bungalow, so he picks up the body. The rain falls as he begins his journey. The moment long foreseen has arrived.

The driver, we may say, is Beale's double come to forewarn him of his own end; he is his mortal self. At the same time, he allays his fears about death, assuring him that, far from being a conclusion, it is a venture into a new life. Like Yeats's soul in 'Sailing to Byzantium' "sick with desire and fastened to a dying animal", Beale is the *pneumatikos* or spiritual man who carries his body, the *sarkikos* or carnal man, with him as his shadow or servant.

Six hours later, at dawn, he stops his truck and falls asleep. A tribe of gypsies passes by. He wakes to an inexplicable sense of guilt, as if he were responsible for the driver's death or for not reporting it or for abandoning his mission. Driving on, he loses himself in a vast plain of paddy-fields. His map is in the bungalow far behind, his watch broken. "Something caved in inside him, a sensation of panic, of an enemy against whose machinations he had failed to take the most elementary precautions" (he had earlier prided himself on "being able to feel the imminence of danger as others feel a change in the weather"). Having always seen the war as a matter of fitness, endurance, muscles; he is now as helpless as the man whose body he carries in the back of the truck.

For a second time, the gypsies cross his path and he drives on into the night. Stopping again, he shifts the body to get at some petrol tins and regrets the indignity of the movement and the discomfort of the ride, displaying a new-found interest in the man and what he left behind. He cleans the corpse, washes himself and falls asleep at the wheel of his truck. Next morning, he drives off again and passes a faun-like group who are going through the bush with their bows. For a third time, his travelling is contrasted to the movements of primitive people. Eventually, he stalls in the middle of a stream which is just then being forded by a tribe of gypsies. He calls for help and they remove the corpse from him. At that moment, he sheds his worldly burdens:

> [H]e was thinking of a page near the beginning of a history book he had studied in the Sixth at school in 1939. About the Barbarian migrations in pre-history; the Celts and Iberians, Goths and Vandals and Huns. Once Life had been nothing worth recording beyond the movements of people like these, camels and asses piled with the poor property of their days, panniers, rags, rope, gramm and dahl, lambs and kids too new to walk, barefooted, long-haired people rank with sweat, animals shivering with ticks, old women striving to keep up with the rest of the family.

It is to this ancient sense of life that he now returns, bare, humbled, driven.

The gypsies offer Beale a sense of community but one very different from the one associated with the orange grove even if it is a community of sorts. Huddling together for survival, they endure without emotion or purpose and without true contact, silent, cold creatures: "Hard stones flung out of Creation's silent matrix" ('Karanje Village'). As Rilke's second Duino Elegy has it, they have found "some pure, contained,/ narrow, human, own little strip of orchard/ in between river and rock!" Indifferent, they move to the rhythm of earth and moon. It is the quality T. E. Lawrence detected in the Arab, "a mental and moral fatigue, a race trained out, and to avoid difficulties they have to jettison so much that we think honourable and grave".

At the end, Beale takes the dead driver's identity disks and paybooks and elects to follow the gypsies. He goes, as C.B. Cox has said, "like a soul to Hades".

> He wished, though, that he knew where they were going. They only smiled and nodded when he asked. Maybe they weren't going anywhere much, except perhaps to some pasture, some well.

The soldier thus bids farewell to the army and his home and sets out to find a new life.

"Well," Alun wrote to Gweno on 8 July,

> time may be short and there is so much refining and evolving to be accomplished — why? Is time short? Does time matter, on that plane? If I grow healthier and more oxlike and tougher and duller for the next year or two, and get nowhere, even lay aside the desire to think — does it matter? Even if it were to end like that, would time end for me? Wouldn't that search, oh deep as childhood, perhaps laid aside in childhood or adolescence or soldiering, the *intermittent* search — wouldn't it be taken up again in the clearer less bounded incorporeal space of endlessness?

There was, then, the possibility of life after death; that much survived.

> . . . I know that there is something indestructible in me — and I've *known* that intermittently and in many moods — in this heavy mood of tired eyes and rain and midnight, as much as in the feverish mood I wrote Lance-Jack in, three years ago. And I'm patient to let it emerge in its proper season. What else can I do?

"Heavy mood of tired eyes and rain and midnight" — these are magical words of evocation, rejecting a religious resurrection in favour of the immortality of the Romantic imagination as mediated by Edward Thomas and the poets who produced him.

Alun was in continuous distress at this time. He described himself to Gweno variously as blank, stubborn, irritated, stoic, loveless, acidulous, without care for the ultimate realities and increasingly susceptible to "Some unstated but compulsive growing pessimism".

> . . . I see life with the eyes of a wizened old man sometimes — no, often these days, as I lean against a tree, mooning in a calm moment during a mock battle, or driving a jeep or holding a drink in my hand with the night all round me and the sleeping camp. And I wonder whether we can keep this *magic*, this youthful delight in the other, and in life; and I know at once that such things are not our concern; we need not and must not worry over the magic and the youth. It *IS*. Amen . . . But oh, the temptation of the wilderness, darling . . .

At the end of July, the Borderers moved back to Kharakvasla, this time pitching their tents on the plateau terracing the hillside a hundred feet above the lake. Alun was granted ten days' leave and told to report to Karachi for a six-week course at the new Military Intelligence Training School in August. He hoped to visit his Aunt Connie in Darjeeling but doubted if he could reach her in time, so he accepted Dick Mills's suggestion and visited Wallace and Freda Aykroyd at Coonoor, some hundred miles south in the Nilgiri Hills in Madras. The Aykroyds kept open house for officers and Dick himself had been there recently. He boarded the train on the 22 July and arrived at Coonoor two days later. A taxi took him up through the bazaar past Sims Park, a beautiful botanical garden, and through the hills to Highfield, the Aykroyds' house, a large, two-storey structure with latticed, columned verandahs surrounded by lawns and bluegum forests. As the taxi drew up, he felt a curious sense of excitement, a vivid, tremulous premonition like a birth of spirit. It filled his heart and head but was without physical point, purpose, foresight or expectation. He paid the taxi and rang the front door-bell. A servant let him in and took him up to Freda, who had been helping her daughter, Gilly, erect a toy theatre she had made for her. She rose to her feet, wondering which of the soldiers had turned up unexpectedly. As the door opened, he trembled as if struck by a sword. Seeing her standing there with the sunlight on her hair "more beautiful than fate", he knew he had fallen in love.

XIV

Death and the Maiden

It was a remarkable turn of events. Not more than a week after 'The Orange Grove' had brought his spiritual exploration of death to a close, Alun discovered a new commitment to life. Just before leaving for Coonoor, he told Dick Mills:

> I'm in a mulish and grieving mood in secret these days — grieving over something I've lost, something unbearable it is. I dream very intensely and do my work with the efficiency of an automaton, whether it's running an Eisteddfod or acting Adjutant for a batttalion move. But I can see *through* the mirror all the time — at the emptiness behind.

Now he had discovered an elation beyond his imaginings and one of a singular kind.

> Beloved when we stood
> And saw each other standing there
> I did not know that all
> The ordinary days
> Had fallen from the earth. . . .
> And did you know then
> How I had been closed
> By the steady expectation
> And preparing of death?
> How did you hope
> That hardness to break

> Of the man who no longer asks
> For love and its ache . . . ?

('The House', unpublished)

Freda was five years Alun's senior. Born in Shropshire, she had grown up partly in London and partly in South Africa, where her father was a farmer; he had served in the Boer War and decided to stay and raise sheep near Potchefstroom, in the Transvaal. When her mother died, he went back to England and returned shortly afterwards, leaving the eight-year-old Freda in the care of an aunt in London. The little girl felt desperately lonely and neglected in a boarding school where bullying was rife. Eventually, she moved to a school nearer home where a kindly teacher inspired in her a love of literature. When she was thirteen, she returned to South Africa to live with her father (now remarried) and stayed with him for two years.

In 1930, she married Wallace Aykroyd, a good-looking nutritional scientist eleven years her senior. He was a quiet, intelligent man with a sense of humour, at once father figure, lover and companion. He was to become the author of several books, though it was his gift for synthesizing research rather than initiating it that took him from the Lister Institute in London to Geneva, where he worked in the health section of the League of Nations. He was not particularly happy there but Freda enjoyed the mix of figures, the drama and music clubs and the chances for intellectual life. Their first two children, Peter and Gilly, were born there. Before long, they moved again to Coonoor, where Wallace succeeded Sir Robert McCarrison as director of the Nutrition Research Laboratories.

Life in the Nilgiri hills was dominated by the army, the Indian Civil Service and the tea-planters. Coonoor and Wellington shared a club round which social life revolved; Ootacamund ("Ooty") lay eleven miles away. Freda was less happy here. Peter had been evacuated from school in England to Canada at the start of the war, there were no proper theatres or libraries and, though she got on well with the military wives, she found their company restricting. Wallace was wrapped up in his work, so she took to painting and sculpting a little, reviewed for the *Calcutta Statesman* and broadcast for All-India Radio. She was a bright figure, full of fun, enjoying hunting, fishing and riding and going to dances, but essentially she was restless. Both by circumstance and upbringing, she was a hostess but by nature she was warm, quick to understand and respond. Of medium height, she was slim but firmly built, her eyes large and set apart, with lazy lids, her face sensual, tawny hair thrown back onto her shoulders. Thanks to her childhood experience (surprisingly like Alun's in psychological outline), she never believed that anyone could love her or, if they did, would not turn against her. Perhaps, like the heroine of Edward Thompson's *An Indian Day*,

> like all intellectual women, she wanted friendship with men; even the dullest man seemed to have *some* touch with life somewhere. She had not realized this so strongly till she came to India. But men's friendship never seemed free from some dominion of the senses. As long as she was young and beautiful, men would throng to talk with her; but their friendship was not the thing it seemed.

A certain gregariousness thus fell in easily with her temper.

When Alun arrived at Highfield, she had just returned from an operation for the removal of an appendix at Nagercoil and the recovery laid her up for two months. Wallace was at a conference at Hot Springs in the United States which was instrumental in establishing the Food and Agriculture Organisation of the United Nations in 1946. (He was to serve as its first Director of the Nutrition Division.) She and Alun were therefore alone and at a dance the first night he confessed to her what he knew to exist between them, a "marvellous feeling of blood relationship, not that of a lover but of a brother, not only a brother". (He was often to invoke Mair when thinking of Freda.) After the dance, she felt faint and he stayed with her on the porch at Highfield in a quiet embrace.

In the days that followed, they went for walks in the woods and tea plantations or picnicked in the hills or by a lake on the Ooty Downs.

> Here with a Loaf of Bread beneath the Bough,
> A Flask of Wine, a Book of Verse — and Thou
>   Beside me singing in the Wilderness —
> And Wilderness is Paradise enow.

The mornings were full of a breathless pleasure. They would stand together under the trees looking into a stream that ran between the eucalyptus trees where, because of the purple iridescence, he said the moles lay, "dappled moles of warm blue sunlight" made by the branches and wind where they cleared a way for the sun to reach the brooks. "I, certainly, for my part," Freda recalls, "felt no-one except Wallace had ever or could ever be so close, so understanding of every aspect of me, my life as it was and had been and what I was and wanted and needed. His gentleness and undemanding love, while he was in Coonoor, was so different from anything I had ever experienced." It was the happiness, she wrote in a poem, of love "given purely/ Simple and free and without stress.// When only the heart stirs, not brain/ Nor blood nor any sensual need".

In the afternoons, they sat together in the garden talking to friends or playing the gramophone or reading poems. Alun read to her from *Raiders' Dawn*, which she had not thought much of when Dick had lent her his copy but which she grew to appreciate the better she understood its author. "There was a frailty about him, a look of not belonging in all the horror and mess of war, that gave his white face and high forehead, his strange, blind-seeming eyes and soft voice a particular pathos," she wrote. Nevertheless, the impression was contradicted by his wiry body and the vigour of his opinions.

Wallace was due back from America within five days, so Alun went to Ratantata, the officers' rest home at Ooty; Freda cried as she bade him farewell. She wrote in a poem:

> But today in the cold and cruel dawn,
> ... the grey light
> Awakened you to your own strength
> And left me to my helplessness.
> As your fingers fastened buckles deftly,
> Efficient and tidy — oh for what? —
> Your khaki jacket rustled stiffly
> As you jerked it down behind.
> Efficient and clean and ready —
> A straw in the wind, a leaf upon the flood.
> As you turned to go I saw your eyes
> And knew my strength was but despair
> And that your own could not prevail.

During his stay in Ratantata, he observed the queer rush temples and gnome-like thatched huts of the Todas and wrote a number of poems. The one which best captures the quality of their love is 'Ways':

> It had been easier, not loving.
>
> I knew I had grown harder than the trees
> In which I held you all the afternoon,
> The tall blue slender saplings leaning
> Each on each, their strength outgrowing.
> And suddenly we two were swaying
> Each upon the other leaning.

It had been easier, not loving.

Grave, tender lines, burdened with sadness. He can hardly believe the miracle that has been wrought on him; it comes with a delicate softness, beautifully captured by the sway of the lines. But there is the perplexity of circumstance, unstated but understood, to shade his new-found emotion. The lovers sway like plants in their embrace yet a sense of reality persists. Hardness is real and will return — and the lovers know it.

> Love being gravel in the wound
> When the silent lovers know
> Swaying in the misty rain
> The old oppression of the burden
> Growing in them as they go,
> Though trees are felled and grow again,
> Far and farther each from each.
> Longing hardens like a stone.
>
> Lovers go but hardly, all alone.

They *can* be parted, after all, since they lack nature's capacity for renewal. How poignant that Alun's love for Freda, breaking the pattern of exclusion that had been his, should be so immediately overshadowed by the threat of separation, should be so brief, discontinuous, powerless to change its course!

> The rock you touched became a stream
> And all reality an ugly dream
> I knew you kissed me in my sleep
> And always, waking or in dream,
> You bend above the blindness in my head
> Raining all your quickness, all your beauty
> On the morose, the taciturnly dead.
>
> (draft of 'Ways')

In a poem she wrote for Alun, Freda expressed her own understanding of this. Here, it is he who weeps and she who stands between him and the world helplessly.

> . . . the grey light
> Awakened you to your own strength
> And left me to my helplessness.
> As your fingers fastened buckles deftly,
> Efficient and tidy — oh for what —

> Your khaki jacket rustled stiffly
> As you jerked it down behind.
> Efficient and clean and ready —
> A straw in the wind, a leaf upon the flood.
> As you turned to go I saw your eyes
> And knew my strength was but despair
> And that your own could not prevail.

For Alun, Freda was inseparable from nature: Coonoor's nature, not Bhiwandi's, cool, remote, upland — the mountain view again. She was the obverse of the dark angel of the lake poems, one more image of the Goddess. In 'Peasant Song' (originally 'The Field'), he wrote:

> The seed is costly.
> Plant it carefully.
> I have only this small plough
> To turn the mighty earth.

His own love, his means of expressing that love and their finding love in wartime apart from other loves — all these are costly, both precious and burdensome, and unlikely to turn the world from its desert ways.

> But if I should go
> And you be left behind
> Among the tall red ant hills and the maize
> Would you hear my plough still singing
> And, bearing endless days,
> Somehow give praise?

What survives? The question never left him. Would the beloved, rising above her grief, treasure his memory and would he still sound with the talent unrealised in him? Does love survive the venom of the snake? (We notice the ironic echo of the opening words of 'Post-script: for Gweno' in the opening line of my quotation.)

In 'Wood Song', he declares:

> The pine trees cast their needles softly
> Darling for your gypsy bed
> And the tall blue saplings swaying
> Whisper more than can be said.
>
> Piteously the world is happening
> Beyond this cool stockade of trees.
> Enduring passions penetrate
> These quiet rides with agonies
> That love can never consummate.

> And we must go because we love
> Beyond ourselves, beyond these trees
> That sway above your golden head
> Till wind and war and sky and dove
> Become again the murmur of your breath
> And your body the white shew-bread.

Love has other obligations and is weak in war. It may try to turn the world to its original purpose but it can never consummate its agonies. As the unpublished 'Map' has it:

> The human passion in me cried
> With the voice of every man
> Who had that wound within his side
> And knew the beauty of the world
> And hated that by which he dies.
>
> But loveliness is no man's bride.
> Your name is mixed with battles on the map.
> And I can lie no longer by your side
> Because the world has laid away the map,
> And I can never lay away the world.

A draft of another unpublished poem, 'Nothing About the Dead', puts it even more forcefully. (I give an edited version.)

> A dream's length, a heart's
> Dream and intuitions go.
> Tomorrow in the jungle and the guns
> The heart will harden, shed its song.
> Love is unbelievable as snow
> And all the cosmos runs
> Like blood away, like blood away,
> And with terror and elation
> My massive hands will tear the day
> And reach the desiccated lands
> That no one goes to willingly . . .
> And what can love or friendship say
> One way or the other way?

Nothing, apparently. So it is he could write:

> The ruthlessness of war
> Holds me passionless and I
> Neither resist nor wish to flee

> The darkness of its inner law
> Nor answer when you call to me.

('In the days when I could choose')

Once more, the beloved is put away, despite the love he feels for her, "more and more love and ever love".

When he returned from Ratantata, Alun carried the poems with him, returning through a wild part of the wood to surprise her. His joy increased with the excitement of having the poems to read, his face alight with achievement.

> Only love me if you can
> Give what no-one else can claim,
> For both the woman and the man
> Wither at the touch of shame.
>
> If you lose too much
> By loving me, forswear
> All I secreted for you.
> Beloved, beware,
> When emotion burns the soul
> Love is already there.

('Beloved, beware', unpublished)

Other claims upon the lovers are separated from the emotion that unites them, something that could not exist with dishonour, giving "what no-one else can claim", a "calm, independent love that endures absence and rejoices in meeting, and doesn't destroy or crimp or cripple".

He was to return to the theme repeatedly.

> I was afraid there'd been a huge destruction, but perhaps there hasn't been, after all. We hanker after one-ness, it's the dominant image — monotheism, monogamy, the uniquely beloved whose face and body is always immanent in distance and danger and despondency & the homeward dream — and I only slowly admit to myself that my whole being has other loyalties or at least other ways of attaining the consummation that Rilke calls a harmony between the individual & the universal cycle of beauty.

Six months before, he had written of the "simplicity" he and Gweno had "achieved in Oh a distant land"; now, she was placed beside other sources of beauty. As he told Dick Mills (without disclosing the precise circumstances):

Yet I'm not a monogamous creature. I know that the guiding force
in me seeks always the leading vision of love and recognises and
desires it wherever it appears and whoever is wearing or bearing
it. How such things work out I don't know . . . . 'Fidelity' is an
expanding not a brittle ideal, I hope.

That this was not simply a piece of special pleading is evident from a
letter Alun sent Gweno from Southend in October, 1942, shortly
before embarkation: "Gweno, we should be happy, really, you and I.
We're a very happy brace of sweethearts and give each other most of
the things we need, . . . I want no other, although I was so made that
there is nothing exclusive in me, and my life is a perpetual search for
new experience and wider circles of consciousness. The unknown
compels. . . ." And yet, he told Freda, "Why should that hurt?
Because somehow it is hurting others: it hurts the possessive in others,
wounds them, distresses & confounds them. And all words, all
explanations are hard & doubtful. I shrink from such words or the
labour of making them audible and cogent."

It was doubtless naive of him to imagine that others would not be
hurt, yet he knew that his quest for "Being" led him into strange
paths. Gweno could not follow this. Her grief in Alun's absence and
her fears for his safety inspired a possessive care which was all the
greater coming from one who was not emotional. She was the essence
of singlemindedness in love, going down deep and slow, straight
down, unwavering, enclosed, and all that winter she was put to the
test, living in "a sort of hourly anxiety". Alun remarked, "[I]t's such a
deadly drain on her spirit, and she must somehow push those black
fears back into the sub sub sub conscious and lock them up, like a
funeral dress. To wear them daily isn't right at all: and to so empty
herself of everything but love: it disturbs me very deeply". Shortly
before embarkation, he had written to her:

> [Y]ou musn't fret like this: all this blackness you hold and hide —
> please try and dissipate it. Make yourself separate from the
> necessities and accidents of the war, as I am making myself separate.
> I can feel myself growing more indestructible, more self-reliant and
> complete and inviolable, and I will *not* let myself be intimidated or
> destroyed — my true self, Gwen, you understand? But without
> separateness separation is dreadful. Can you feel what I mean? It's
> very important, darling, to feel this difference between oneself and
> what happens to one.

She must have a proud existence separate from himself, as he would
with the army.

Like Alun, Freda longed to escape into aloneness the better to love. Being divided herself, her love for Alun was steadfast and single but always with the proviso of her marriage, "of the anchor, of the substitute father, family, sibling; of deep and quiet belonging. It is so odd that all that can exist side by side with the passionate certainty of LOVE, romantic, found-at-last, never-thought-to-be-found love. There it is." In her time with Alun, he showed no importunacy; they could feel without grasping. Alun wrote to her:

> I've growingly had the sensation this last year of the separateness of each one, of the *necessity* for each one to be separate and not try to be identified with someone else. This I mean in terms of personal relations, not political — in politics we must join. But individually, let us be separate, I say. It's so very painful for Gweno, to suffer separation without this separateness. Every letter has this awful foreboding in it, dread of loss, anguish at the fear of death — my death. It gets on my nerves to think of her having that feeling all the time and I try & tell her to be *herself* — not crudely that, but to become indestructible as I am becoming slowly . . . . the *real* music is in being thrillingly & sensitively aware of the separateness of the other one with whom you share love and who is in your arms or in bed with you or five thousand miles away from you.

If one were not separate, one could not distinguish oneself from all that happened to one. That is why, when Freda said she wished to be alone, he

> answered 'Yes yes yes' with my whole heart, but my voice said 'No' aloud. Because I was afraid of the thoughts that would come, and become a resolve ultimately and after that become words spoken to someone else, someone very very important & easy also to hurt. Yet the deepest longing *is* this aloneness that we need, and I gladly go into it, very gladly, although I fear it also. I fear it for the simple reason that it isn't final, that one cannot stay there, but must emerge, and *must obey* what it insists and I've always refused to submit to a rule — Jesuit, Anglican, Nonconformist, military — out of fear: and I've clung as long as possible to the freedom that does not decide and scarcely has an opinion, that suddenly acts from an overpowering conviction that appears to be simple intuition, and acts always *in* the situation, and not according to rules that one applies to the situation.

A Keatsian revelation.

As Alun prepared to leave Coonoor for Karachi, he and Freda took a last walk into the woods. They both wept. He tried to express his love for her but failed. Ashen-faced, he rose and put his head back in a proud gesture. "Well, I can take it if it has to be like that. I would

never have written a line if it were not so." (He always associated
Yeats's 'Solomon and the Witch', one of his favourite poems, with the
"broken rhythm of the wood" in Coonoor.) A dinner, an evening's
conversation, a kiss on the railway platform, and he was gone. Soon
afterwards, Freda wrote a poem expressing her pain at their parting
and the strength she believed would come from it, its secret joy. It was
a poem Alun said he would keep by him for ever.

> It matters little that you are away from me
> I do not seek to measure time nor yet to see
> Eternity lying between this little soul of mine
> And that great coldly flashing star.
> I do not seek to hold its light within my hand.
> That it shines and you are in the world
> Is all I understand.

A curiously Alun-like complication of imagery.

At Arkonam, he wrote a letter to her headed 'The first day':

> . . . I'd gone and you'd gone. And in that caved-in sensation was
> also the other knowledge, that sometimes the night plagues and tries
> to obscure, that I — & again it's hard to say, — love you, love you,
> love you . . . .
>   . . . this morning the day is lovely & a bell is ringing in the town &
> the day has come very softly and unobtrusively on us and I can see &
> feel & hear you and speak to you, but not here, nor these words: but
> instead in your own woods, where the moles lie in the sunny water
> and you smile and, for all the world you know of, yet you are shy and
> very young, and innocent in a way you cannot hide. . . .
>   Freda beloved, things were queerly reversed and in a way it was a
> pity for yesterday which hurts in me more than the finger with the
> blue nail coming off. [He had caught it in an electric fan.] But it was
> bitter, perhaps, for now there is no pretence in any sort, but only a
> beginning from the beginning, darling, and not from where I left off
> in life with certain achievements.

Two days later, on 4 August, he reached Poona. He drove a lorry
down to Bombay to collect furniture and materials for a reading room
he was making and then continued his journey. Floods had closed the
line, forcing a detour via Delhi and Lahore (where he arrived on 9
August), adding another two days to the journey. At Lahore, he
contacted the family of his Hindustani teacher aboard the *Athlone
Castle*, Lieutenant Khulla, and arranged to visit them again on his
return.

All the time, he enquired "ruthlessly" into "the basis of the
tranquillity" Freda had filled him with. "I find myself throwing up all

sorts of answers & charges, none of which go deep enough. That tranquillity was so deep, I can't fathom it, and that ecstasy so unearthly that I can't answer it with the ordinary answers". He was, he told her, "involved utterly & entirely in what is happening, and I know that more depends upon it than just life; yet I am somehow as impartial as a battleground, and I wait as best I can. Another part of me actively seeks you, plans to meet you, fixes a time & a place". The larger tide of fate carried the smaller current of his will and he was content to await the outcome "within the situation".

The poem born of this emotion, 'The Way Back', is one of his finest.

> Six days and two thousand miles
> I have watched the shafted rain
> Feminise the burning land,
> Cloaking with a green distress
> The cerulean and ochre
> Of the season's ruthlessness.

It was as if Freda's impact on him were comparable to "the season's ruthlessness", his the "green distress" after months of burning on the land. Once more, water falls and induces in him a special mood of creative destruction.

> Soldiers quickened by your breath
> Feel the sudden spur and rush
> Of the life they put away
> Lest the war should break and crush
> Beauties more profound than death.

The tranquillity he associated with Freda — indeed, the tranquillity *was* the ecstasy — called to mind a picnic they had taken together by Malmund lake, he breasting

> with exquisite ease
> The foaming arabesques of joy
> And in the sarabande of trees
> Of guava and papaya
> And crimson blown poinsettia,
> The millrace of my blood
> Beat against my smile,
> And were you answering my smile
> Or the millrace of my blood?

(the last is an image he had first used in 'Beloved, beware'.) Repeatedly, swimming in lakes meant something special to him,

"when I'm nearest to complete *being* with the universe". As he told
Freda, "Wherever I see a lake or river or a bay whose beauty pierces
me, I merge with it, become it. In the activity of living I know now
that I've always wanted and longed for another illumination, to
encounter and know and merge with the same living stream in
whoever it flows. In you, and you, and you." It is what had happened
earlier that year when he woke up near the zareba of dead thorns, but
the experience of 'The Way Back' is more brilliant. The language is
decidedly exotic: "cerulean and ochre", "arabesques", "sarabande".
We are as far from the severity of 'Water Music' and 'Shadows' as it is
possible to be. Here is no Rilkean harmony between individual and
universal cycles of beauty but a Yeatsian rapture in which love
destroys "this foul world". In 'Beloved, beware', he had written
(directly echoing Yeats's 'Among School Children'):

> When you look at me
> Do I not answer
> As if you were dancing
> And I your dancer?

Eventually, the "golden" realm of his swimming and her smiling
and hiding her face, shy with the newness of love, is interrupted by the
"gladiators and levies" who recall the soldier to his task. The
flourishing diction of "gladiators and levies" lends a quite surprising
martial glamour to the war (as does the phrase "iron beasts", a
mixture of the allegorical and concrete). Indeed, Freda's "golden
gate" is made to seem as much an introduction to it as an alternative,
related to her and the season's 'ruthlessness'. Once more, the goddess
is shown to be two-faced, benign and malign. (Compare the "deep
gates" of the darkness that bids the soldier enter alone in 'Burma
Casualty'.) Like the predestined voyager, the hero leaves his beloved
for some cataclysm which will engulf his spiritual self:

> And in the hardness of this world
> And in the brilliance of this pain
> I exult with such a passion
> To be squandered, to be hurled,
> To be joined to you again.

Here is a terrible explosion or wasting which also reunites the lovers.
Alun once described poetry as "an act of daring, always daring, to
plunge and tear and enter" and he repeated the language in describing

Freda's impact on him: "concussed", "pierced", "broken down", "pain as well as joy". The impulse to join the loved one merges with the impulse to join the earth (thus repeating the image of "feminising" in the first verse and the sexual suggestiveness of "shafted rain"). The emotion of the lake scene here yields a specifically sensual meaning which runs excitedly to its supra-sensual conclusion in the bold rhetorical phrases of the finale, brilliantly shortened and intensified in the closing two lines. Passion mixes with the destruction of soldiering and is converted through love into an euphoria of joy.

"Oh Frieda," (Alun retained the correct spelling of her name, altered by her parents at the time of the First World War to make it seem less Germanic)

> do you know how deeply you have pierced in me? How everywhere you have restated, revived, broken down and compelled in me, so that, as I gradually encounter the beliefs I had, I find one after another is changed, maybe replaced, maybe just lost & nothing yet in its place? And now I am hunger & thirst and effort and this strange intense joy that really is pain as well as joy, not because it is complex but because it is commensurate with life, and with all that the imagination has ever explored and identified and known. . . .
>
> Darling, don't let yourself think of me as a little youth. Nor as a poet nor as a writer. I am something much harder, more obstinate and vulnerable and devoted and blindly determined than any of these people. I am just an instinct when it becomes real and there are no embellishments. It is that instinct I want to give to you, I want you to feel inside you. . . .

'The Way Back' embodies that instinct, recalling the "wild communion" of the "final union" when "my flesh will turn to clay". ('The Ploughman', a poem of 1938 echoed again in 'Peasant Song'.)

The writing of 'The Way Back' marked an important stage in Alun's life bringing to a head his sense of satisfaction with his recent writing, from Poona hospital on, and it led him, for the first time, to reflect on what writing meant to him. On the train to Karachi, he read Virginia Woolf's biography of Roger Fry and it made him realise how much he, like Fry, had made his career against the odds. In his sixteenth, seventeenth and twenty-second years, "there was nothing to be said, nothing", but he had discovered "the clue, the almost invisible clue" and followed it more ruthlessly than he had realised.

> Christ, don't I *loathe* the bloody war? I hate it with my guts, because it's just plain rottenness and it has no satisfaction at all, either to the

living or the being killed. But my tapeworm, my writing bug, he's alright. He's alive & obdurate, no matter how many other ways I fail. And I've got his courage to discard all death forms that these times seek to impose. And when I thought, reading old Roger Fry, of the long novels & plays I've written and thrown away, the blind persistence & humility of hammering at my typewriter in my mother's house while she dusted and cooked, & the utter lack of disappointment when I realised that 300 pages of typescript were no good — then I do know that I was right in trying just that, that, that, that.

For the first time, he discovered that, however much he submitted himself to the war, it no longer held any purposeful meaning for him.

To his parents, he now announced the completion of a second volume of poems, better than *Raiders' Dawn* but "it must be *different* as well as better. *Raiders' Dawn* was young and passionate. These poems must be steadier, more general, more in line with fact and universal experience". He described the earlier book to Freda as "poor little *Raiders' Dawn*. It's not a bad book, is it?, but it's a very young one. Full of seed, every page is seed; no harvest, only seed, seed, seed". The new collection was to be called *The Voyager* and was divided into four sections: 'England', 'At Sea', 'India' and 'The Land of the Heart'. The last contained the poems to Freda which, he told Gweno, did not belong to any specific time or place: "Wherever I am Love relates itself softly to the physical influences of the land and when the mood and the place are fully integrated I write and send you the poem" (including the geographically-revealing opening of 'The Way Back'). The poems, he said, were a queer batch written in queer moods over a long period, transplanting himself from India to Longmoor and Burma and "never never Land" and living "more lives than one so they're a sifting of imagined lives and other people's experiences as much as my own". Eventually, though, 'The Land of the Heart' poems were mixed in with the Indian poems and the logic of the progression lost.

"I write always *against* the tug of war & the horror & tedium of it:" he told Freda, "and all I'm trying to write is love". He saw his stories as acts of "steadiness & recognition, of *myself where I am*. Is that true? I value the stories myself because they stick to things the poetry sweeps above or below. They authenticate the poems: pay for them in cash or sweat or patience or guts". Again:

> You say things about my poems & stories that I do not expressly answer . . . because I am content with your saying them simply.

Mostly I let the things I've written pass away from me. If they have merit I don't want it for myself. . . . The only thing I respect in myself are the poems & stories I haven't yet written. These I work for with all the power I can gather, fiercely as any mother. I don't worry even what other people are writing, the new tricks, the modernism; I read them with pleasure and a thrill of something new & exciting, but I don't try to be like them or like anything or anybody, in the same way as I've never tried to meet any of these people, preferring to go my own way & be that hardest of things, my-self. Nobody & no thing has succeeded in preventing me, not even myself, though many powerful beings have tried, often not intentionally. The sensitiveness to criticism or the desire for praise you speak of is very real, it's fundamental really, yet it's only the word from the very *near* person that one wants, to be fertilised thereby: the critic's opinion is a pale thing with no more warmth to warm or burn than the moon has. But mother's quiet support was everything I needed, & daddy's inarticulateness was like a shadow all over me so that I avoided him: it's the same as you say. Except that one does go on & on, praise or no praise.

To Gweno, he wrote:

Usually I don't know anything about a poem or story until suddenly I discover that it's written itself, and I'm left with a slightly incredulous and pleasantly surprised tiredness. I feel more & more that my métier *is* writing: that that's the only real thing I can do. [My memory is now] discarding everything it doesn't need to write & dream upon. It retains the bare necessities of soldiering: otherwise it forgets. All the stuff I learnt at College and Pengam has gone by the board, & it tunes itself more and more to the simple human materials of life and of itself . . . . It's going native, quite definitely, and all its reasoning is done from a human standpoint. My longing is more & more for one thing only, integrity, and I discount the other qualities in people far too ruthlessly if they lack that fundamental sincerity and wholeness. So I only hope that I will be able to write, for I'm sure I won't be able to do anything else half as well.

Freda did not realise how good a writer Alun was until she read 'The Way Back''. Then she knew him to be a real poet and wrote to tell him so. He replied,

I hadn't read it since I wrote it — I read it this afternoon and it seemed strange that it should be there, clear and hard as a lump of coal. . . . I imagine a mother looks at her child in some moods and is incredulous that she has borne it. I like best to abstract my own self out of a poem & feel *I* didn't write it. It was only my hand that wrote it. It wrote itself, being a spontaneous action in the world of thought.' And similarly to submit myself to a poem, offering it hospitality, and respect; if it wished to be written by me I'll help it. Often I think of Love the same way. . . . The other, deeper existence, is it not a purification & submission?

'The Way Back', then, expresses a sense of achievement and it comes from the full man in a way none of his other poems do. It is sensitive and shapely, carrying his hopes and fears; it is the very breath of sincerity and modesty, yet magnificently rhetorical, too.

The achievement was answered promptly and extraordinarily by Karachi. From 11 of August, he was immersed in the tactics of the Japanese army and Japanese life in general (the first time these had been studied in the Intelligence school, which had previously concentrated on the German and Italian armies). He lived in Old Government House and kept regular hours, with time off at evenings and weekends. It was like a grown-up OCTU, altogether luxurious after his period of beach training, but it reinforced his belief that "the only place worth going to is the Jungle". There was little time for writing save for a revised version of the poem 'The Journey' and 'By the Gateway of India, Bombay'. Then, one evening, he cycled down to the Boat Club carrying three of Freda's letters with him and wrote to her from there:

> Oh such wealth, great caskets of sunlight unlocked pouring all over me like the water in the lake — *all* your letters — three envelopes of your letters — all waiting there today. . . . There isn't anything I can do with this fullness except feel and bless it — do I need to *convey* it to you, darling? . . . There are situations, obligations, yes, yes, yes — but not now: nor when we meet again. . . . I dream of this other time, of deep freedom — . . .
>
> I do grieve. I know that. I don't let myself hate because hate spoils — it withers & shrinks like socks in salt water, but grief pours gentleness liquidly round everything and it's a natural expression for the love & the melancholy that almost, I think, I like best. . . .
>
> Don't worry about my love, will you, or your own love? Hands are safe, are gentle, are kind.

Even in the midst of his excitement, we hear the presence of the beautiful singing sexless angel, her hands "so soft you scarcely feel her touch/ Gentle, eternally gentle, round your heart". Accordingly, beneath the explicit tension between Freda and other "obligations" (rendered in the unpublished poem 'Love' —

> Unbearable ecstasy, how can I answer,
> Possessed with your splendour, having no choice,
> That other bitter agony

> That other broken voice?
> Am I not cruel as you are
> So to rejoice?)

we discover another, deeper tension, expressed in 'What is love?' (also unpublished):

> What is love at least?
> A way of dignifying death.

When Freda expressed her fears for his safety, he replied,

> You say it almost as if it would be my fault, for being clumsy, or not worldly wise enough. There's a devil of a lot of very skilful and wise people gone clean out of existence since 1939, they're a company not to be ashamed of. And I'm not clumsy and I am moderately wise to the world, wise enough to know that there are a lot of risks I can't avoid, and wise enough to know I don't want to avoid them. I *want* to run the gamut; and it's quite a mature wish, too: — it isn't for the thrill of it nor for the horror of it, though both these attract. It's for two reasons — to have authority in the long fight of peace, and to share the comradeship of a war, and of death. Sounds very British Legion, to write it: still, it's sound enough. As for death, it's a matter of luck. I'm no weakling and if endurance or one's own resources are all I need to get through any particular spot of murder I'm confident I can do it. But I *do* think of death a great deal, and I think life & human relationships have grown more & more precious & warm and urgent to me because of this thought at the back of everything.

He was now reading the Bible — the Song of Solomon and the life of David: "there's something wishing to take shape in me and write itself," he told Freda. "But I can't do anything except lie open to the sky for it & reject the dances & the clubs so that it may have the quiet it desires." He waited for 'this poem, for you, for whatever happens inside me" and it happened on the evening of 23 August.

> One huge thing happened to me on Monday night when I was all alone — I sang it to myself, the thing that happened; the room was empty & I was naked splashing water over myself & singing this enormous & dreadful joy that came up to me so casually & said something quite final & terrible to me & I laughed and sang it back. It was in my sleep, too, & when I woke, yesterday morning & this morning, and I'm delighted that I can sing it & not shudder over it.

He gave a fuller account of the experience in his journal.

There are many sadnesses, justified & inevitable & established:
why should I make another? I make no sadnesses — and last night I
was singing and there was my death quite clear & familiar at last after
all the groping & revulsion and I sang of it in my tuneless man's voice
Did she be close unto thee, Billy Boy, Billy Boy? Yes she lay close
unto me as the bark is to the tree And me Nancy tickled me fancy oh
my darling Billy Boy: and the places on the map faded away from me
pleasantly & the jungles of Burma came towards me & flowed round
me familiarly & I could count the days that remained neatly, in a neat
pile on a white cloth, and I knew that this little gesture, this joy of my
pen writing this word, is the good spending of one of my days.

Though the world be wrong & commit men's blasphemies and
deadly enemies against itself I will not add to those lecheries in the
days that remain, nor hope less or love less, but more yea more &
more love & ever love, & be less & less the nothing that does not exist
& cannot breathe.

I am glad & I am in love and I don't care.

The singing voice that had been calling all the year (as in 'The
Journey') is finally internalised and the certainty of death made clear,
flowing round him, like the beautiful angel, with "dreadful joy". At
that moment, love becomes more precious to him: he will have
nothing to do with the mortal world and its errors but write for love,
be in love, in the time that remains.

Immediately, there was an attempt to versify the thought. (I give an
edited version.)

> Sadness manifold, ineluctable and established
> Grow as the rough grass everywhere in India.
> I shall not add another, this is singing
> Counting my days upon my fingers
> Neat pile of days on a white napkin
> Now after all the groping and revulsion
> Come clear at last entertain my death
> With singing Did she lie close unto thee?
> Yes she lay close unto me
> As the bark is to the tree, my billy boy
> And my nancy tickled my fancy, Billy boy.
>
> The innumerable places on the map
> Fade from me pleasantly the jungles wind
> Their mortal coils about me dulcetly
> And this sweet joy of writing is the right spending
> Of one day that remains me out of ninety.
> Though the world commit countless blasphemies
> I will not add dismay to its treacheries

> Nor love less, but more and more love
> And ever more love, growing less and less
> The nothingness that exists not, cannot breathe
> This I write to you love, to whom the stones
> Are the river's songs. . . .
> India, torn by a century's wilderness,
> Many good men have entered. Now be brave.
> Bear as a child within you your huge error.
> Endure what all must suffer
> Be healed without miracle, without saviour.

So his pen ran on, the original "seventy" days left him being altered to "ninety", thus taking us to the late autumn, when the Borderers were expecting to see action in Burma. The identification of Burma with Alun's death is now complete.

As if in response to this revelation, he composed the following scene:

> Fields of golden sesamum, pollen trickling in untidy yellow streams down your green overalls & leaden boots, snakes of the earth in 50 yards of deep yellow flowers & you kneeling away among them listening to the order of a man you hate — listening coldly & obeying coldly & exactly because hatred takes away warmth. And later your heart is hot with an unforgiveable sorrow kneeling over a man you love who has bled away in your hands, hiding swiftly his horrible wounds and gently slowly reluctantly his unresponsive face.

A remarkable passage, embodying the consummation foretold by 'The Orange Grove' and 'The Way Back'. At last, the double hinted at by the end of 'Ward "O"3(b)' makes his appearance. There is a death or execution, performed reluctantly by one who obeys orders, soldier-like. They come from a man he hates. Afterwards, he kneels over the body of the man who lies bleeding to death in his hands and tries to hide the disfigurement he has caused. It is a measure of the love he feels for him, yet his sorrow is "unforgiveable" because culpable. He is the cause of the thing he mourns. It might be a Japanese soldier who is being described here, the "dreaming German soldier" of 'War Wedding' and 'The Patrol' updated, but both the setting and the remorse expressed make it likelier that the quarrel we are witnessing is an internal one. One side of the man comes to tell the other what he is going to force him to do — and what the result will be.

An early ancestor of the scene in the sesamum field is to be found in the journal Alun kept during his Manchester days. This, too, personifies the death instinct in him and goes thus:

When I lie down, above me the sky
Is vast and still
Two words for one quality,
And instead of the thrush's wild music
Or the sublimation of the skylark
That makes the mind follow
It upwards till it is spirit
And the body an unneeded
Precipitate, the spirit's dregs,
There is nothing but the slow
Strong pulse of silence
The throb of waiting in silence.
Then comes the tread of feet, the
Clatter of mattock and spade
Over me,
The living man with a purpose
That must be performed upon me.
And the silent bell screams
Out as his hand tugs the rope
Which he pulls till the bell,
Tormented, beyond bearing,
Turns over and swallows
Its tongue and suffocatingly falls.
And when I at last dare
Lift my terrified eyes to
Confront the sexton
I know the features, the eyes,
The mole by the drooping
Mouth, the white uneven teeth,
The twisted grief
The terrible presence of the
Lover
Whom I do not love.

Edward Thomas has a story called 'The Attempt' which is relevant here. It tells of a man's attempt to kill himself in anguish at the suffering he causes his wife and daughter.

> [O]n this day, the arguments for and against a fatal act did not weigh with [Treharon]. He was called to death.
> He was called to death, but hardly to an act which could procure it. . . . Death was an idea tinged with poetry in his mind — a kingly thing which was once only at any man's call. After it came annihilation.

As he prepares for the purpose, he sees another man hallooing him in the wood half a mile away. "Treharon had been watching the wood with soul more and more enchanted by the soft colour, the coldness, the response. The cry rescued him." He puts the revolver to his breast, touches the trigger lightly and throws it away.

> For a moment he dreamed that he had succeeded. He saw the man who found him pick up the revolver and examine it. Finding but one cartridge in the chambers he concluded that the dead man was a person of unusual coolness and confidence, with an accurate knowledge of the position of the heart. Then, for he was cold, Treharon moved rapidly away. . . .

This mysterious scene is the ancestor of Alun's description of the sesamum field. Treharon postpones the shooting for a later occasion and goes through the motions, anticipating the act he hasn't yet the courage or the ability (or the necessity) to perform while the double appears to tell him not to hasten. He will reach his end in due course.

In the Karachi journal passage, the deed is performed calmly. The very detachment increases our sense of grief. In fields of golden sesamum (preceded by a description of Alun's swimming in the river at the Boat Club, laughing and feeling virginal and "exquisitely alone", the water, as ever, ridding him of his longing and worry), pollen trickles over clothes and boots, the yellow flowers spreading their light for fifty yards around. Here is the realm of the snake, venomously beautiful. The use of "sesamum" rather than "sesame", derived from *The Upanishads*, adds a note of archaic dignity, as of an ancient rite faithfully performed. At the same time, there is a hint of a magical release into plenty. We are as far removed from a realistic battlefield as it is possible to be. The poet sees his body in a strange region of time and space shot through with the brightest effulgence, an experience related to the Poona hospital poems earlier that year. All is peaceful, tragically so. Death has become a means of attaining a state of repose, secure, inviting, serene, fulfilled.

"Frieda darling, you must be gentle and not blame me for being all the things that happen to happen. . . .," he wrote. "I know there is a way — and intuition says the way is through Burma."

> . . . all the time the malaise has grown and I'm sick of it hammering away, hammering, hammering. I need your real presence & that is all I need. Otherwise I only ache for oblivion, the desert, fighting & the laughter of a spirit grappling with brutality. All bad things: it's ugly, this silken fascination that evil has some times. Writing of it releases me from it.

He pleaded with her to meet him in Bombay as soon as his course was over, though he reminded her that he loved Gweno "very deeply":

> I can feel her love all the time, its reality and its deep tides. She worked miracles for me, not once but many times. There were terrible nightmares & sterilities in me & sometimes I got unbearably lost & parched & stunned in them, & frightened so that I cried & cried, cried my heart out: and then she was always strong enough to make the terrible journey herself. Sometimes it was a real journey, by train: sometimes it was in bed, whether before we married or after. It would be impossible for me not to love her. . . .
>
> The trouble is in the conflict of two tides of loving. I hoped devoutly there need be no conflict; perhaps later there won't be, perhaps my being will grow enough to understand the coexistence of things: but now it's trouble in me, trouble in the mind & in the body, and I don't know, I just don't know, darling. Do you know? Can you tell me? I'm so weary with wanting your hands & lips and aloneness. I'm so worthless, too, beloved. You have asked me to be careful of our love. Love is one of the few things we can't be careful about. It lives & dies in its own nature. Care can not foster it, nor lack of care kill it. All it asks is honesty. That is all I'm trying to give. Honesty and love.
>
> And I can write this to you, yet I couldn't write it to Gweno. . . . I couldn't tell her that I love you, though I can tell you much more easily than I thought I could.
>
> Frieda, I'm not asking you for advice or to do anything. I only want you to know. If you know it will be infinitely happier for me. I can love you if you know how I am made. Perhaps there is nothing new in this to you. I think of you saying Yes, you knew it all. Does it alter anything? Will you still come, and will you know that the love I give you is true love?

Gweno, to whom he had returned all his recent poems prior to publication, had grown alarmed by their sexual content, just as she had grown restive at the profusion of death images in his earlier poems. She wanted to believe that he would find his impartial self in India and write the better for it once his anguish had been subdued. Alun tried to mollify her:

> I was delighted with your vituperation . . . against the sexual preoccupations of my typewriter — breasts, breasts, breasts, you roar in a splendid presbyterian wesleyan rage. Well, unfortunately the world is full of breasts. I can't help it any more than you can. And where there are human beings, there's sex. And I just write how I see things and I see a lot more sex than I ever write. And as for the Welsh miner's son — I'm sorry you're cross with him. (There's a delightful little tree squirrel running down the fire escape, quick and beady.) He may be a bore, but he's authentic . . . . I make no apology for

repeating myself any more than I would blame D.H. Lawrence or
Spender or Hemingway for repeating *them* selves. It's unavoidable.
So if you want to sever connection with the firm of Lewis and Lewis,
well, solong!

Even so, he did change two lines in the original draft of 'The Way
Back' — "Like a lark within its nest/ Laid my hand upon your breast"
— before omitting them altogether.

The officers at the Intelligence School were impressed by him, so
much so that they offered him a captaincy and a staff officer's job. He
turned them down on the grounds that it would be presumptuous of
him to accept before he had been to Burma. Even before the offer,
however, he had told Freda: "I want to be with my own gang when the
bad dreams become a series of reverberant facts. So many of the men
are from my own home, were taught by my father or delivered
groceries to the house, or worked with my Orphean uncle in
Shepphard's pit or Brown's pit. I do belong to them and I always
think of the peace in terms of their jobs & their kids. I always feel glad
when I'm part of them." Yet he knew that the promotion was "a
temptation. If I was reasonable — but not, it's obvious. I can't do any
job till I've been in action and come out of it. All else is cowardice and
inferior and would be shameful to me". Something "very sad and
unargumentative', kept him with his "Welsh boys", a crying
emotional loyalty and inner challenge. In any case, he believed
regimental life offered him greater opportunities for writing than a
training school would and he looked forward to rejoining "the solid
realities of troops & guns & marches & blisters & sweat & action. I can
write there because I live in a spiritual tranquillity and clarity more
than I can here. I wrote Orange Grove in a spiritual Parnassus in the
centre of a physical hurly burly. I love it when it's like that — it's a
thrilling synthesis of living & writing, thought & deed, wrong & right.
It's like being in love". On leaving Karachi, one of his instructors told
him, "You're the most selfish man I've ever met, Lewis. You think the
war exists for you to write books about it." He told Gweno, "I didn't
deny it, though it's all wrong. I hadn't the strength to explain what is
instinctive and categorical in me, the need to experience. The writing
is only a proof of the sincerity of the experience, that's all".

Alun and Freda met in Bombay on 21 September. En route, Freda
saw Dick Mills at Poona. Going from her bedroom to the dining room
in the hotel, she suddenly felt sick. Instantly, she knew she was
pregnant — that was what her faintness on the first night of her
meeting with Alun in Coonoor meant. She was in a turmoil. Delight at

her and Wallace's success in conceiving again after ten years mingled with apprehension. After her ten-day enchantment with Alun at Coonoor, she was still shy of him and fearful lest they be seen together so far from home, yet she longed to receive his sympathy again and give him the solace he needed. Whatever the circumstances, nothing else mattered as much as that.

When Alun greeted her at the station, he felt his life "swing into a single orbit". Freda was again moved by his gentleness and youth and by his purposefulness in taking their situation so resolutely onto his own shoulders. Later that night, she told him of her pregnancy. It was, he told her afterwards, like "a kind of forest fire in my body", likening himself to Philip Bossiney in Galsworthy's *The Forsyte Saga* when he was out roaming in the fog and Soames was the lord of creation with Irene. Nonetheless, his hurt quickly gave way to compassion and for five days they lived together in a little guest house overlooking the sea. It was there that their love was consummated. Every morning, they would wake to a little boy selling lotus flowers. At night, they watched the world go by. He was a prince again.

The only sad note was struck when he read Arthur Koestler's *Horizon* essay on Richard Hillary with Freda. The essay dwelt on Hillary's foreknowledge of his own death. "[He] wanted to find out why. In fact he had deliberately chosen a course of which he knew that it could not end otherwise but by his death." After suffering extensive and painful injuries in an air crash, Hillary returned to the R.A.F. after his face had been remade patch by patch, his hands and eyes barely able to perform their tasks. He was a walking skeleton, inspired, like T.E. Lawrence before him (Hillary was very conscious of his debt to Lawrence) by the comradeship of his fellow officers. "His days are numbered", Koestler wrote, "he has but ten more to live."

> The fraternity of the dead has its peculiar etiquette; one has not only to live up to one's form, one has to die up to it. But then again, there is the writer's curiosity which forces him to feel his own pulse, to jot down . . . the minutes of his agony; there are the nerve-tearing oscillations between cant and introspection, acceptance and revolt, arrogance and humility, twenty-three years [Hillary's age] and eternity. . . . When all isms become meaningless and the world an alley of crooked query marks, then indeed a man's longing for the Holy Grail may become so strong that he flies like a moth into the flame, and having burned his wings, crawls back into it again.

Alun wept at this, so deeply did it touch his own concerns, though he struck a different note with Gweno: "what twaddle of Koestler's about him being wilfully led to his fascinating death! Poof." Standing in the window of their hotel room, "high and unassailable and perfected", he and Freda created an allegory of themselves as two "yellow-eyed beasts that go their own way and in some clearing near the jungle sometimes come upon each other and become thereby sublime".

> There was the sea moving against the seawalk along a curving league
> And the pleasure parks where time is killed by playboys and the more
> fresh-air sort of whores,
> And two loving each other, linked in the spying crowd,
> Their bodies radiating and fulfilling each other from a window
> To which a chokra child brought lotus every day.
>
> When the world entered the minds of these lovers
> It more nearly attained its peaceful potential,
> And ugliness achieved its long-refused transcendence
> Over suffering as authentic as the strata of mountains.
>
> Naked within their love in a bed in a window
> They made the end an image of their love.
> And the end was death,
> Not for them only, but all the time for someone
> In a bomb or bullet, malaria, cholera, sunstroke;
> And the end for these two lovers began away back in the beginning, . . .
> [Growing] Into a wider, deeper, more general prevision —
>
> Envisaging a slim spaced forest, a gladed darkness
> Fretted with fireflies and the touch
> Of long cool grasses each on each,
> And through the scrub the instinctive trails and spoors,
> The opaque yielding awareness of animals,
> Wild beasts, smooth and evasive, tawny-eyed complete creatures —
>
> And in the deep familiar darkness the loving elements conjoined
> In the endlessly desired mutation of decay and generation.
>
> ('The Transmigration of Love', unpublished)

The lovers join the eternal round, between one birth and another, decay yielding to generation which yields again to decay in their transcendence.

XV

Waiting for the Pistol

Back at Lake Kharakvasla for a fortnight, Alun was lost amidst "sensations and images and echoes and recurrences" of Freda. He was engaged in a variety of field exercises, assault landings, staff conferences and the like, all unbearably fatiguing, and found himself unwilling to resign himself to them against the great love imprisoned in him. "It *is* uncanny," he told Freda, "how we seem to think the same things, quite independently. It isn't telepathic. It's because we are in the same place in eternity: our alonenesses are identical, our spirits have the same callousness and the same ferocities, and the same vulnerable sides".

> I know it was something more than either of us, that it is a directive force which will achieve itself in us whether we oppose it or not, whether it brings pain or not. And I am content perforce to wait. Some things one dare not force. . . . Frieda, beloved, the untamed wilderness is away in the jungle about its own ways & we must let it be so. It's the only really fundamental truth we mean. It's the only miracle over which we have no control. And if we could control it it would no longer be a miracle. Let it hide, beloved.

What had happened to him was so swift and beyond him that he felt like a clod with "the old childish hankering that I haven't outgrown, the hankering for a continuous happiness". Even the lake failed to cheer him up.

Freda, shaken by the realisation of what he had brought into her life, still clung to the safety of Wallace. Before, she would pace the garden every morning awaiting his letters; now, she felt a new sense of helplessness as she thought of the baby.

I loved him always, always. Never for a second, ever, did I not love him — . . . . But I drifted, unhappily, away in the practical world I lived in, as he had to through the war involvement and all he had to do. Love remained in both of us, but ailing, sad, though hope always remained, however faint, until just before the end.

In a letter, Alun told her that he was like a collier child or peasant with

an 'old' feeling that is queer to me and makes me try to laugh it away — in vain. . . . I knew you were upset when I told the man we were going [after Bombay] and when you said 'It seems such a wrong & so wasteful that we must go different ways'; I heard my oldness saying clearly to you 'No, it isn't a pity, Frieda'. And then he shut up, because I'm very conscious that this oldness is precocious in me and isn't supposed to go on parade. But I *have* experienced that dreadful inevitability long ago, darling. A year ago it came to flower in me, a dark flower like D.H. Lawrence's blue gentians, and I bled and bled inside me and then I healed myself lying awake in the troopship listening to the ceaseless throb of the engines and accepting the hurt to my being that the remorseless engines inflicted with their indifferent and steadfast purpose. *And I knew I had gone.* That's a tremendous truth, darling, to know one has gone. I wrote myself off then and I shall never go back to before that again. And when it happened again, sweet, it happened in the morning darkness when I was unprepared & without defence, . . . and I was lucky to be in your arms in the darkness because with you I can do impossible things, I can cry. So when it came to the arrangements of going I was very mature and there was no desperation in my simple wish to leave fresh flowers where we'd been so happy, but just a sense of rightness and order. And I make my own order where I can, for there's none in the world.

Parting from Freda, as when he had left Liverpool on board the *Athlone Castle* a year before, was more than just a separation. It was a stage of his descent into the darkness, like Lawrence's 'Bavarian Gentians' whose "blaze of darkness" (a very Lewisian term) marks the soul's wandering in the spirit's geography. He knew they would have to be alone, which is why he cried that last morning in Bombay; their "beginning" of things was "not even beginning to begin" and would never do so. At Poona station, where they parted, Freda saw something of this deeper fatalism in him.

Love had been such an enchantment — yet more: so tender, close, fraternal almost. . . . But we moved on, myself into another, different love, domestic and demanding, he further and further into the other extreme: that of life ending, love and living joy, all living things for him ending and he entering into it while I remained, joy gone out like the sun at evening.

Yet there was also joy for her coming baby.

> I grieved about him, fretted . . . but this joy in the baby, this sudden
> and unexpected return to motherhood, protected me from the pain I
> would have felt without it, a protection denied to him. I had felt that
> implacable drawing towards the void in him for so long, but I didn't
> understand what the voice that called him was. I think understanding
> of something frightening, some haunting in which I was not
> involved, touched me as I stood in the departing train at Poona and
> he, unable to look up, stood with his head lowered, despair shaping
> his hunched shoulders. Something more than bereavement at
> parting — for the last time, as I knew — possessed him while my
> heart broke.

The first of Alun's preoccupations when he returned to camp was
the struggle in him between Gweno and Freda. It tore at him. To
Gweno, he wrote, very shy and nervous of hurt:

> Darling Gweno, I'm sorry you had to go and marry me. It would
> have been so much simpler if you'd been charmed away by a fireside
> faun with a job of national importance such as doing statistical
> research or editing a literary magazine. Anyone rather than me,
> darling, for I'm just some animation the world has set flowing and
> compelled to develop into and out from itself. I learn new things
> everywhere, all the time, new things form in me & bud & flower and
> flow out over the streets & deserts & roofs and fishing boats and
> beggars and poems I encounter or rather find myself amongst. And I
> know they are necessary & vivid, all these things, and they do
> something to me and in a queer deep unchained way I belong to them
> & feel with their eyes & nerves. And also in a queer deep unchained
> way, I've made my peace with life and am willing to go on and into
> and through and beyond. The only thing that prevents me is my
> body, which grows tired, and my mind which grows dull, and my
> heart which has a grief and a love that these things, these perpetual
> heres and nows, do not permit to exceed them. And it gets conscribed
> and crowded.

To Freda, he wrote:

> The problem is so utterly simple, darling, and so utterly insoluble. I
> would come to you through all evil elements and death-surges; and
> yet I cannot come to you except when I am with you. (This isn't
> true.) When I am with you the problem has ceased to exist. *We are.*
> That is complete. At all other times this love is a cruelty to the other
> love I receive and have given, which so powerfully shaped and
> directed me that its compulsions & recollections are as normal and
> real as my daily answers to the daily tasks & situations in which I live
> in the army. You knew all this. . . . And I would not have imagined
> that this also could happen which happened to us, nor that we could

enter in of ourselves into such liberty and such untrammelled ways. It was bound to be restricted in many ways. The most obvious is the impediment of time. . . . And the other obstructions lie inside us and sometimes they choke me. I've fought very hard you know, darling, since I met you, very very hard. Really fought and fought. And when it's been very hard I've made myself endure the hardness & not try to end it in some false way. And I know we need a long time for ourselves to be understood . . . I am not afraid of you or of me. There is only one fear in me at all. That is *for* Gweno. I love her and can hurt her too much. I would prefer to lie or die or not be born than hurt her like that. Oh Frieda darling, I don't know what all this is going to become. Do you, beloved? . . . Don't call me conscience-ridden. There's never been guilt in us, thank God, never from the beginning of time have we — you to me & I to you — had guilt.

The second of his preoccupations was his relations with Colonel Cresswell. It is the Colonel, the second in command, the Intelligence Officer and the Adjutant (together with the Orderly Room Sergeant) who act as the battalion's nerve centre, so that a good working partnership between them is essential. Alun Gwynne Jones (the Adjutant) and Alun got on well and respected Major Moon, the 2nd i/c, but Cresswell was a different matter and during that October something of the discrepancy between them became apparent. For eleven days, the Borderers took part in a large seaborne exercise among creeks and mountains, one of "those macabre and faintly mocking rehearsals of dire events that only take place in war . . . . The imagination projects itself carefully, and withdraws from the rough prevision of reality like a snail whose horn has touched a hairy leaf". One of the problems was Cresswell's habit of seeing things for himself rather than relying on what he was told. If companies had to attack, he preferred an approach which offered him a vantage point rather than concealment, a risk evident in one exercise which claimed several casualties. He was a blunt, straightforward man and his clash with Alun came at a time when Alun felt most uncertain of himself, weak and lonely. As he told Dick Mills:

I've been reading Richard Hillary's Last Enemy (Death) lately — he did many things I foresee myself doing — insouciance to danger, melodramatic personal relationships in interludes of dying — even the serious thought of life & people is melodramatic in so far as Death prompts it & dramatises life — that is, puts it on a stage & spotlights it. He was conceited and tough and he never 'got' there. He learned to suffer physically — he never got beyond that. That in itself is the beginning of a man: he never had time for the rest. I don't think it

would have come if he had lived. He's like Lawrence — something
vital lacking: I don't compare my own petty self with him or T.E.L.
but I am conscious of the same lack & it worries me. I need more
energy, more resilience, more faith. And more — the word was
'sincerity' [' = wisdom' interleaved].

Like Popham, Cresswell was a disciplinarian but without his
predecessor's purposive, protective quality. Like Popham, too, he
had no intellectual or artistic pretensions, being at once loftier
(perhaps because of his great height, six foot six or so, long and lean)
and less awe-inspiring. Popham had a native acumen beneath his bluff,
staccato exterior — "a shouting and petulant C.O.", Alun called him
— and an instinctive understanding of the other man's point of view,
though he often chose to disregard it. Cresswell was more rigid, less
solid and forthright, with the professional's tendency to look down on
non-regulars. It is a nice question whether his suspicion of
complication in Alun failed more than Alun's demands on him,
demands which led him to expect that others would respond to him
and show it — that and his genuine foreboding, which made him
determined to fulfil his duties to the best of his abilities. He was well
aware that the lives of others depended on him. All men must question
themselves at such times, but Alun thought longer because he thought
that much more deeply.

To some, this manifested itself as a want of resilience, and one can
only speculate why Popham should have made him Intelligence
Officer instead of, say, giving him command of a unit. Perhaps it was
because of his very concern for the men, which exceeded the
paternalistic quality the army can best appreciate. Alun was
unquestionably well-suited to intelligence work; he was a good
organiser and had an accurate mind and nimble mastery of detail as
well as the patience and resolution to succeed. Yet the same
preoccupations that pronounced him unsafe to some also made his
removal from the immediate line of fire advisable. The Adjutant and
the I.O. are the two men in the battalion who do not feel the sharp
edge of soldiering: they have a professional job to do and do well.

Alun worked into this a kind of guilt, as if leadership were an
evasion of duty rather than an indispensible responsibility. His gentle
temperament struggling to adapt itself to an antipathetic way of life
collided with men who could not always appreciate how much the
effort might cost him or how it could be best accommodated. On the
Borderer's first night in India, when a thunderstorm turned a ravine

into a raging torrent, he swam across with a rope rather than wait for the water to subside. He always loved a dare; now, he did things as if to show that nothing could frighten him. He was encouraged when an officer with twenty years' experience asked for his help in surveying a stretch of ground for field firing but hid the natural vacillation he felt, being always one who was prone to see the other side of a question. To most people, he gave the appearance of being a popular, cheerful man, clean-living and devoted to his wife. Cresswell thought him an excellent Entertainments Officer, good as an I.O. but only adequate generally. It was not an assessment Alun would have disagreed with. "I can be a moderately good soldier," he told Freda, "but not *very* good because I have too many scruples and a certain detachment from it all that tends to undermine my physical energy and enthusiasm".

That detachment had grown markedly by the autumn of 1943. Alun's appreciation of the inequalities of the social order in India made him question what he was being asked to defend. For all their poverty and squalor, he felt more akin to the Indian peasant than the British Army.

> I've got very interested in the war in the East, not only as a purely military problem, but also because these countries and peoples are a constant source of wonderment to me: so strange and individual and unlike our closed swift little Western world are they. Every time I look at an Indian peasant, I feel tranquil, especially when we are on some fantastically strenuous exercise, for the peasant is so utterly different and settled and calm and eternal that I know that my little passing excitement and worries don't exist in his world and are therefore not universal and will disappear.

As in his poem 'The Peasants', the greater reality of the Indians dwarfs the British soldiers and the tranquillity this induces in him recalls Freda's peace or that of the cool upland states of his anaesthetic vision in Poona hospital. And precisely as his affection for the peasant grew, so his disaffection with the army grew. He sensed the mockery and hostility of the ordinary Indian to the soldiers and regretted that there might have to be conflict between them. On 9 September (the day of Italy's surrender) he told Gweno:

> There *is* such a thing as freedom, and in Europe *we are* liberators at the moment. In the East it is less so, alas. Liberty isn't the point at issue, and neither side offers it. That's what makes it so hard to accept. Personally I think it's the pure adventure and enormity of it and the technical military problem that keeps me at it. And the desire

for experience and for the scales to fall off completely that I may
return and write of it.

The larger purposes for which he had joined the war had vanished; in
their place was the narrow expediency of the everyday. This marks a
very great disillusionment, and it was eventually to spread even to the
everyday.

As his relations with the army deteriorated, so, too, his ties with
Gweno weakened. In 'In Hospital: Poona (1)', sixty degrees of
longitude are said to vanish as he and she are reunited in the dark
hours following midnight, proving that time and distance cannot
break the heart. On 12 September, immediately following his
reflections on the fall of Mussolini, he wrote to her:

> It's Monday afternoon with you, 10 p.m. with me. Six hours
> difference, that's all. I can almost reach across such a little time —
> only that I know when I read your letters that time is unbridgeable,
> enormous, endless. . . . Your longing stirs me darkly and grievously,
> I long futilely to soothe you, sometimes to shake you and rebuke you
> (with all the gentleness in the world, though) at other times, and I feel
> a dark and melancholy confusion rise in me like a turbulent mist. . . .
> Thank you, Gweno darling, for so much love and thought: but oh
> Gweno, PLEASE be easy. Don't fret at it like this, sweetheart,
> please, please, please.

On 8 October, 1943 (almost a year after leaving her at Liverpool) he
wrote:

> . . . in just a fortnight it will be the saddest anniversary of my
> sheltered and fortunate life. I've still got the pass entitling Lt. A.
> Lewis to go from the docks on Saturday and Sunday. It was a
> mysterious and miraculous event, that. My dark dreams breaking
> into the real flesh and sepal and heart and touch overnight. Now it
> seems very sad to me. Why, Gweno? Why should it seem sad? It
> shouldn't be, it was beautiful, which is more than sadness. Beautiful,
> and now impossible. But the sadness has grown with time and
> distance and the weariness of this long journey you and I have had to
> make.

It is the same sadness that fills his poems to Freda, as if he sensed he
had lost her even before he got to know her. That is why he could say
that he had made his "peace with life". He had gone beyond.

It was in this atmosphere, fraught with tensions large and small,
that the autumn of 1943 passed. Cresswell tended to treat his I.O.s (of
whom he had a good few) somewhat less than respectfully; he was
hypercritical on principle. His prickliness may even have caused Alun

to doubt whether he was doing the job as well as he could or whether he could ever do it well enough to satisfy him. He yearned a little now for the post at Karachi. As the weeks went by, his vulnerability became more pronounced and invited the reprisals of the other. Raised voices could be heard coming from Cresswell's tent. The word went around that the C.O. had a down on his I.O.

"I dread the next six months of sterility and heat," Alun told Brenda Chamberlain, and, beyond them, the four or five years he thought the war would last (an estimate based on the American intelligence he had gleaned at Karachi). As the perspectives closed, he felt a strange poetic recession taking place in him, a withdrawal to some fastness, one of "those cyclical expeditions that take place and take me willy nilly with them". He was about to enter the most despairing period of his life. His inspiration dried up. He was in agony. He knew there were "several deep water poems swimming about below the surface. And there's a whale of a story in the air, something big-boned and definitive, placing objectively the balances that swung in the monsoon of the Orange Grove". Perhaps this refers to the project he had worked out with Freda in Coonoor for a play with prose interludes about the effect of the Burma campaign on the British hill-top communities, an echo of an idea he had earlier toyed with of writing a play for Lynette Roberts at Longmoor, but nothing came of it. Without the army, without love, without writing, he plunged into depression.

> I hate this wandering life and fear the caprice of experience: yet I know in the loneliness of my bones that it's my way . . .

As 'Lance-Jack' had predicted, joining the army had created the negative conditions for the writer's emergence but the writer seemed unable to capitalise on his opportunities. "I'm not busy, you know," he told Gweno. "I'm just at something or other all the time." — a desolating observation.

> How hard it is, how hard. My heart has grown a crust so that I can't break but it leaves my body leaderless and it just dodders and bustles alternately and everyone else is an object encountered en route and circumvented . . . I'm angry at all I've wasted. You waste nearly everything from which you withhold your heart and my heart has withdrawn itself for weeks now from my dead here.

Of the few poems written at this time, 'Pastorals' is the most significant. It looks plaintively at the world that might have been his — seed, with millet fields, sons to inherit and "love and pride".

> But I stand here instead
> With dry earth in my hand,
> And death in my head
> Crying Treason! Treason!

Famine — there was a serious famine in Bengal at this time — , warfare, corruption: "What harsh mosaic plague do we engender" ('The Everlasting Ultimatum', an unpublished poem).

To Freda, he wrote of an experience one night when he heard himself shouting, "NO NO NO": "I tried when I heard that voice crying, I tried to find a reference — what was it denying, darling?" What was it denying but the forces dragging him away? It is the voice of Edward Thomas or the singing in the shower at Karachi and it provoked in him an intensely human protest very different from the charmed mystification that greeted its earlier manifestations. He was now powerless to resist, and wrote to Brenda chamberlain:

> There's a maniac in me that cries out only to be sensitive to hurt. He's more concerned with poetry than normal human happiness and patience and drives me to odd places. I let him, too. I'm dull and platitudinous when he's away from me and I welcome his return with a secret exultant trepidation, although I know now that he has no intention of allowing me to retain the deep happiness of body & mind that Gweno brought with her when at last she came to me. I thought life could stand still on that foundation. But I was wrong. Life moves & moves and I change and change. If happiness survives it will be because it alters itself also. I'm different already from what I was a year ago. And as the war folds round me out here I know I'll become someone much harder & shrewder & more daring than I was as a young immediate husband. I try to mark the change so that I don't burn my boats, but I don't care what happens so long as I am continually myself.

It was the nearest he had come to telling anyone what had happened to him and the context suggests why. Brenda Chamberlain had written to say that she and John Petts had separated and this allowed him to broach the subject with her. Using the imagery of Karachi and before (particularly the "folding" of the Poona hospital poems and the Edward Thomas poems), he confesses to the presence of a "maniac" in him, one who draws him away from his loved ones as from his human self towards somewhere "where I can at least and at last *breathe*" (a word often used in the letters with connotations of the mountainside). Tragedy has no curtain; he would find his renewal:

> . . . the dagger in the heart
> And the ghost in the soul
> Lean on each other suddenly
> And the darkness grows whole . . .

('Renewal')

A — self-inflicted? — plunge into darkness and completion is attained. He tried out the idea again in 'Lady in Black':

> Lady in black,
> I knew your son.
> Death was our enemy
> Death and his gun.
>
> Death had a trench
> And he blazed away.
> We took that trench
> By the end of the day.
>
> Lady in black
> Your son was shot.
> He was my mate
> And he got it hot.
>
> Death's a bastard
> Keeps hitting back.
> But a war's a war
> Lady in black.
>
> Birth hurt bad
> But you didn't mind.
> Well maybe Death
> Can be just as kind.
>
> So take it quiet
> The same as your son.
> Death's only a vicar
> Armed with a gun.
>
> And one day Death
> Will give it back
> And then you can speak to him tidy
> Lady in black.

An astonishing anticipation of Sylvia Plath's manner, adding strikingly to the metrical variety of Alun's work. The penultimate line, speaking "tidy" in prosodically untidy form, is a perfect piece of poetic wit. ("Tidy" in South Wales has a particular meaning, roughly "decent", "conscientious".) The lady herself is both the grieving mother and dealer of sorrow, the many-faced goddess who promises death and rebirth.

He formulated the idea a third time to Freda:

> I had a swift dream as I read [your letters] — one second perhaps — of being posted as missing believed killed & coming back and fetching you and being with you afterwards all the time and writing under a new name & being more utterly & completely ourselves than we could ever be before that death.

He knew there was a lot of hurt ahead of them — "It's trite to say so. It's so bloody obvious" — but he felt they would survive it. "Perhaps I'm most 'jumpy' about the physical danger — it's like a horse race you can't guarantee to win: the rest I'm sure about. I mean that it will work out its own salvation, that is its own justice".

Alun's grief at the conflicting claims in him between Gweno and Freda was eventually resolved the more he learned to separate them in his mind. In Gweno was all his attachment to valley and township, in Freda his yearning for mountains and lakes. With the former he had found "nearness and friendship and solicitude and love", the "real" things of life against "the big cloudy gulfs of time and impersonal submissions to history". With the latter he had discovered an emotion defined by the Nilgiris: "up in that brilliant cold mountain country I was dissociated somehow from anything before or after and I lived in a strange new way — angelically almost. I had no cares; no future; no duties; no past". It was the rebirth he had longed for. Strangely, two loves had arisen to answer the deep division in his life. To Dick Mills, he wrote: "[Gweno] says I work either on romantic wishful-thinking or an obscure disbelief in myself, and so she says I'd better disregard my own judgement & take that of the nearest normal man — meaning hers." About Freda, he wrote, "She's always got the deep complex of being disregarded or maltreated by those nearest & most important to her — . . . she'll never outgrow it now, and it gives her much of her wildness and freedom." Gweno knew there was part of him she could not reach:

> If he was sometimes pre-occupied, desiring solitude and the 'deep brooding silences that are necessary for this trade of poetry', if he was a selfish and wilful lover, if he allowed himself to be carried by the

cross currents and tides of chance, wanting more and more experience — all this belonged to the creative side of him, the dark side — which he called his alter ego.

At the end of October, he was shaken by a new experience and told Freda about it.

> I've been indifferent to love this week, it began on Sunday afternoon. I could even tell you about that. I've been working pretty well all day for the last week & I haven't had any time to consider my self except when I stole two hours on Sunday afternoon. I went down to the lake and swam. On the way down through the long cotton grass whose ears are thorny parachutes that prick your ankles as you walk I aided three Indian boys in chasing an iguana. It was a beautiful beast. They had cornered it in a currant bush & I saw it break cover & I shouted & pointed to the swaying line of grass and they chased it and stoned it and killed it. It was like killing Lawrence's snake. An obscenity. My only motive in disclosing its escape was to know what beast it was. It was a beautiful huge three foot lizard, a soft sleek brown. Its body was very tranquil in death. They cut off its tail, which has an aphrodisiac secretion in a gland. I went on then to the lake where I was quite alone & stripped by the brown flood water under the bushes and let the sun smooth my body & my genitals. And my body was thinking of you & me. But my mind said very remotely, like an arbiter, 'Body is captivated, but the mind is not at one with the body.' And at that antilogy the body withdrew its thoughts & the desire as if rebuked & I went & swam my body and came back wet & fishlike & insentient. You were *NOT* there; and my mind said it so implacably: the world has harsh and final demands which I must fulfil. The rest is not possible until the demands of the world are admitted & executed. I hate this passionately, passionately, passionately. I accept it coldly, with the calculating coolness of a man betting at the races. I hate betting at the races. But this gamble is a necessity. Damnation.

In a way, as important an episode as the one under the showers at Karachi. Freda is put away and the war accepted, its consequences being hinted at in the encounter with the iguana. As in the sesamum-field passage, the body is forced to accept "harsh and final demands". In D.H. Lawrence's poem, 'Snake', a man denies his own instincts, refusing what is greatest in him in favour of "control". And so it is here. Ever since the meeting with the Vishnu, Alun had been drawn to images of calm and the iguana offers just such another, an Edward Thomas-like conjunction of death and beauty, the aphrodisiac touch adding an ironic note in view of the debate about sensual attachment. The other source of peaceful imagery — lake water — is also put to use here. It was in the hospital pool that Lt. Weston first divined the appeal of something moving "like a series of temptations in the wilderness". This idea is fully developed in the stream in which Capt. Beale surrenders his driver's body and the Malmund lake of 'The Way Back'. Now, the association of Freda and lake water is broken. The swimmer emerges from his bathing "insentient".

Alun was ill at the beginning of November, in a delirium of malarial fever. He returned to Poona hospital for a week prey to "depressing thoughts" and "morbid reasonings". All purpose seemed to have deserted him. "I feel sometimes as if I'm to blame for the whole world," he told Gweno.

> I knew I needed the reverse treatment to lying in a hospital bed and rotting in my mind. But happiness is a rare bird these days and I don't see it often: it flashes away and hides in the distant forests and I fret in vain for it to return before its own good time. You're quite right in taking me to task about my grandiose remark about 'having made my peace with life'. Maybe I did, for a tranquil hour. But I've forgotten what it felt like. Oh I suppose it's because one gets so absorbed in taking the endless strain of estrangement and uncertainty and preparation for fighting — it's a long nausea. Never mind. We must take it as we can . . . . I'm in such a poor state to judge my own work impartially I'm prepared to damn it all. I feel very angry with myself. I want something to happen. Silly boy.

He asked her for a photograph, saying he couldn't remember her face. Exhausted, he felt "negative, null, void, done for, discarded", like "the horrible slump and no man's lands I used to stray into" in his early twenties. He wrote to Freda:

> It was simply the lack of toughness of my mind which I'm afraid isn't half as strong as I'd hoped and has really behaved very bad of late. It has been without conversation and without solace: a kind of deliberate impoverishment of all living streams, a shrinking and a despairing. I don't know why. But I've never been so cast off, so worthless, purposeless, unresponsive. I loathed myself for it and was anxious about it, too . . . . It's a long time since my ancient enemy made such a determined assault on me. Damn his bleary eyes.

She up in her forest of saplings high on the hill was separated from him and they seemed to be "spinning one of those bitter webs of Greek legend, like traumatic subjects of a broad and indifferent destiny whose mind has long been made up".

Back in camp, he tried to write some poetry but without satisfaction. Midnight after midnight he finished poems that in the morning he found himself scorning. "I'm trying to simplify not deepen nowadays," he told Lynette and Keidrych Rhys. "Everything is very complicated. India is a horrid entanglement of routine complications. So is the Army. I seek the natural forms, the bare shapes, the ultimate & initial innocence. I hope to find it in an ocean farther east". The poems he had sent Gweno didn't seem "very good" to him now and he condemned his recent efforts as "a lot of half finished and half baked morbidities", a weary wrestle with "unnecessary poems". "The last story I *really* wrote, that wrote itself in me & out of me, has found its way into *Horizon* ['The Orange Grove']. I find myself too haggard an interior to create and talk the essential equipoise and joy that I believe must exist in the creative act, of whatever nature it is. . . . I've deteriorated into something hard & wary and expecting savagery, a homnecule in an animal's skin".

When he next wrote to Freda, he enclosed his signature in a series of wavy lines, as if he were trapped in a watery maze. More than ever, she found herself worried about him.

> I know that at some late stage I thought painfully that if I could go near enough to be with him even for one meeting . . . I might comfort him. But one did not attempt that sort of compassionate undertaking during war . . . and, furthermore, I was expecting the child for whom we had waited for ten years. I was anxious about Alun, loving him in the romantic, isolated way that was our own, and at the same time preoccupied with the coming birth of the baby. Thinking of it now it seems incomprehensible. All I know is that I *was*. It wasn't all happy either. I worried. There were worries. Awful medical arrangements in India, a Cesarian-like scar recently performed. . . . I tried to comfort him in my letters, to give him hope of some sort of solution to our divided loyalties — I tried very hard — but in the end I, too, lost faith in there being any solution.

As she prepared to go to Tellicherry for Christmas with Wallace and Gilly, she received this letter from him.

> I'm very far away from you — do you mind if I quote a poem I wrote the last winter I was in England? It always soothes me.

> > Absence & distance soft as snowflakes fall
> > In long silk skeins on this unearthly night,
> > Effacing and gathering up all that resists.
> > Somewhere your curtain falls against the light.

> [Ironically, this poem, 'Love Letter', was originally addressed to Gweno and dates from his period of service on the East coast in early 1942. It was published in *Call Wind to Witness* but has been

unreprinted since. Originally, the last line read 'lifts before' for 'falls against'.] Oh Frieda, did you hear me sigh then? Can you feel the leadenness, the persistent oppression that I'm trying to accept and wear and hide? . . .

I try to look at myself obliquely & analyse it down to something rational & explicable. I say 'It's because you've been three years in the Army & *it* still delays & doesn't happen & you go on waiting & waiting & naturally you get a bit rotten & downcast.' Then when that fails to help I make myself go more fully into the other things — go & watch A Company playing B Company at Soccer, or go & umpire a hockey match, or go & play some records in the reading room or go & talk to somebody. But I really think that I am escaping not resolving the trouble by doing that. It's in my head and in my heart: and I can't help it being there. It's not malignant sometimes, for years. Then it becomes a force in me, disrupting and corroding, & I've got a real fight then. It's always manifested itself in an intense awareness of the *waste* that I'm causing or suffering: Today has been wasted in me, Now is wasting away in me. And what is waste? I think it's the feeling of dissatisfaction with one's deeds, the feeling of incompetence, of being hustled into inefficiency by the daily rush of trifles & duties, none of which give any feeling of accomplishment or fulfilment.

The war which had once seemed to him a necessary defence of democracy now appeared increasingly futile and the harder he tried to restrain his doubts, the worse everything became.

Sunday gone! Oh damn it, damn it. What else might I have done? Might have had a deep thought, might have thought of an exciting phrase or felt a run of ideas catch fire one from the other and the crackling line develops into a conflagration of thought, might have gone down to the lake and contemplated the water. Didn't though . . . When will I have time (and the mind and the peace of mind) for all that is suppressed, jockeyed and heckled and spoilt? Oh hurry up, sweetness of all that and heaven too.

He found himself irritated by "the coarse swearing ranting violent and shallow atmosphere" that had come into being in the battalion and the mess since July.

I was very conscious of the hotchpotch we make of life in an Army, the bad way we do a lot of jobs because we're doing them all at the same time and for a purpose that is intolerable. And I had a wicked sense of dissatisfaction with everything I put my hand to, & in consequence did them worse than I needed to, because I had no faith in myself doing them. And I'm clumsy & dreamy in matters of memory & administration. I forget details or slur them, and condemn myself like a Dickensian Bumble.

Increasingly, he found himself going "under a surge of bungled violence and released irresponsible harm. Have you ever heard a battery of artillery laying down a barrage of shell? It's a terrible experience philosophically and morally, all that crushing dreadful arbitrary violence. Physically, it's just a bloody row and a reflex fear or shudder. But to think of the impersonal evil it implies is terrible."

Sleeping or waking, he felt "a universal pining and regret that scarcely has any context or reference, so wide and purged is it". Every thought turned rancid. He tried to tell himself not to worry; he had felt like this before — indeed, ever since he could remember, the forces of darkness had gathered in his head; "like water in a sump. They are the determinants: and it's always been a hard fight for me to keep myself as an individual integrated against these forces". They had grown in him "quietly and persistently" ever since 1939, whatever temporary alleviations there may have been since then. They were his "death in life, the black water", his Doppelgänger. He was sorely taxed and wanted to cry out in sorrow and hurt.

> At other times in these long inadequacies I suffer I think I want it to go a little further, a little further, that I might explore the fields of insanity. That is a temptation that attracts & repels with like force & I don't act towards it; it's just a thought in me, not an impulse. I know it's danger: but it's very closely connected with the bit of poetry there is in me, the writing and creating mystery that wants to break down the last barriers and explore the deep involutions of trouble and complexity & relationship of things. But I don't really know whether the great poems were really written in madness. I think they were written in intervals of sanity. Madness I fear is chaos, a greater bewilderment, a worse darkness. Has any apprehension of the mystery of everything and the mystic varieties & interconnexions of the universe ever come to anybody except in a moment of exalted lucidity? I don't know.

Increasingly, he turned to letters as to what Freda has called "a faith-keeping act". In one letter, he told her:

> You were afraid of something that might turn into resentment in me: and of something in me that in cowardice and for peace of mind would shut away this love, this burning image and deep reflection of you in me & in the world. But it would only happen like that if I died also within myself: and I need to be as terrified of that as you, oh more than you. . . . I know how I lose & fail back into time & the impotence of time: but I don't think these small stumblings & wounds & disasters in time can really matter much one way or the other to that great freedom that one can only leave alone. Because it IS. That's all. It IS.

As 'A Fragment', one of his "midnight poems", has it (he sent it to her in a letter of 22 November and to Gweno on 3 December)

> Where aloneness fiercely
> Trumpets the unsounded night . . .
> [I] feel your anguish beat its answer
> As you grow round me, flesh and bone.
>
> The wild beast in the cave
> Is all our pride; and will not be
> Again until the world's blind travail
> Breaks in crimson flower from the tree
>
> I am, in Thee.

Three summers before, he had said that Gweno was "a singing rib within my dreaming side"; now, the positions are reversed: he is in the beloved (c.f. "But I am still in you" in a letter to Freda).

At this time, he told his parents:

> I regret my lack of Welsh very deeply: I really will learn it when I come home again. I know more Urdu than Welsh: it's very sad - it's the price you pay for an M.A. in medieval history at an English University at 21. If I could live my life over again one of the things I'd do would be to learn Welsh: another to do an English degree at Oxford or London, a third to work underground for a year, a fourth to marry Gweno. Well, perhaps none of these mistakes are fatal, and I may still pull things together.
>
> When I come back I shall always tackle my writing through Welsh life and ways of thought: it's my only way: but I must get to grips with the details of life as I believe I haven't yet done: the law, the police, the insurance, the hospitals, the employment exchanges, the slums: I've always enclosed myself in an impalpable circle of seclusion, turning away to the Graig or Traeth Bach [a bay in Penbryn reachable only at low tide] for the aloneness that is somehow essential for youth to breathe and grow at all. But I hope I can breathe in crowds and in business when I return, for all these fields of human life — the greatest part of people's lives in fact — is scarcely known to me — I mean in sufficient force and familiarity to write of it.

It was a brave effort. "Daddy", he told Freda, "is the rock of love, she's the wind about it. He would grieve but not break. She would be desperate. He's been very good to us always always, but sometimes he was too stolid for mother. I knew all that since very early, long before I knew anything about sex."

By the end of November, he was thinking of a new story, "a sort of symphonic arrangement of people and moods and antagonisms within a battalion round the posting of an officer away from the unit just when they're due for action. I want it to be lighthearted, satirical and varied — not moody and rapt like the others I've written out here". He also had an idea for a story about a subaltern who refuses promotion, but nothing came of either. At the same time, he tried to persuade G.H.Q. to let him act as a war reporter but to no avail. Feebly, he was trying to gain what Karachi had been all too ready to offer him. "I shall be glad to be rid of the battalion I couldn't bring myself to leave," he wrote. "Otherwise I am doing nothing except read, write letters, sit & think, worry, do odd jobs, wait for the pistol. Only I feel I'm rushing it."

Robert Graves had read his poems at his request and sent him a detailed critique. Alun felt reassured but convinced that he was "still waiting for my big moment, my big word. It's still in seed and won't flower till it has a mind to. I can't hurry that up". Instead, he turned to a short story based on his reunion with his brother Glyn in Poona early in December. Written three midnights running, it gives us a valuable insight into his state of mind at the time. It is all feverish and jumpy. Glyn, a private, had travelled six days from the other side of India in a fanless third-class compartment with only a wooden rack to sleep on. He reminded Alun what India was like for the majority of soldiers. Alun was particularly shocked by the disparity in pay: Glyn got forty rupees to his two hundred and fifty or so (one reason why he turned down Karachi, which offered nearly 1,000 rupees). The two brothers stayed in the Napier Hotel, where a noisy party took place next door which Alun gatecrashed at two a.m. to ask for silence after the hotel manager had tried and failed. "I had everything a writer wants in contrast, social implications, decline and fall of empires & individuals — everything except character," he told Freda. "I couldn't create character: and that is due to lack of energy in me."

'The Reunion' is elliptical and hypersensitive to atmosphere: the animal heat of the sun, the crush and noise of Poona, the talk in the hotel room (reminiscent of Conrad's globetrotters in *Lord Jim*), the memory of the squalor aboard a troopship, the empty bustle of the streets at night. Eric, the older brother, waits for Vincent to tell him about the fighting in Burma from which he has just returned wounded, and it is the intrusion of Burma into the story which gives it its fretful quality. After retiring for the night, Eric senses a coldness inside him instinct with the horror of Burma. "I can't settle down. I can't sleep, life is being wasted in me, going round and round on its empty repetitive journeys, avoiding the encounter, identifying itself with nothing, avoiding love, refusing socialism, rejecting a better world because my self is worse, worse, worse, but doesn't matter, my self doesn't matter". There follows the imagined encounter with the enemy, described in theatrical fashion thus:

> He could have shot me, but he didn't. All the time I was crossing the clearing he could have got me with his pistol. But he didn't. He waited until I was right by him, till he could make his magnificent thrust. Then he leapt out of the brake and his sword was raised above his head.

This is a battlefield but it is scarcely a realistic one. We recall the ceremonial execution of the sesamum field and Alun's fascination with the "blow and counterblow" of knives as far back as the story 'Grenadier' and his troopship sonnet to Gweno, together with the more recent "dagger in the heart" of 'Reunion'. The encounter ends with the firing of a pistol (the first time this means of killing has been mentioned since 'All day it has rained . . . ') and the swordsman dies. In agitated mood, Eric tells of his punching his way into the party next door (which in reality was a peaceful affair) and the beating Vincent receives there. The story ends with his screaming, "I'll kill . . . I'll kill. Kill now. Kill.", the whole hotel awake by now. Nothing captures the quality of this furore better than Edward Thomas's definition of melancholy: "A sort of nervousness, a continuous palpitation and sense of something approaching that never comes. . . . I don't mean a sense of approaching good or bad luck, but merely a sense of *something* coming, as if I had heard a report and waited for the other barrel".

Alun's sense of drift prevailed and with it his agony. His meeting with Glyn only proved to him that the world was getting worse. Every morning he would wake up reluctant, uneasy — a sure sign of depression. "I wish I hadn't this capacity for pain," he told Freda. "It so wearies me. I wish I was strong like an oak. And less aware of the waste and the going wrong of things and mea culpa in it all . . . . I must let go of today now, let it go. I don't want to. I want to mark each day with my nails or my lips, but I have to let them go as they come, these days." We notice the allusion to Edward Thomas's 'The Glory': "I cannot bite the day to the core".

Just before Christmas, he was sent out on a three-day mission to the jungle and was delighted by the experience.

> The jungle really is another world. Cold, enclosed, private, willing to keep you for ever and ever, letting you go on your own way if you can

> find it, indifferent to your trouble if you can't. Its inhabitants wear the
> same strange outlandish coolness. . . . In the nights it was silent and
> starry, no sound but the howling bark of monkeys coming to see what
> the light was all about. In the day the bamboos creaking in the breeze
> like a door on unoiled hinges — I was very happy in there, unworried,
> unpreoccupied. And I'm looking forward to a larger experience of it.

With his acute sensitivity to place, he had found a refuge to succeed
mountain top and lake. The bamboos curved like cathedral arches, the
villagers seemed eternally isolated from the soldiers' obligations and
distractions. "I'm simple again," he told Freda, "& like a stream, it
may be deep, it may be still or swift, it has its own nature. Oh God,
how lovely it is, this interim of peace." He had found "a separate
world, remote, unperturbed, indifferent, serene". Returning to camp
made him "impatient to have a showdown with fate. I've lived a queer
unnatural life these last three years. I depend far more than I like upon
the simply physical excitement of movement and newness. . . . It's
not good for me: I pay for it. I've paid for it these two days since I
arrived — a nervous depressive dissatisfaction which turns furiously
& cruelly upon myself. I am my own scapegoat".

Gweno, once again disturbed by his state, sent him a secret message
to calm him down.

> You chide me for being downcast and bedraggled of soul. I'm sorry
> for being like that. But I must go the way my imperative leads me —
> and I feel that this long trial and strain on my spirit is likely to be
> decisive for me. I believe I'm being true to the realities in feeling this
> way: India is really a great purgatory and so is the war, and so is the
> future we are facing. And if I could be light hearted and tranquil
> about it as I sometimes can be I'd be very glad. But just now the
> burden of it weighs hard and steady. I'm foolish. I've not got much
> responsibility and I don't work hard, yet I don't write and my brain
> isn't active. And how can I be one of the young writers etc unless I
> wake from this slough? Its only familiar feature is that it's happened
> in me before and I know it must be accepted. But I'm sorry that its
> shade falls across your own light.

"My main reason for living is to write," he told her, "and I've got a
very strong feeling that I could have done the job better in the ranks.
But I'm not interested in pips and crowns, and all my efforts are bent
otherwise and at present inwards where all the battle is." The last
phrase is a striking one.

At Christmas, he asked Freda for a ring and she sent him one.

> . . . Gweno, Frieda, And love that cannot and will not submit to any
> of us. How I scorn my weakness: and pity it also. And the weakness is

that I know fear. Fear of two great wonders uniting in a third which is not me but infinitely more than me.

Frieda, it doesn't matter who is more than who, does it? It's as irrelevant to ask Are you more than Gilly or less than Gilly? Am I less than thee by overmuch? . . . But what has happened is us. . . . I can hardly bear to imagine it. It *did* happen, darling, it *did* happen. It was thus & thus, beyond speaking.

He could have asked for leave now but did not; he felt it would be too much of an escape. The battalion had received battle inoculation and was busy adapting to jungle warfare. The amphibious operations of the early summer had come to nothing. By the autumn of 1943, Lord Louis Mountbatten had established a separate command in South East Asia under orders to engage the Japanese in a decisive battle, thus drawing some of their troops from the Pacific. He took over from India Command on 15 November only to discover that the proposed amphibious assault on Burma had been superseded by Operation Overlord, the Allies' planned invasion of Europe, which would require most of the resources available, especially landing craft. Since the Germans were the main target and the principal theatre of fighting against the Japanese was in the Pacific, he had no choice but to give way and fall back instead on a plan devised by General Sir George Giffard for operations in the dry weather-weather period of 1943-4 on a front stretching across the North East border between India and Burma. A second thrust would advance down the coast from Cox's Bazar to recapture the Mayu range peninsula and Akyab at its southernmost tip. The directive for this attack was issued early in January, 1944.

By New Year's Eve, Alun was with an advance party in the jungle some two hundred miles from Lake Kharakvasla preparing for a field exercise. He carried with him Freda's letters ready for burning.

I'm afraid of the fighting when it comes. I'll loathe it so utterly, & be so faithless to Life, beloved Life. It is spoiling me already. Yet I refused the chance to escape it. I half think I want it to happen to me to activate the submerged instinct of humanity in me. I'll fight much better for peace than I ever can for war. I'll write better, too. When it at last comes my slow way.

A fortnight later, on the day before the battalion was due to arrive, the party was recalled. The Japanese, realising that their defences were insecure, had launched an attack on Imphal, thus forestalling the Allies' own offensive. As a feint, they sprang a subsidiary attack on the

Akyab front, pinning the Allied troops down there. The battalion hurried away to fight in a war it had never been trained for. The irony was not lost on the men.

Alun's experience of the jungle marked him deeply. Whether making bamboo beds and shelters or plaiting coconut leaf matting or foraging for edible roots and fruits or hunting the sambur (the Indian elk), he was "content with the green oceans in which I was lost so completely that I found my simple and honest self without any complexity". In his "absurdly unreal little elysium", the people were clean, quiet and unshy for once, the animal life fascinating: tiger prints in the sand, panthers and elephants, wild deer and diamond-skinned vipers. With Jack Gush, he witnessed a ritual ceremony before Gunpati (god of good fortune) and found himself attracted as he had never been before to any Western religious ceremony. He swam in a river of long, idle pools near the camp and experienced "all the coldness and pride of nature". One more phase of his life was ending: "the climacteric is near. I'm glad, and I feel something working bluntly towards a position from which it can see and plan and have faith and work enduringly, not among things that crumble as they are made and are meaningless in history and in the heart".

From these various elements — the threat of danger, the appeal of the jungle, the need to reassert enduring values, the social and political ills of home — he fashioned his last poem, 'The Jungle'. Here was "the big word" he had been waiting for. It is divided into four sections; the first is set at a stagnant pool visited by the soldiers, who come "To quench more than our thirst — our selves". Immediately, a sense of tension is established, "quench" playing on "refreshment" and "extinguishment". The jungle is a place where one is restored and a testing arena in which all previous convictions are stripped from one.

> this mantled pool
> Where sleep exudes a sinister content
> As though all strength of mind and limb must pass
> And all fidelities and doubts dissolve,
> The weighted world a bubble in each head,
> The warm pacts of the flesh betrayed
> By the nonchalance of a laugh,
> The green indifference of this sleep.

As in 'The Way Back', the pool offers a fertile destruction. The "warm pacts of the flesh" — reminiscent of "the warm ones about us" — give way to a careless happiness, "green" indifference recalling the "green" distress of 'The Way Back', though the stagnancy of the pool offers a vivid contrast to the energy of Malmund lake. We are nearer the Lake Kharakvasla of 'Water Music', "where the last light trembles", musty, mildewy, rotting: "In whose grey bed black swollen leaf/ Holds Autumn rotting like an unfrocked priest." It is a witty Audeneque conceit and it exposes the collapse of idealised beliefs. A great spiritual occlusion overtakes the soldiers as they come to the pool, Narcissus-like, to meet their secret selves and receive its sinister sedative balm. (Is "content" accented on the first or second syllable?)

> Wandering and fortuitous the paths
> We followed to this rendezvous today
> Out of the mines and offices and dives,
> The sidestreets of anxiety and want,
> Huge cities known and distant as the stars,
> Wheeling beyond our destiny and hope.

The panoptic style is Auden's, too, though done without his characteristic levity. How painful now the distance from home! The brilliant phrase is picked up — "the humming cultures of the West" — and their bankruptcy itemised in Alun's finest generalising style. Here is a farewell to the Thirties done in Auden's own voice, a conscious critical mimicry akin to the use of Edward Thomas's voice to describe the view from the Downs in 'To Edward Thomas':

> . . . Shadows ride from precipice to plain
> Closing the parks and cordoning the roads,
> Clouding the humming cultures of the West —
> The weekly bribe we paid the man in black,
> The day shift sinking from the sun,
> The blinding arc of rivets blown through steel,
> The patient queues, headlines and slogans flung
> Across a frightened continent, the town
> Sullen and out of work, the little home
> Semi-detached, suburban, transient
> As fever or the anger of the old,
> The best ones on some specious pretext gone.

In Jack Jones's *Rhondda Roundabout*, Uncle Shoni tries to persuade his nephew not to take charge of the local chapel on the grounds that the Rhondda is no place for a young man like himself. His wife protests: "All you and your sort want is to drive all the best away from us". It is a phrase Alun must have heard many times and he recalls it now that he, too, has left the valleys. Once more he takes up his detached vantage point to describe the scene before him, but now from a far greater distance and with a desperate sincerity. What was once shared (or part-shared) is discarded as it is described. Lost on his spirit's journey, he begs pardon from his loved ones for his desertion of them. Alun always understood that, to write, he would have to sacrifice the tender side of him and that is part of the complexity he sheds when he enters the jungle. All that remains is a fading humanitarian indignation and an even greater love of beauty, abstracted into an ideal to replace the old ones, an embodiment of spontaneity and perfection unconcerned with human misery, which Alun now believes can never be remedied.

> But we who dream beside this jungle pool
> Prefer the instinctive rightness of the poised
> Pied kingfisher deep darting for a fish
> To all the banal rectitude of states,
> The dew-bright diamonds on a viper's back
> To the slow vituperation of a meaning lost
> And the vituperations of the just.

The kingfisher embodies the appeal of nature to "dreamers" disenchanted by affairs of state. It is associated with the cycle of life and death, and darts for its fish just as the viper awaits its prey. All that matters is the being, effortless, rainbowed or diamonded — and then the not-being. Everything pursues everything else for its existence, like the crocodile of the first section and tiger of the last, beautiful but deadly. In 'In Hospital: Poona (1)' Alun had asserted that love would survive the venom of the snake; now that we are in the realm of the snake, life is but for the instant and all values subverted.

In the third section of the poem, he gives the more personal complexion to his suffering, complementing the catalogue of social and economic ills in the second:

> The vagueness of the child, the lover's deep
> And inarticulate bewilderment,
> The willingness to please that made a wound,
> The kneeling darkness and the hungry prayer;
> Cargoes of anguish in the holds of joy,
> The smooth deceitful stranger in the heart,
> The tangled wrack of motives drifting down
> An oceanic tide of Wrong.

> And though the state has enemies we know
> The greater enmity within ourselves.

The manner is reminiscent of Eliot's 'Gerontion' as we trace a universal sense of wrong which has its origins in the self; the battlefield in Alun was assuredly internal. The description of the failure of each individual to attain his fulfilment is reminiscent of the similar catalogue in 'On Embarkation' and precedes the failure of community; the war only carries the process to a conclusion. That is why (like the grinder in the prologue to *Raiders' Dawn*)

> Some things we cleaned like knives in earth,
> Kept from the dew and rust of Time
> Instinctive truths and elemental love,
> Knowing the force that brings the teal and quail
> From Turkestan across the Himalayan snows
> To Kashmir and the South alone can guide
> That winging wildness home again.

Lines of great beauty, turning to a non-human agency to lend the soul deeper direction.

At this moment, the poet begs pardon from all those he deserts.

> Oh you who want us for ourselves
> Whose love can start the snow-rush in the woods
> And melt the glacier in the dark coulisse,
> Forgive this strange inconstancy of soul,
> The face distorted in a jungle pool
> That drowns its image in a mort of leaves.

Alun here out-Audens Auden. The pool is a medium of dissolution, "mort" playing on "death" and "great amount" but also on the hunter's call (an idea first mooted in the schoolboy stories). It is a Narcissus-like reshaping in pursuit of the self.

> Only aloneness, swinging slowly
> Down the cold orbit of an older world
> Than any they predicted in the schools,
> Stirs the cold forest with a starry wind,
> And sudden as the flashing of the sword
> The dream exalts the bowed and golden head
> And time is swept with a great turbulence,
> The old temptation to remould the world.

Gravely beautiful rhetoric, gathering the familiar images of cold planetary movement into a final statement. The "orbit" of 'Lance-

Jack' denoted the power of life which the soldier was tempted to disregard in pursuit of brutality; here, it is the deathly perfection he is forced to choose. We sense the shedding of a huge burden. A sword flashes — like that of the assassin in 'The Reunion' — and the "bowed and golden head" attains its consummation. The image suggests both ennoblement and decapitation. (Are we in the sesamum field again? It is, at any rate, another Narcissus pose the soldier here adopts.) It may be that one of the men at the trestle-table is suddenly stirred by "the old temptation to remould the world", a line which recalls the old Lewisian compulsion only to cast it aside.

John Lehmann recalls the impression the poem made on him when he first read it:

> I remember how struck I was by the sense of old certainties dissolving under the pressure of some deep upheaval of the spirit [and the] — to me unforgettable — lines
>
> > A trackless wilderness divides . . .
> > The old temptation to remould the world. . . .
>
> I think you ought to remember that Alun Lewis started off as a convinced, proselytizing socialist, in order to understand the distance he had journeyed to 'The Jungle'.

In a letter to Brenda Chamberlain, Alun wrote that India was "a world I wouldn't have believed in if I'd stayed at home. It's infinitely more wasteful, vaster, fundamental, and tragic than the closed & highly organized world I left. Its poverty is deeper & more imperviable, its people more various & simple, its extremes more extreme, its perfidies and selfishnesses more obvious & blatant". He understood how a young Indian might be tempted to act, just as a young Russian might have done in 1917, but he could do no more than "observe in a detached but warm way the flux & reflux of it all and it profoundly affects the way I think and the things I wish to write". To Robert Graves he wrote:

> England is 'easy' compared with India — easier to corrupt & easier to improve. There are few deterrents at home: the inclination isn't continually opposed by the cosmic disinclination, the individual isn't so ruthlessly and permanently subject to the laisser faire of the sun and the sterility. India! What a test of a man!

It broke him. Generations rise and fall, insects on the sea of time spinning through the ages. Nothing matters; everything is unreal.

Like the grey monkeys, the soldiers avoid the "human, near".

> A trackless wilderness divides
> Joy from its cause, the motive from the act:
> The killing arm uncurls, strokes the soft moss;
> The distant world is an obituary,
> We do not hear the trappings of its dread.
> The act sustains; there is no consequence.

The soldiers, relaxing their "killing arm", exist in a perpetual present, without before or after; they are "ghosts", free to go their way without reference to any previous conviction and sustained by no more than the compulsions of the instant. They have been dehumanised and care little for what they do. The last lines build quietly to a close.

> The bamboos creak like an uneasy house;
> The night is shrill with crickets, cold with space.
> And if the mute pads on the sand should lift
> Annihilating paws and strike us down
> Then would some unimportant death resound
> With the imprisoned music of the soul?
> And we become the world we could not change?
>
> Or does the Will's long struggle end
> With the last kindness of a foe or friend?

For a last time: what survives? Would the soldier's death resound with his unachieved creativity or would it lack consequence? The blankness of death is steadily contemplated. Death is evidently a release from frustration, which is why, whether it come from friend or foe, it is "the last kindness". 'The Jungle' has a strange, laconic calm, outlining its argument in a severe, restrained way yet lyrically, too, with the natural majesty of elevated utterance. It is a forbidding achievement (and, in view of the time in which it was written, a brave one, too).

On his return from the jungle, Alun revised his poems hurriedly (not as much as he wished to) and chose a new title for the collection from Job: *Ha! Ha! Among the Trumpets*. Its subtitle was 'Poems in Transit'. He returned them to Gweno and asked her to send a copy to Freda. He now thought them better than *Raiders' Dawn*, "more objective and the words have more balance" yet also less "poetic", less young and passionate. The title gives the flavour of the collection. He explained it to Freda by quoting the bible's words about the battle charger "who smelleth afar off the shouting captains & the din of battle. Lovely lovely words. God is speaking them, the bible says. But

I don't think he is. I think it's a man speaking them, with an understanding of beauty & a longing in him". Like Job, the poet is cast out into the darkness and cries for his release. He knows he is blameless yet is treated as one of the wicked, suffering the torments of the unjust. Like the horse,

> He mocketh at fear, and is not dismayed;
> Neither turneth he back from the sword.
> The quiver rattleth against him,
> The flashing spear and the javelin.
> He swalloweth the ground with fierceness and rage;
> Neither believeth he that it is the voice of the trumpet.
> As oft as the trumpet soundeth he saith, Aha!
> And he smelleth the battle afar off,
> The thunder of the captains, and the shouting.

He laughs sardonically as he goes gaily into battle. It is, Alun said, "an expression of sorrow by antithesis", a careless defiance.

The book is divided into three sections, 'England', 'The Voyage' and 'India'. The subtitle takes its immediate bearings from the second, which describes the journey from England to India, but it refers generally to the theme of spiritual wandering. In Matthew Mead's opinion, "The transit was from love to death". As Alun told Robert Graves, reviewing his thirteen months in India,

> [p]eriods of spiritual death, periods of neutrality, periods of a sickening normality and insane indifference to the real implications of the present. . . . [T]hen for a brief wonderful space, maybe every six months, a nervous and powerful ability moves upward in me. India and the army tend to fortify the negative & passive phase . . . . I think I'm most completely normal when I'm roaring across the country on a motorbike, aware of the flow & the tradition in the peasant's life . . . . I've felt a number of things deeply out here; perhaps the jungle has moved me more deeply than anything else, the green wilderness where one has nothing but one's sense of direction and there is no alarm because there is the sun & there is your shadow & there is time. . . . I want to go East & East & East, faire le tour; there is a consummation somewhere: after it is over, then I can be particular and exact; meanwhile I learn to fire a revolver with either hand and try to suppress the natural apprehensions of the flesh at a thing so long delayed & postponed & promised & threatened. . . . I'm as restless and fidgety as a man on a deserted platform.

It is the journey "East & East & East" that *Ha! Ha! Among the Trumpets* records. It shows how far back he had gone in India, "into origins whose roots are like snakes".

The poems of the first section strike the least depressed note in Alun's poetry, and much the same can be said of the second, which expresses no more than the doubts and fears appropriate to each situation. (The photograph of the apparently full-fed and contented author that appeared as a frontispiece was taken in Southend in 1942.) The best poems — and the core of the volume — come in the last section, 'India'. As Keith Evans has pointed out, the poems prior to this are almost evenly balanced between free (or blank) verse and rhymed poems. Here, all but three are rhymed. The order is deliberately achronological, ending with two poems, 'A Fragment' and 'Midnight in India'. These are poems of farewell, the first to Freda, the second to Gweno (written some time in the spring of 1943). The man achieves life in one woman, remembers his achievement with the other and bequeaths his body to her. It is the witching hour: moonlight lies in pools, pain soothes dry lips that seek quenching; the loved one bears a "calm white face". Everything bespeaks the presence of the Goddess.

Two poems were omitted at Gweno's request: 'Letter from the Cape' and 'Letter from a Long Way'. "I couldn't decide myself," Alun told Graves, "— they are too much flesh of my flesh for me to pretend to assess them: and I've left it to Gweno to exclude them if she chooses. I myself feel that they are necessary to the book: they establish certain things about myself which are organic to the poems as a whole. In these days of clinical critics, I feel it's as well to tell the world I'm not suffering from a castration or an Oedipus complex & that I'm not writing my head off about thwarted sex-images. The degree to which a volume of poems should be autobiographical is always different for different people. For myself, I don't claim as much hold on the universal as you long ago possessed, and I consider my poems as expressions of personal experience". It is the qualification he had entered for all three of his books.

At the same time, he wrote to Freda:

> . . . I can't look at the future — I can't see any distance at all — Oh well, the time I've wasted, dreadful. . . . I am conscious all the time that a whole life is being thrown away all the time we are denying & are denied each other . . . . I've finished so many things these last days, it's got me down. I've packed all my kit, & sorted out my papers, revised my poems & sent them off to Allen and Unwin, — burnt all your letters, darling, oh with such trembling & gentle but fierce sorrow, made arrangements for my accumulated raw pees [sc. rupees] to go to Gweno: I've made everything so tidy. And it

shouldn't be tidy like that — it should sprawl along healthily & confidently into the future: not detach itself from the future so neatly and circumspectly.

He asked her to mark all her letters "*If undelivered return to F . . . A — Highfield etc.* . . . Lest they go the weary round of effects to be disposed of and break a heart in the end". He also burnt some letters from Dilys Western dating from 1938 which he had with him. The two had been in correspondence ever since they had broken with each other and he now wrote her a very private and loving letter "from a strange wilderness". To his parents, he confessed to owning a "phlegmatic humour"; "the only reason why I've written poetry, I think, is this painful ease with which I feel the anxiety of a world at war".

Apart from a last story, untitled and unfinished, the period before Burma was a time of waiting, both a limbo and a purgatory. At the end of January, he met Dick Mills at Poona and confided some of his troubles to him. Shortly afterwards, he told his parents: "I'm not going to write any more till the foulest day is behind me. Then I'll tackle a more massive fruit than any in the Orange Grove". He told them his depression had never really lifted; every morning, he would wake to the "crazy machinery of anguish".

> I don't know why I'm so preoccupied these days — I seem to live with hooded eyes. I ought to say Ha ha among the trumpets and dash off and swim, but somehow I don't contrive.

Preparing for battle only served to remind him how poor a soldier he was. "You know the cloud that comes over the mind:" he told Gweno. "I'm in a useless phase now."

> I've put a huge burden on you always, through my poems, which have spoken more openly of the danger and the jeopardies than either of us could or would with the living voice.

He went on to reassure her that he would come back in the end after all.

To Brenda Chamberlain, he wrote:

> God knows where happiness & spiritual safety lies: not here, not with me, not now. . . . I'm on a hard rein, blinkered, mettlesome; I watch lest I bolt, and I look at the froth & the sweat of my noisy & clumsy living and I sigh very quietly and regret myself & let it all go on in its inevitable crashing drive into the headlines and the oblivions of this mammoth world. . . .

The snap was taken when I was very happy — I was on leave last July — the only leave I've had — and I stayed up in the Madras hills, the Nilgiris, with a delightful family and I was as deeply and innocently in love with life as I've ever been. Since then I've gone steadily downwards and a growing obscurity & introversion has come over me. As usual with such neuroses we don't do anything to stop them until the 'thing' has a very strong grip on you & then your realisation has a quality of hysteria in it and you tend to go wronger instead of righter. . . . I talk lightly as I can of a bad business: not the first time it's happened: but just now I can't afford to have it. It's a critical period in my little existence and more depends on my balance and brain than ever has before. So I don't mind sacrificing my writing & the wilder genius that wins itself out of these catacombs if you stay deep in the toils. I want to emerge straight and new, at whatever price. I'm telling you what I haven't told anyone else . . . because I must talk. . . . I am grappling & clinging a long way from the safe & fructifying life Gweno made about me & I made about her. Dick Mills says my mind is tentative in everything, and being tentative is a heavy disability in the Army. It can either be the pliant grasp or the stammer and falter, depending on the climate of your soul & thro' the soul, the nerves: And on the pressure of circumstance & of others. Others — a strange word for those who have entry into me, live in one's thoughts & being, — yet 'others' is right in part, for much of the most powerful things within us happen *alone* in us. I've lived in vacuo too long & I want no more of it. But I'm not my master.

Shortly afterwards, he wrote to Freda:

I don't mind what happens now: I've got myself in rein, I think I'll be what I am expected to be & do what I ought to do and that in itself is a scriptural simplicity. For the rest, I feel that it's out of my hands now: and I feel no distress at having to go unresolved as it were. . . . And the accent is so heavily upon work and duty that I can let it be more easily. Something nearly died in me last week: I was horrified with the sense of loss and vainness. But it didn't quite die. . . .

He felt he wasn't doing his job well "because I plan inwardly and not objectively".

I've still got to prove myself satisfactorily. Maybe I will this time. I've finished with the fear & loathing and failure of it, I hope, & my nerves have stopped spinning & getting dizzy & wearying my body with the insistent fretting of the guilty & trivial in the mind.

As for his emotions,

I can either be positively alive and in love, or I can be negative, an element as unresisting as air, through which people can walk . . . — this collapse of myself & the painfully fortified values is something which prevents one from ever saying certainly 'I belong' for worthlessness belongs to no one.

But it was to their love that he returned.

> Oh, the *thrill* of myself to thyself, sweet swordsman, the dancer & the dance, the wind & the cry of the wind, & the child making its way into the world through you; and Gilly in the world wondering and knowing; and the hazards between & the long cycles of returning to the revelation and the incarnation. There is no end to all this, except the accidental end, the bulb fusing, the mind failing, the body ceasing to function, lungs & heart & eyes. Don't be fretted with loss, Frieda; I feel wonderfully happy whenever the certainty moves in me that I have lived indestructibly in thee. And in mother, and Mair, and boyhood, and Gweno, and words sometimes joining in flame. So I try not to shiver when a cold gout strikes me, and I feel a collapse in the nervous clocktower of my being. . . .
> I'm glad with all my heart I've finished with waiting & shilly-shally (though I've no expectations). I've had enough of a life of routine & soccer matches in the evening.

His mind now went back to two memories and merged them, first, his "swift dream" of October in which he saw himself missing believed killed and returning to live with Freda under a new name "and being more intensely and completely ourselves than we could ever be before that death"; and second, his return to Highfield after Ratantata walking through the blue gum trees, the poems in his hand, excited to meet her again.

> For you I wanted to come & see you first, but it will be very wonderful to come in the end. Don't worry over the hairs on my head. May you not be tried harder than you can bear. And I'll surely come up through the trees to the lawn, to the splendour & the homecoming & the child & Gilly and us.

> Ever, Alun

When she received this, Freda was alarmed; it seemed to her more than the usual soldier's farewell. Yet she felt there was nothing she could do. From the start, a sense of doom had accompanied their love, colouring everything and lending their joy a keener edge. 'Wood Song' had spoken of the agonies that "love can never consummate" and one such was upon them now; the animals had met in the glade, clung, and parted.

On 13 February, 1944, the Borderers joined a troop train for Calcutta at Poona; Colonel Popham was there to see them off. (There is a mysterious reference by Alun's mother to the battalion doctor ordering Alun into hospital just before "to rest and build up his sadly depleted store of nervous energy" but I have been unable to confirm this. His only recorded mishap after his second stay in hospital in November was a razor cut to his finger which necessitated a stitch.) The journey was hot and uncomfortable, the train stopping to allow the cooks to file up to the engine and fill up their dixies with water from the boilers. They would then prepare the food (porridge and soya sausage) at the side of the line to the accompaniment of hordes of flies and the troops would gobble it down; the bugle would sound and off they would go again. After three days of stopping and starting, they boarded a ship for Chittagong on the other side of the Bay of Bengal, which was reached on the 24th. En route, Alun wrote to Gweno saying that he was still "trying so hard to be me" and that he was "at the start of something and the beginning of something else". A few days later, he told her that she had rid him of the "black mood and the distress of mind I've been labouring under. I'm just steady and square now and give as good as I get". At Chittagong, the men embarked on the coastal steamer *Sir Harvey Adamson* for Cox's Bazar, which they reached the next day after a difficult voyage up river, clambering onto flat barges for the landing.

From Cox's Bazar, Alun wrote to Gweno again, describing their world as

> alive with sunlight & growth & health. The darkness & threats are from another part of ourselves. And the long self-torture I've been through is resolving itself now into a discipline of the emotions of you and me . . . , and I can feel my reason taking control and working carefully and methodically. . . . I feel that my grasp is broader & steadier than it's been for a long time. I hope it's true, because that's how I want to be: and the rest of me, is invulnerable. I want you to know that, Gweno, sweet wife. . . .
>
> I must run now, darling. Sorry I am to go. And god be in our heads & in our eyes & in our understanding. Buy me a typewriter when somebody has one to sell and I'll buy you a beautiful beautiful emerald or maybe a sapphire or maybe something neither of us know. For keeps for you for love. All my love: Alun.

This was to be his last letter to her. Amphibious vehicles motored the troops to Reju Khal, a concentration area several miles inland. From there, they marched to Bawli Bazar on a track made up of twelve inches of fine dust; eyes, boots, noses, mouths and water bottles were filled with it. Alun was in diffident mood, fretting about his pistol (a .38

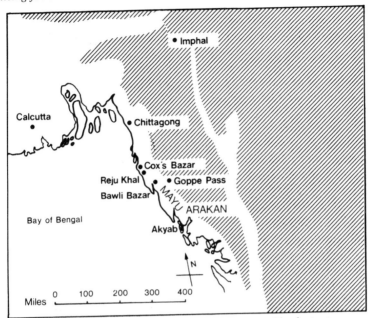

3. The North Burma Coast, showing locations named in the text.

Smith and Wesson) and irked at having to pass the time playing cards with Colonel Cresswell. He regretted the civilisation the West had brought to India with its cheapening mechanical influences and incitements to the flesh, thinking with particular revulsion of the "coquettes" who lifted their skirts for the men to see.

The battalion reached Bawli on 26 February, where they remained in reserve. They were fifteen or so miles behind the front line, all save B Company who, under Major R.O. Crewe-Read, were posted on the Mayu Range a mile or so away to guard the Goppe Pass a thousand feet up. Alun remained with Battalion H.Q. in Bawli Bazar. The Japanese offensive had been beaten back by 14 February. On the 24th (the day the Borderers reached Chittagong), it had been abandoned. A week later, the Japanese pulled back. The furthest north they had penetrated had been Taung Bazar and Briasco Bridge, about five miles south of Bawli and Goppe. It had been a fierce battle and it cost the XV Corps 3,506 men and the Japanese over 5,000. The Arakan was not a very important part of the Burmese front, yet it proved to be decisive for it marked the first occasion when the Japanese were beaten. They now fell behind their main line to prepare for the XV

Corps' expected offensive, which was timed for 5 March. The Borderers' arrival, therefore, coincided with a lull before the storm. There were a few reports of scattered enemy shots but no actual contact, save for a few prisoners who were brought back.

Alun now appeared very agitated. He wanted to join B Company at Goppe Pass and, though it was not necessary for him to do so (the I.O. assesses and disseminates information but does not gather it himself), Colonel Cresswell thought it understandable that he should want to go out on patrol; the experience would do him good. As if by an ancient impulse, he was being drawn up the mountain again.

He joined B Company on the night of Saturday 4 March. The next morning, he was woken by his batman, Harry Tudor, at 5.30. The men took up their usual defensive positions against any possible dawn attack for an hour. Loaded weapons were carried, the order being to shoot anything that moved; silence filled the misty air. After stand-to, breakfast was served. Harry Tudor brought in some shaving water and, while Alun shaved, fitted his equipment ready for the patrol to Goppe Bazar, due to leave at 9 a.m. Alun was in an excited mood. Years before, he had written: "Waking up in the morning is the worst time. It always had been with me. Unhappiness swells to the proportions of nightmare at that time and it is hard to overcome it enough to get up and shave and wash and be active". Again, on 8 October, 1943, he had written, "When Tudor wakes me in the mornings I say 'Alright, Harry' and go to sleep and wake up too late for breakfast. I hate waking up."

After shaving and washing, he left the hut carrying his revolver (loaded arms had to be carried at all times) and made for the officers' latrines on the hillside. A shot was heard. Tudor ran towards it and found him lying about five yards down the slope. The revolver was in his hand; he had been shot in the right temple. He ran back to call for help. Major Crewe-Read met him and they returned to the body. The pistol had one empty case and five rounds. They carried the body back to the medical tent. Lieutenant Qureiohi, of the Indian Army Medical Corps, was called. He found Alun unconscious on a stretcher with a first field dressing to his head. He took it off and examined him. There was nothing he could do. The body was taken on a stretcher by jeep down to the casualty clearing station. All that morning, he lay dying, Ariel in the dust. Thousands of miles away in Mountain Ash, Gweno was working on the poems, which had arrived the day before, checking their order against the list of contents.

At 1.25 p.m., six hours after he had been wounded, Alun died. He was buried later that afternoon at Bawli North Military cemetery in a shallow grave alongside the river near Bawli Bridge. The ceremony was conducted by the regimental padre. He was twenty-eight.

XVI

What Survives?

On 31 March 1944, a court of inquiry was held under Major Moon. Captain D.M. Morgan, from Aberdare, and Lieutenant D.M. Drummond (both friends of Alun's) sat as assessors. In his evidence, Major Crewe-Read said that Alun was "normal" and keen to go out on patrol. Lieutenant Qureiohi said there was no "charring" on the wound at the point of entry and that, in his opinion, death could have been caused by the revolver going off when he fell down the hillside. The entry wound was in the temple, the exit at the back of the head; there was no massive disfigurement. There were no witnesses to the killing. Colonel Cresswell noted a report that the gun was found by Alun's side (which was not, in fact, the case; it was in his hand) and concluded that the shooting had been accidental: Alun had fallen down the hillside or "khud", the hammer of the revolver striking a stone or branch and discharging into his brain. The battalion diary entry for the day accordingly reads: "Lt. A. Lewis (214565), Battalion I.O., died as a result of an accidental G.S. [gun shot] wound received when on duty with 'B' Coy." The death certificate reads: "Killed as a result of an accidental revolver shot wound of the head".

In the Battalion Roll of Honour, Alun's name appears under the heading "Died from Battle Accidents" (though there is a separate section called "Battle Accidents. Not due to enemy action"). He was awarded three medals: the Burma Star (for service in Burma from 18 February to 5 March, 1944), the Defence Medal (for three years' home service from 16 May, 1940 to 24 October, 1942 and one year's overseas service from the last date to his death) and the War Medal (for service during the emergency). Gweno received a pension.

Professor Bernard Knight, head of the Forensic Medicine Section of the Institute of Pathology of the Welsh National School of Medicine, has reviewed the evidence for me and comments: "Obviously the whole point is the differentiation of accident from suicide". He draws attention to two stigmata of suicide: first, recognised "sites of election", of which the temple, mouth and chest are classic examples, and second, closeness of discharge.

> By and large the whole story to me smells of suicide but on the information available I would not think it justifiable to make any firm decision. If we had a better description of the wound and especially as to whether there was powder blackening rather than charring then interpretation would be easier. To the best of my knowledge I have never seen an accidental death with a revolver, though they are common with shotguns. One reason for this is that the wide spread of a shotgun blast is far more likely to kill anyone in the neighbourhood because of the wide zone of injury, whereas a revolver has a single small projectile and therefore obviously the chances of that projectile hitting someone in a vital spot are far less than a shower of hundreds of shotgun pellets. I feel strongly inclined to think that the statistical chances of a single shot from a dropped revolver hitting someone in the temple are very remote indeed and that deliberate self-infliction is far more likely.

Amongst the Borderers, it was universally assumed that Alun had killed himself. In the absence of any other obvious reason, they blamed his relations with Colonel Cresswell—a remarkable assumption. The War Office telegram reached Gweno on 14 March. Both Popham and Cresswell wrote letters of condolence. The former remarked, "Alun I considered one of my best officers and from the day he joined the battalion I recognised in him a man who would make his name anywhere". Philip Unwin was more affected than by any other of his authors' deaths. He had such an interest in Alun's work and such high hopes for the future. "One felt that character, passion and atmosphere were all there, waiting for further development; but it was not to be."

Alun had not provided a dedication or introduction to *Ha! Ha! Among the Trumpets* so Gweno inserted one herself, "from me to him". Recalling the time when she tried to teach him some German folk songs and remembering that he had called her "Kamerad" once before and often thought of her as a companion and friend, she added the following epigram:

Kann dir die Hand nicht geben,
Bleib du im ew'gen Leben
Mein guter kamerad!

It is a German soldier's song from a ballad by the nineteenth century poet Ludwig Uhland usually sung at military funerals—a brave enough gesture to one who had fallen in World War II even though not in the immediate battle against the Germans. Nevertheless, it has a certain aptness, for had not Alun written of his "dreaming German soldier"? The lyric tells of two friends who fight in battle side by side; one of them is killed but the other cannot help him because he is firing his rifle. "I can't give you my hand, but you must remain in eternal life my good comrade."

Ha! Ha! Among the Trumpets was published in August, 1945 with a foreword by Robert Graves, whose eldest son had also been killed in the Arakan. It lamented Alun's death as the passing of one of the sacred trinity of poets, groves and kings, one of those with whose "well-being and well-doing the prosperity of the kingdom was magically bound up. . . . Alun Lewis's presence conveyed this same sense of power. . . . I was his friend only by correspondence, but from the start became aware of the power and knew that it lay in his poetic integrity". When Gwladys Lewis wrote to thank Graves for his words, he replied, "Like the Welsh poet of the fifteenth century, when the Prince of the Air carried him off, he snatched at the apple-bough— i.e. poetic immortality—and so escaped".

Gweno told Christopher Cheney about Alun's death.

Alun just fell on a narrow path! He was unconscious when they picked him up & remained so till he died. . . .

His death was swift & unexpected & sometimes I think it is better he died like that. You see he was 'intelligence' & ran a greater risk of being taken prisoner & questioned.

Freda wrote a letter of condolence to Gwladys Lewis, who replied:

My only comfort is the thought that he didn't fall into Japanese hands and that it was clean and quick; that he had no painful foreknowledge and that he didn't suffer at all. I like to think that a kindly Providence intervened to save him from worse.

But what a waste it is! . . . I am so perplexed about so many things that seem to have stirred you too, that I wish I could talk to you. Sometimes I think that both he and I had some foreknowledge. I don't know and I am very troubled.

The same theme occurred in a poem she wrote for him:

Such Aching

When you cried in your cot,
Afraid of the dark loneliness,
I took your tiny hand in mine
And blessed sleep returned.

This was your Talisman
Through all your early years.
Your hand in mine
Resolved your childish fears.

And then you grew
So gently kind,
So understanding and informed
That I had learned
To lean on you
Not questioning your word.

What fun we had!
How much we laughed
Those days!
For what pleased one
Pleased both,
Being alike in ways.

And when with prescience
You felt
The shiver of impending doom,
Its passing tremor
Rarely touched
Our happiness with gloom.

I am now the small child
Crying in the dark.
If only you might take
My groping hand,
I should not ache
Nor feel so desolate.

To Leslie Sykes, she wrote:

> . . . a terrible thing has happened to our family and we shall never
> cease to mourn for Alun. He was exceptional as a son and with me he
> had a very special and close relationship that had always existed from

his earliest days. I feel as though a limb had been torn from my living soul. Huw says 'Alun was more than a brother to me, he was a way of life.' And I'm sure that is how we all feel about him. Our memories of him are unclouded and I think now it had to be so, for we were to enjoy his company for such a short while. I don't know but sometimes I feel sure Alun knew he wasn't coming back and I think I felt it too, ever since he went abroad. There always seem to have been the pointing finger and then the inevitable accident.

Freda herself had received the news from Gwynne Jones and from Quartermaster Stan Thomas at second echelon, whom Alun had asked to write in case anything happened to him. In a poem, she wrote:

> Another death is in this death.
> This grief
> Beats black wings throughout the lonely night
> And hangs, a stale despair, in each awakening.
> The lonely hours drag, the sun's unmeaning light
> Reflects an empty world.
> It is that you were there,
> In everything, and now are not
> So naught has meaning. . . . Time,
> Oh time, stand still, return!
> Let this moment be
> The one before I knew the dread
> To be a truth, before I knew that he
> Is forever dead.

Again, in another poem she wrote:

> Speak in me—
> Oh speak within my listening heart.
> I have waited on your teaching,
> Served so long your gentleness of thought.
> Silent, with love green-growing in my mind,
> I hear your voice, but far so infinitely far.
>
> Today the Spring has moved the earth at last
> And alone and longing, I cry out
> Oh speak in me.

Her sorrow had a further dimension.

Alun must have suffered the appalling experience of grieving for his own death. It is possible: one grieves for all that is lost or unfulfilled in the dead; how much more would one grieve at knowing the loss and unfulfilment in one's own certain death? No-one quite believes he will ever really die except the suicide. He knows he will. Or part of him, the suicidal part, knows.

His death was fitting, she thought, a kind of transcendence, Romantic, Shelleyan. Perhaps, as Virginia Woolf wrote in *Mrs Dalloway*,

> A thing there was that mattered: a thing, wreathed about with chatter, defaced, obscured in her own life, let drop every day in corruption, lies, chatter. This he had preserved. Death was defiance. Death was an attempt to communicate, people feeling the impossibility of reaching the centre which, mystically, evaded them; closeness drew apart; rapture faded; one was alone. There was an embrace in death.

Divided within himself and conscious always of the good being wasted in him, with his loved ones not so much denied as out of sight, the ties loosened and he came to contemplate himself as an object caught and limed by the flesh. Only when he was rid of it could he be free.

In a broadcast, Dylan Thomas mourned the death of "a healer and an illuminator, humble before his own confessions". W.D. Thomas lamented the passing of "a very noble spirit moved by the deep and grand things of life". Keidrych Rhys spoke for the many who had found in his work "some sort of guide through the turmoil of this war. Indeed, all his writing was illuminated by this healing light and suffused with a quiet, deep and warm humanity. . . . He was a man in every sense, mature of outlook, yet with a poet's knowledge of death, a curious streak which some may put down as the common death-wish of some of our most sensitive writers of two generations. . . . It was also an encouragement for him to have no difficulty in placing his work — important for him — as his terrible premonition-impetus pointed".

Of the artist, W.D. Thomas wrote in a review of *Ha! Ha! Among the Trumpets*, "The personality which he showed his friends in private was a more varied one than his verses have scope to reveal. The happy lad with his merry gaiety, the athlete eager and strenuous in play—they are not here. . . . His nature, as we become aware of it in his poetry, was eager, grave, independent and resolute. It was free from both arrogance and pretence. His art was spent on making an intensely true thing clear. Ornament, affectation, pettiness, whether of word-play or of sentiment, he rejected, and his style is hard, clear and very personal." *The Sunday Times* carried an anonymous review of the book which declared:

A hospital ward, a village funeral, a troopship in the Tropics, he writes on such subjects as these, but always relates his theme to the central issues of life and death, which Lewis believed were inseparable. This belief gives a grand though sombre unity to his work as a whole. In this acceptance of ordinary life he differs from Rainer Maria Rilke, who influenced these later poems, and whose abstract sense of pity and tenderness reappear in a less passive idiom.

Gwyn Jones wrote in his obituary notice:

> His term in India had clearly produced a new Alun Lewis—the poems are there to prove it. They are not happy poems, nor can I think him a happy man out there. [In a letter on Boxing Day, 1943, Alun wrote]: 'I've grown older and humbler out here, and expect less of life than I did once.' He was always open to the impulse of pity— for the weak, the broken, the exploited, the dumb and suffering millions of all creeds and colours whose unheeded lives and deaths but dung the roots of history. The comfortable assumptions, if he ever held them, were gone; he saw a continent of four hundred million people where Nature's indifference and Man's stupidity made life as cheap as dust. It was a cosmic revelation for one who believed so passionately in the dignity and inviolability of the individual. . . . He was a brave and splendid young poet, and his death, like the deaths of all such, is a limb torn from the living.

(The last image is borrowed from Gwladys Lewis.) Alun's death, he thought, was

> probably the heaviest single loss sustained by English letters during World War II. . . . What he had done is remarkable; what he would have done is a speculation at once thrilling and saddening . . . He wrote . . . without acrostics or pretentiousness; the enigma arises from the subject, the consciousness of different levels of meaning from the height and depth of the poet's mind. . . . To read him now is to be left sadder and wiser, and, I think, better, too.

Professor Jones's emphasis on the "new Alun Lewis" was echoed by a little-known tribute paid him by R.S. Thomas in a memorial poem which refers to him as one whose thought was "not born of our climate" but in "the sun's glare",

> Harsh as the land, whose white bones prompted
> An alien creed, that wakened in you the soil's
> Naked perception of the rain's worth.

The last image is particularly striking in view of 'The Way Back'. Here again is the theme of Death and Beauty, what Elizabeth Drew has described as "a poetry steeped in that heightened consciousness of life which is created by the immanent presence of death". Professor Jones's reference to the enigmatic quality of Alun's poetry captures very well the coded quality of his work, so transparent on the surface yet mysterious beneath, causing you to go back and re-read him, very different from the "decent sententiousness" which is all that some have found in him (no doubt guided by the edited form his letters have appeared in since his death).

To those who still think of Alun primarily as a prose writer, *The Times*'s obituarist had something of interest to say. He noted his

> rigorous economy in the handling of words and an ear for those influences that sing finely in the heart. His outlook was tragic . . . but it was often penetrated by moments of radiance . . . . Last year Lewis produced a volume of short stories, *The Last Inspection* — a book of promise in realistic fiction; but in prose the author had not yet attained the concreteness, the directness, and depth of his poetry.

Had the obituarist had a chance to read the last stories, he might have revised his opinion, but these were not published in book form until 1948, when Gweno authorised the release of a collection called *In the Green Tree*. This consisted of two parts, 'Letters from India', comprising edited extracts — sometimes considerably rewritten — from the letters to herself and Alun's parents as well as six short stories, a preface by A.L. Rowse, a poem by Vernon Watkins (which the publishers tried to exclude) and a reprint of Professor Jones's obituary (which Gweno tried to exclude). Several drawings by John Petts were featured, notably a portrait of Alun in profile done from memory which tried to capture something of his yearning, dreaming quality. The letters were first published in somewhat fuller form in *The Welsh Review* and subsequently in a limited edition by Professor Jones's Penmark Press as *Letters from India* in 1946. It was from a brief introduction to the latter that the War Office insisted on the deletion of the following paragraph: "Whilst preparing to go on patrol before dawn on March 5, 1944, he was killed accidentally. The last communication from him, probably sent the day before, was a gay birthday greeting [to Gweno]".

Two reviews of *In the Green Tree* and one of *Letters from India* are worth mentioning. Assessing the letters, Alun Llewelyn-Williams wrote in *The Transactions of the Honourable Society of Cymmrodorion*:

> The letters read like a chronicle of a pilgrimage, undertaken in search of a fatal secret. The strange thing about the book is the impression it

gives of the inevitability of the final result; not that the poet himself is aware of this — he is conscious only of the overwhelming fascination of the quest, of his danger, too, of course; but we who now read the story that he has recorded so faithfully, are disturbed by a realisation that the writer is being carried inexorably nearer to 'the ultimate purposes', to the problem which perhaps has only one answer. . . . Alun Lewis's search was, of course, for something more enduring, that which survives death . . . This is the ageless human quest.

In the *New Statesman*, Walter Allen praised the prose above the poetry. Stories like 'Ward "O" 3(b)' and 'The Orange Grove', he thought, showed "an imaginative understanding and compassion for human nature which raise [his work] to an altogether higher level than any other English writing inspired by the war that I know". The letters drew even more generous praise.

[I]t may be that these letters will ultimately take a higher place than either the poetry or the stories, for, like Keats's, they point to a maturity beyond anything their author had been able to express in his works, and they make the sense of loss one feels at his death all the keener.

A remarkable verdict, considering that Allen had seen only the tip of the iceberg.

The Times Literary Supplement's reviewer drew attention to Alun's imaginative power. Few poets, he thought, were more robust than he.

We feel it about his work and about his character, in so far as we know what it was like: the air of the long-distance runner only just settled down into his stride. Whether he would have found his way from the short story to the novel is only conjecture. It seems probable. But in any case he would still, surely, have been writing poems. . . .

The chief impression [the letters] leave is that of a greatly likeable man, sincere, adventurous, warmly affectionate, observant and tough. The grace that enables one man to please with self-revelation, where another maddens, is of course humility — never to be confused with modesty, that agreeable, minor virtue which doubtless Alun Lewis also possessed. . . . No sprig of Bloomsbury could ever have written [as he did], so unsuperior in acute observation, so warm in intelligence.

In 1958, Gweno visited the Taukkyan War Cemetery in Rangoon, where Alun's body had been reburied after an earlier reburial in the Akyab Military Cemetery. On his headstone stands an epitaph from his own 'Song' ("Oh journeyman, Oh journeyman"):

> And what's transfigured will live on
> Long after Death has come and gone.

. . . I need ten years at least to work out my spirit in writing. I have a lot to say before I stop!

to Jean Gilbert, 26 December, 1939.

It looks as if several years will have to pass before I convince myself I can't and wasn't meant to write.

to Christopher Cheney, August, 1939.

I want to write poetry. It would be such a relief to write. I wait and hunger for the relief & the poetry.

to Freda Aykroyd, October 1943.

I sat at my improvised table for hours, from dusk to midnight, wrestling with poetry, achieving something *perhaps*, but no satisfaction. Writing poetry does not satisfy, it exhausts. I don't know when one experiences pleasure: there is no place for pleasure in the process of writing poetry as far as I can see: yet one would rather write poetry than do anything else on earth. Strange, isn't it? But there are few creative processes which have a positive content of joy. Love seems to have it all, far far more than its share. And yet, perhaps not. Love has more than its share of tragedy, too.

to Freda Aykroyd, 8 November, 1943.

Oh, I get so angry with myself. Who am I? A strange uncommunicative creature. Let me just Be — 'the only minds worth winning are the warm ones about us' . . .

to Gweno Lewis, 5 January, 1944.

APPENDIX A

The Caseg Broadsheets

After spending a weekend with Lynette and Keidrych Rhys at Llanybri in November 1941, Alun wrote to Brenda Chamberlain:

> A matter of policy I thrashed out with Keidrych. He believes — & it is SO true — that the living must be helped before the dead. The Cymmrodorion publish Taliesin & the old literature: nobody publishes the new. You know the hardship of trying to get your work published. All the young writers are the same, & we must help them to find a platform & a public. Later, after the war, we'll start a Review — but now I think we must have living & dead — so will you, if possible, spread out the old Welsh ones . . . ?

He proposed the following programme for the broadsheets:

No 1 and 2 — as printed

      —————

No 3   War in Wales
             Welsh and English

      —————

No 4   The Welsh Peasant
             1) Iolo Goch (one extract)

[In a note, he said they might have to omit the Welsh Original of Iolo 'but I think it's worth it — I don't want too many bilingual sheets — I fear falling between two stools, you see; most of our support will be from *English* - Welsh. I'd prefer to have the *tradition* shown by printing the dead & the living on the same sheet.]

2) Prys-Jones
3) Keidrych Rhys 'The Good Shepherd'

No 5   Dylan Thomas in Memory of Ann Jones
[in a shortened version prepared by him.]

No 6   Lynette's *To a Welsh Woman*
Brenda's *Green Heart*
        Love Songs I and X

No 7   Glyn Jones Choirs (Fortune Press)
Alun Lewis The Mountain over Aberdare or River
Rhondda (*Life and Letters*)

No 8   Welsh Epitaphs
[He suggested they consider his own poem, 'The
Defeated', for inclusion if there were room.]

No 9   Williams Parry Sheet with translations

No 10   Vernon Watkins, John Pritchard, Huw Menai.
[He wrote to all these for poems. He wanted Pritchard's
'Swansea Bay'. Vernon Watkins sent 10/- 'in goodwill'.]

He also drew up a rough draft for a prospectus which announced the venture to the public.

Alun continued to correspond with Brenda and John after joining the Borderers. The following letter concerns the third and fourth sheets:

> ... the idea I have is that the sheets should work forward all the time, beyond individual love or failure or defeat, & should speak for a whole nation, all humanity in their small way. That is why I prefer the cosmic mood of 'these carried bitter tears to the sea' to 'A man has drowned my pride'. The latter is terribly true and *real*: but I want the great flow of earth & water and emotion of the second to be the closing harmony which opens a window onto the world, & does not nail trouble and anguish to its root.

In the event, the following broadsheets were published. I am indebted to John Petts for the details.

In the event, the following broadsheets were published. I am indebted to John Petts for the details.

(1) *TWO POEMS* by Alun Lewis (Raiders' Dawn and Song of Innocence). With a wood-engraving (Debris Searcher) by John Petts.

November 1941.

(2) *PENILLION* (traditional verses) in an English translation by H. Idris Bell. With two wood-engravings by Brenda Chamberlain and John Petts.   December 1941

(3) *WAR AND WALES* Three texts from Taliesin, Peryf ap Cedifor and Gwalchmai translated by H. Idris Bell. Illustrated (half-tones) by Brenda Chamberlain (Study after Leonardo) and John Petts (The Slain)

March 1942

(4) *TO A WELSH WOMAN* and *THE CIRCLE OF C* by Lynette Roberts, from The Green Heart and from Lovesong by Brenda Chamberlain. With a wood-engraving (Snowdon Ridge) by John Petts.   March 1942

(5) From *IN MEMORY OF ANN JONES* by Dylan Thomas. With a pen drawing by Brenda Chamberlain.   June 1942

(6) *SPRING (GWANWYN)* Translated from the Cynfeirdd by H. Idris Bell. With a wood-engraving (Flower of the Bone) by John Petts.

June 1942

UNPUBLISHED (proof copies only exist):

(7) *CHOIRS* Poem by Glyn Jones. With a pen-and-wash drawing (Geese over Eryri) by John Petts.

Designed 1942, proofs by Gomerian Press

(8) *HEDD — PEACE* Poems by William Llŷn, translated by H. Idris Bell. The whole sheet is a wood-block, the figurative work engraved by Brenda Chamberlain and the lettering of the two verses engraved by John Petts.

1942, proofs by Gomerian Press

APPENDIX B

3 Kent Terrace

In the autumn of 1953, two writers, Reginald Moore ("Graham")
and his wife Elizabeth Berridge ("Lisa") were members of a small
group experimenting in psychic communication. One night, their
leader announced that someone called Alun Lewis was coming
through. Did anyone know him? Graham and Lisa did, though they
had never met him. Graham had founded *Modern Reading* in 1941 to
cater for the growing wartime interest in the short story. *Selected
Writing*, a reprint anthology, and *Bugle Blast*, a Forces anthology co-
edited with Jack Aistrop, followed. Alun appeared in a number of
these: 'The Madman' (a poem) in *Selected Writing* in 1941 (chosen by
Tambimuttu, who was responsible for the poetry section that year)
and three stories, 'Private Jones' in *Bugle Blast*, 1943, 'Grenadier' in
Bugle Blast, 1944, and 'Night Journey' in *Selected Writing*, 1944 (all
chosen by Jack Aistrop). Lisa, of part-Welsh extraction but a
Londoner by birth, read these as she had read a good deal of the work
of her contemporaries and had been in brief business communication
with him in April, 1942, when she sent him a copy of *Selected Writing*
at Felixstowe with a cheque for his contribution. He wrote back to
thank her, adding: "I don't think I'll have any new stories by the end
of the month, I'm afraid. I'm full of unwritten stories, lacking time
and typewriter. If I do manage one, I'll send it along." Ironic words,
in view of what was to follow.

One Sunday evening in her flat in Regent's Park, she sat down with
Graham and found herself writing "Alun Lewis" several times. The
next afternoon, Monday 19 October, she was alone. She put on a

record and waited for him to come through. When he did, he told her he wanted to write some stories and poems. She agreed to copy them, so urgent was he, though she was not without misgivings herself. She feared that, being a writer, she might colour whatever came — worse, was getting involved in something fraudulent or mad. Was she joining the lunatic fringe?

Before long, she began to write without thinking. It was a soundless exchange. There was no voice to hear or figure to see; she was aware only of a presence near her by the bookcase. It was like being in a car that is slightly out of control, in a skid one can guide but not master. Evidently, nothing could break the flow. She wrote easily, not pausing except to punctuate a line or take up a new piece of paper. Alun asked her to copy down two poems which he said were for Gweno and asked her to send them to her. This caused her much anxious reflection. Not being a developed psychic, she was not sure about the material she had transcribed and hesitated before intruding on Gweno's grief. She feared the effect such a letter might have. Eventually, however, she wrote and told her that she was prepared for a show of "indignation, grief, incredulity" and explaining her and Graham's "growing interest in — I hesitate to say the occult — rather the lively realisation that there are whole planes of existence beyond this one, so that life does not end on the edge of darkness. We have been investigating various phenomena coolly and speculatively, meeting the trustworthy mediums and checking up on their statements from as many sources as possible". She continued:

> Very recently, I have discovered that I have the power of automatic writing. . . . You know, you sit down and try to 'blank out' your mind and see what comes. I did this, and found that I had 'Alun Lewis' several times. A message then came through 'Will you write to Gweno and tell her I am happy.' This seemed so extraordinary that I tried to get some proof that it was in fact Alun Lewis who was doing the writing. *My* mind was completely blank, I had not been thinking about him. Again the message came 'Tell Gweno not to weep for me, love'. I expostulated, saying that it would upset you, even if you had a belief in life after death. He said you did not believe, but to write all the same. I asked him why he came through me, and the message came 'You are a writer'. The proof I tried to get was this: I asked how many children he had. He said a son. I asked his name. He said Curig. I asked when he was born. He said 1944. I asked his birthday, he said June 21st. I don't know whether these facts are correct or not. But you will. I asked if you were still in Wales. He said yes.

It may be difficult for you to understand — or accept — but he told me he wants to start writing again and cannot until he has reassured you as to his well-being.

I do want you to know that this is no idle hobby of mine and that I write off to people with fake messages! This is the only thing that has ever happened to me and I was in a complete dilemma as to whether to write or not. Then last night an urgent message again: 'Be a dear girl and write to Gweno tonight'. I feel there will be no peace for him wherever he is until I pass this message on to you, whatever your reaction. It will be damnably painful, I expect, and you will curse me . . .

Do please forgive me if I have made you unhappy, and believe me when I say that this is quite the oddest and most compulsive letter I have ever written in my life.

The poem Alun wanted Gweno to have recalls their walks above the tree-line in the hills behind her house in Mountain Ash.

> Above the trees she lingers. Not for me now
> As of old she hesitated in the grass.
> Wedded now to bracken and to ash
> She leaden walks the paths upon the hills
> My gay and gallant one, my girl of joy.
> To greet you tardily my verse now comes.
>
> At home nowhere, nowhere to rest
> My phantom head upon your solid breast.
> No more the robin on the gate
> Will sing us his warcry. For too late
> I'm gone, another warcry fetched me forth
> And left poor robin on the bitter earth
> To dig, to sing for worms
> I shall not dig.

This recalls the penultimate verse of Bequest' (written at Easter, 1943, but not published until 1966, so it was unknown to Lisa at the time).

> I leave you in their company,
> The winter snow heaped on your door,
> In the dark house in the mountains
> With a robin on the floor.

A further extraordinary coincidence arises from the mention of "Curig" in Lisa's letter to Gweno. There was, of course, no "Curig" born to Gweno and Alun — he fantasised with the names "Sian" and "Nevin" in his letters to her — but Wallace and Freda's child, a girl,

was born on 16 May, 1944. She was called Juliet. As it happens, St
Curig, one of the minor saints, was venerated in conjunction with his
mother, with whom he was always associated. Her name was Juliette.

On one early occasion, Lisa wrote half a story called 'The Lost
Man' (I give the text at the end).

> This is only a sketch, Lisa, to get my hand in. It fails as a story, I
> think, what do you say?
>> (I said that I felt rather the same. It was top heavy, somehow, the
>> end didn't support the analytical beginning. But it was an
>> experiment.)
> It is. I never thought it would be. Sorry.
>> (Were you here when Gweno and Mair came?)
> Yes. I'm so glad you liked her. I want to try to get through to her.
>> (I said Gweno would try to.)
> Good.
>> (I asked whether he thought direct contact important.)
> Not now she knows about me. Can't try. Proof is hard.
>
>   (signed) Alun Lewis

Gweno had visited several mediums in London and called on Lisa
after receiving the letter from her. In a later session, another story,
'The Boychick', was copied down (again, I give the text at the end).

> Monday. November 9th [1953]. 11 o'clock.
> (Signed) Alun Lewis. Where's the story?
>> (I've typed it. I'm going to send it to Gweno.)
> Yes.
>> (Gweno sent me this card. She says whether you would like to say
>> anything about it.)
> We always liked it. It reminded us of a bay in Wales.
>> (Any particular one?)
> No.
>> (Where did you get it?)
> In London when I was on leave one time. I saw it in a window and
> bought it for Gweno. I like it, do you?
>> (Yes. Oddly enough, we have one as well!)
> Gweno is better now. She isn't so desperate. Quieter, happier, I
> want her to come up again. Will you let her?
>> (Of course. She wants to speak to you through Paul. Direct voice.)
> I'll try that, but it isn't easy to do. Can I write now?
>> (Of course.)
> Here's another one for you. I hope it will turn out better than the
> last one.
> [Several attempts at a title.]
> Never mind. Some other time. Let's get on.

(As he started to write the first paragraph, the words 'The Boychick' kept coming insistently into my mind. So I put them at the head as the title. I did not see how very apt this was until the story was a quarter through!)

The stories and poems soon came to an end, but Alun continued to communicate with Lisa for another year before disappearing altogether. He seemed particularly concerned about Gweno.

I try to take care of Gweno—she does need a rest poor darling. . . . Gweno knows I am with her but also she must lead her life in her own way. There is nothing more I can tell her or do, really. . . . Lisa thinks I ought to speak to Gweno through a medium. Believe me, that would never satisfy her. She would want to probe and become immersed in it or disbelieve completely. I feel she must be left alone.

Life, he declared, "is all a complicated interweaving of passions, actions, reactions—like sound waves spreading out into the atmosphere widening, thinning but never dying completely away. . . . I am glad to be free of that parcelling up of time". The Moores found this quite comprehensible. They believed that earthly life is but one of many and that the physical body represented only a temporary shelter for the self, which inevitably moves through many planes and different existences. This movement has its obligations, however. One cannot leave anything undone in any one manifestation. In particular, one cannot leave anyone behind in grief; amends have to be made.

Lisa was relieved when Alun disappeared in December, 1956. She did not want to become too deeply involved in the "other world". She had a young family to consider. Moreover she felt she could not practise as a medium and be a creative writer at the same time. Her brief experience left her convinced of the authenticity of the communication but scared and inadequate nonetheless. Nothing she had transcribed was remotely like her own style or subject matter or handwriting, for that matter, and since she had not been reading or thinking about Alun at the time, there was no question of unconscious influence. There was, however, one strange, indirect connection with him. Her and Graham's address in Regent's Park was 3 Kent Terrace, which represented the upper half of a house owned by the poet John Hall. It was to 3 Kent Terrace that Lynette Roberts came with her two children after divorcing Keidrych Rhys in 1948, having spent the intervening period in Hertfordshire. The date was 1952. She rented rooms from Hall after the dissolution of his own marriage and was therefore living in the house at the time of the events I have been describing. She and Lisa never became friends. They met casually at parties but neither remembers talking to the other about Alun Lewis.

During one of their sessions, Alun dictated the following into Lisa's copy of *Raiders' Dawn*:

> Alun Lewis, in memory of one who is kind and gentle and takes trouble over the so-called dead and salutes Lisa and Graham Moore, 1953.

A month after his death, Freda also visited a medium in Coonoor. There was a single exchange: 'Don't go my way, Freda'.

Transmitted October 19th, 26th, [1953].

The Lost Man

He stood outside the door of the house, not liking to enter. He was a very new officer in the regiment and had been told to call on the Colonel's wife for drinks before dinner. He was a tallish man, dark and lean, with greying hair around his temples and a full mouth. He was no longer young although he thought of himself as a bit of a youngster still. He was inclined to drink more than he enjoyed because he wanted the other men younger than himself to think well of him. Not long out from England he was afraid of not doing the right thing and this made him nervy and unsure of himself.

Now he hovered on the porch. In England this porch would have been covered with some sort of rambling rose; here it was empty of trellis or flowers, and was bare and dusty from the baked earth that covered it from the scanty patch of garden. Sunbaked by day and cool and bare by night; that was the Colonel's garden. And his wife, waiting to let this new officer into the hallway, hoped he would be presentable. For she yearned for a man to be pleasant and to be bored with. Here was a possible specimen, she thought, as the boy ushered in the new lieutenant.

"Lt. Manners, how very nice of you!" she said in a small high voice, a voice that belonged to dry places and sun-baked gardens.

"Mrs. Morton, the Colonel said I could call. Very kind if you don't mind my saying such a thing."

"My sister will be here directly, so let's have a drink before she comes in," her sleeve dipped against his cheek as she passed him to mix a highball.

"Look at the moon, oh what a sight!" exclaimed Lt. Manners, suddenly spotting it through the window. It rose. It was huge. It dominated the room, the woman, the tiny bare garden.

"I don't like it," she said, shivering. "It's too big and vulgar, like a neon sign in Piccadilly."

"Oh, d'you think so?" Manners didn't at all care how she found it, and the conversation lapsed. Luckily before the drinks were finished the door opened and another woman came in. She matched the moon in largeness and splendour and Lt. Manners felt he understood why Mrs Morton hated the moon outside. She was obviously the lesser luminary.

"My sister, Miss Susanna Field," said Mrs. Morton with a certain thin irony.

"Oh, how do you do? My name is —"

"*His* name is Lt. Manners, and don't you think he will be an excellent addition to our rather mundane Mess?"

"How do I know, not having had a word of conversation with him yet?" smiled Susanna. Lt. Manners felt as if he were suffering from prickly heat. This woman affected him. She exuded a sharp smell of sex. How true, he wondered, were the stories that pig Bastrell had spread round? You never could tell with a man like that, of course. He lived in his own swill of filth.

He longed for the Colonel to come in and break the tension. Manners had never been easy in the company of women, and now he was so much at a loss that he was quite dumb. He felt the regard Mrs. Morton may have had for him at first meeting slip away, and he knew why. She had divined his wonder at her sister. *Did* he want her, then, this big flashy Susanna? That was an odd name, Susanna. Where—ah, Susanna and the Elders? That picture in his aunt's room—a naked girl cowering away from peeping wicked eyes of lascivious old men. Had this latter day Susanna ever cowered? He would like to know.

The Colonel came in through the big windows. Good God, had he been watering his peas? He would have, in Surrey. Poor devil. A dry man, the Colonel, dry and unseeded. Dry like broom on a ripe hillside and like a ridged shell high up on a cliff. He was not yet as grey as Manners, being not such a worrying type.

He walked quickly towards them, a hurried man who went through life in hasty preoccupation. He greeted Manners with the polite form of words necessary in such an instance and took a stiff whisky from the bamboo table by the sofa.

"Well, how's life with us all?" he asked in a forced and jocular manner. His wife laughed.

"Oh, how could life vary?" she asked, her eyes on their guest.

"Life is always changing, my dear. No one moment is exactly like the next. Ask Susanna here." His eyes slid furtively, with a sort of dry wonder to the immobile figure of his sister-in-law. She raised her glass to him in what was meant to be an ironical gesture, but only succeeded in being over-large and florid like a tipsy barmaid. How exquisite you are, thought Lt. Manners, like a hollyhock, tall and crude but somehow essential.

The Colonel, it was evident, wanted to get rid of Manners, so he gave him a lukewarm invitation to dinner the following evening and said heavily that he supposed he would have to be getting back now. Manners, dismissed, rose to go and hoped Susanna would speak at least one word to him before he left. She did.

She offered to show him the old wonder of the Colonel's garden; a pergola, a fountain court, very Indian and exotic if he liked that sort of thing. He did. He would have liked anything she chose to show him. But he affected a cool assent and avoided the Mrs. Colonel's ironic eye as they left together and went out into the blazing night.

For some time they went along in the curious silence that seemed a habit between them, then she said, "Here's the fountain court. Do you like it? Do you find it impressive?"

With courage he was able to reply, yes, it was, but she was more so. She did not laugh. Only sighed—gusty breath.

"Perhaps that is why I have never married," she said, half laughing. Oh, a terrible embarrassment took hold of him. What was he supposed to say to that? Divining his reaction, she sat down on a stone bench out of the way of the fountain's blown, delicate spray and reached up for his hand.

"Come, mon lieutenant — how is it with you, then?"

"Oh," awkwardly, "I'm not married. Perhaps I'm too unimpressive!"

Surprisingly he laughed. He felt released. There was no fumbling as he kissed her and found it good. "We'd be quite a pair then. What would people say, do you suppose?"

"People always find the worst things to say. Why did you kiss me?"

"A — salute to a woman of parts — will that do?"

"Oh, is that all?" she pouted. She expected something more. A compliment to her beauty, to the irresistible place they were in, away from the Colonel and his barren wife and bare dusty garden where no one could water his peas.

"Let me come to you tonight," she said, making amends for her private thoughts. "Where?"

Lt. Manners was alarmed. Kissing the moon was one thing, possessing it another. Oh, quite another. She would flame in his being and burn him up after the heat was over.

[The transmission ended here.]

Monday. November 2nd. [1953]. 11.15. (I feel overtired tonight). (Signed) Alun Lewis. Let's go on.

They sat on for a time until she began to feel cold, then he got up rather stiffly and said he must be going; Susanna rose with him and they walked across the hot dark garden to the gates. "Tomorrow then?" she queried, not repeating her offer to go to him. Relieved, he agreed. Tomorrow may bring its own excuse.

Next day he was ordered to go to a station some way off and he only saw Susanna once more. She was talking to one of the other men, enigmatically gazing into his opaque, stupid eyes. "I have to go to Basra," said Lt. Manners, when the other officer had moved on. "I may not be back for some months."

"Oh, the rains will be starting. Life is too like Somerset Maugham to be believed then," she laughed, not caring. Not caring? How could it be when those moments they spent in the fountain court had come to mean such a deal to him? Some people, he thought, had the key to significant living. Even if they were in themselves insignificant. This odd thought stayed with him until he was shot crossing a flooded river. Then he found his own moment of significance and it was only death.

Susanna barely remembered his name when the Colonel came in shaking his head one night.

"Lord, that boy," she said, and laughed.

"He wasn't a boy," corrected the Colonel, frowning. "Not a boy at all."

The Colonel's wife remembered him a little longer. She said he sat on the edge of a chair like a man called in to sweep the chimney and being offered an unexpected cup of tea.

The end.

The Boychick

He was not too big from birth but compact and neat as a bantam. Never a cheep out of him of discord, his family said. They lived in a small village dusted over with coal, and many of the men there felt this same dust in their lungs as they neared the fifties.

Dai Denry was an odd boy out in the school room and later on when he went down the mines he was the same. He took his place like the others in the cold dampness of the mine's passages and plunged there every dawn in a lift that squealed its hatred of the early morning. Only one man liked Bantam Dai and he was Big Twm the overseer. Man and lad he'd worked the jealous seams of black stuff that the earth held close as a lover his girl against the chapel wall on soft summer nights. Big Twm could not say what tied him to Bantam Dai. Smallness of bone was not in itself a recommendation in the valleys. Most men were wiry, lithe and full of spunk, but if it was necessary for them to be so, Dai did not feel it to be so for him. He denied courage and had not even tried that peculiar form of pride small men attempt. He pretended no amazing adventures among the girls of the valley. He preferred to any of them fat Maggie of the Black Swan, and she knew it, by God. Maggie knew it and also knew she was no bantam hen to take this valley cock for her own.

Dai and Big Twm worked the damp seam together right enough, but Maggie was not to be shared and Big Twm said as much as they sat over their boxes eating bread and paste one day.

"Keep off Maggie, Dai lad," said he, bulging over the bread. "Keep off and away, lad. Black Swan aint no place for 'ee."

"And for why?" Dai ate neatly and with economy. No bulges. Nothing spilled. Neatly he lapped up cold tea and spilt not a drop. He smiled as a small man should, tidily and with concern. "Fat Maggie is a woman," he sighed, grinding a spare bit of coal into dust. "Big woman and jolly and full of pleasures."

"Not for you, Bantam, she isn't. Pleasures in plenty from other women, but Fat Maggie's to be mine." Jovial he was, but oh so definite. Dai felt his heart sink into his clumping black miner's boots. Risk Big Twm's hatred he couldn't, not now he was nicely on an easy shift. Back-breaking it would be — and was — without that man's hand steady at your back to help the heave of a shovel. Other men too, pick on a small chap. Bantam Dai gave up without a struggle. Big Twm was better meat to him in his daily work than was laughing Maggie on his rare nights of pleasure. Fine pair, too, they'd make, with no inches but the right ones to spare between them.

All the same he still went to the Black Swan. Homely it was for him, a lantern lit in the dark of the mine and a fire in his own darkness of mind. Nowhere else perhaps was there a pub so warm, so glowing, so full of talk and ease after a day or night ground in the earth's dark bowels. But drink flared him into a different bantam, a cock o' the walk bantam, and so he fell foul of Big Twm, not meaning to, see.

It was like this. Full the pub was of cries and jeers and the old darts players.

"Come then, bantam," cried someone, "throw a dart with us."

"He's too busy with other kinds o' darts," laughed one other. "Too busy by half, eh!"

"Who said that?" Bantam put his fists up in pride and a brief glory of clowning. "I'll knock that man's head clean off his shoulders if he'll say such a thing to me outside."

Roars of laughter. Oh how loud and how deafening for a poor wee laddie not up to her shoulder! Maggie bashed a pint mug down on the counter. "Argue wi' that, Twm Griffith. Argue wi' that, I say, ye bullying mountain!"

"I've said nowt," mumbled Big Twm, hurt. True never a word had he said, but sat at the bar cradling his mug as he wanted to cradle Fat Maggie's breasts.

Square on his toes danced Dai Bantam, shunting and weaving and somehow comic to all except Fat Maggie.

"Let's get on with our game! Leave off, Dai Bantam. Crow in the farmyard, not here, man."

Then Big Twm got up slowly from his stool and threw his beer clean over the little man in his dance of titivation and preening maleness. When the cold beer drenched his skin his spirit went out black as a lamp and just as sudden.

"Hi and ho, fallen into a beer cask?" roared out a wag by the fire. But Big Maggie dived forward over the squelching counter and drew him up strongly in her two great fists.

"Come then, my mannie. Come then and change," she crooned, glaring at Big Twm whose mirth had shaken him into a helpless jelly. Natty still and small as a dwarf tree was Dai Bantam between Fat Maggie's hands, and dripping she pulled him onto his feet with outrage melting into pleasure as she pushed open the door back of the bar and edged him through it.

"Bar, Simon!" she called up the narrow back stairs and then set herself to pull off her wet mannie's coat.

"Fat Maggie," said Dai Bantam then, straight out. "Strong as an ox ye are, but so am I, taken right. Let's be married then, and you shall boss the pub."

"Ho, ho," Maggie laughed, her big hands on her knees, "and who'll do the throwing out? Tell me that, you up to me shoulder and that's all."

But she looked at him kindly and with a certain calculation, for he was steady and sweet, that much she did know.

"Hand me me coat and I'll topple Big Twm off his stool," said Dai Bantam dead in earnest.

"Not in my pub!" retorted Maggie strongly. "Over my dead or alive body you'll topple Big Twm!" Dai straightened up and flexed his arm muscles. "Then I'll topple you first, Fat Maggie," says he and by jingo, so he does, getting a Jap hold on her arm and flexing himself in some way so that she goes right over his shoulder and lands bang on the rug by the fire. Roaring like a bull she scrambled for him and clawed out. Again he got that hold nimble as a cat with steel muscles and threw her again. This time he didn't wait, but opened the door and vaulted straight on to the bar right amongst the glasses. Straight onto Big Twm he jumped, toppled him off on the floor, let him stagger up fighting mad, then threw him neat as a sack of coals over his shoulder on to the floor.

Darts stopped. Drinking stopped. Arguments stopped, for here was something to argue about. And there was Big Twm on the floor in a puddle of spilt beer and there was Fat Maggie out of the door back of the bar, her hair coming down, her blouse not decent, laughing and beating her fists like a demented child at a Punch and Judy show.

She married him soon after, for what woman could resist a man with a few surprises up his sleeve? And never a night's trouble was there in the Black Swan, even with Big Twm, after that.

> There's your story. D'you like it?
> (It's splendid!)
> Well, good. I'll go now, bless you. Next week. Same time. 10.30. Nos da, both, Alun Lewis.

November 16th [1953]. Monday 10.30 p.m. (Signed) Alun Lewis.

Well you wrote now well
[I did not quite know what he meant, so said nothing. Then told him we liked his story last week.]
Good. I'm glad it came off. [pause] 'The Mountain'.
[This is a story I was struggling with today. I was in bed with a heavy cold. I told him I did not think it came off.]
Not yet. Will if you do it over. Remember every writer who had to rewrite.
(Yes, I know, I'll go over it and rewrite tomorrow.)
Good that's the stuff. . . . Moore is off.
[Graham in chair looked as if he were asleep, I noticed.]
Here's a new poem for Gweno.

Tell not the fearful piper I am dead
Tell him I live to love again
The rose's station and the moss.
Say that I live and living yet love one
To my content and not her certain loss.

Love we today the hours are not so bold
That loving can be nurtured by the old
Tomorrow birds and roses bring
Reminders that all winter follows spring.

[Pause] Cut out that second verse please. It's awful. Let me go on.

If she my bride of green and silver be
Like lichen fond or slender birch
Let her come privily and fondly come
My garden girl, my mountain-crowned love.
Above the trees she lingers. Not for me now
As of old she hesitated in the grass.
Wedded now to bracken and to ash
She leaden walks the paths upon the hill
My gay and gallant one, my girl of joy.
To greet you tardily my verse now comes.

At home nowhere, nowhere to rest
My phantom head upon your solid breast.
No more the robin on the gate
Will sing us his warcry. For too late
I'm gone, another warcry fetched me forth
And left poor robin on the bitter earth
To dig, to sing for worms
I shall not dig.

I like this pen, it's easier for me. My name is more like my signature now. Let
Gweno see it.
  [Pause while I agree.]
  Read the poem out please.
  (Do you want to alter anything?)
  Not now. Will you send it to Gweno with the story?
  (Yes.) [Graham now rouses himself in the chair and asks about vibration.]
  Everything is done by vibrations, Graham. I could not get through unless
Lisa's were right for me. Poetry is a finer one. It came off better than I thought.
Here's a short one for you.

Time is no stream to get fixed in
Sink or swim, time will carry you along.

Its tides are swift, its motions wonderful
And altogether lovely are its moods.

Time is no stream to partly paddle in.
Time will take you knowing or unknown.
Its currents are in harness to the stars' waggoner
To drag you protesting over many fears.

(signed) Alun Lewis.

Will go now. Two poems are good enough and you're not well. Next week 10.30.
Nos da, Alun Lewis.

NOTES

References

1. Published books of Alun Lewis:

RD   *Raiders' Dawn and other poems*, London, 1942.

TLI   *The Last Inspection [and other stories]*, London, 1943.

HH   *Ha! Ha! Among the Trumpets, Poems in Transit*, London, 1945.

LI   *Letters from India*, ed. by Gweno Lewis and Gwyn Jones, Cardiff, 1946. The text of the letters is unreliable.

IGT   *In the Green Tree*, London, 1948. The text of the letters included is unreliable.

IH   *Alun Lewis, Selected Poetry and Prose*, ed. by Ian Hamilton, London, 1966.

SP   *Selected Poems of Alun Lewis*, ed. by Jeremy Hooker and Gweno Lewis, London, 1981.

Misc   *Alun Lewis, A Miscellany of His Writings*, ed. by John Pikoulis, Bridgend, 1982.

LW   *Alun Lewis, Letters to My Wife*, ed. by Gweno Lewis, Bridgend, 1989. The text of the letters is unreliable.

2. Other published work:

(i) Of Alun Lewis

KL   'A Sheaf of Letters from Alun Lewis, 1941-1943—First Selection. One Modern Poet at War', *Wales*, VIII, 28, February/March, 1948, pp.410-431. (The letters, in fact, date from 1940; there were no further selections.) Addressed to Keidrych Rhys and/or Lynette Roberts.

RT   'The Young Historian: Some Letters from Alun Lewis', *The Anglo-Welsh Review*, 40, Winter 1969, pp.3–21. Addressed to Reginald Treharne.

TL   'The Timothy Lewis Collection: Alun Lewis Memorabilia', *The Anglo-Welsh Review*, 48, Winter 1972, pp.48–53. Letters to Timothy Lewis and his family.

PW   *Poetry Wales* Special Number, 3, 1975. (Includes a selection of letters to Gweno Lewis as well as various articles.)

(ii) Others

TEL *The Letters of T.E. Lawrence*, ed. by David Garnett, London, 1938.
AL *Alun Lewis My Son* by Gwladys Lewis, Aberystwyth, n.d.

3. Unpublished material:

Letters to
AD Andrew Davies
BC Brenda Chamberlain (These letters were in fact addressed variously to Brenda Chamberlain and John Petts and kept by her. They are referred to in her *Alun Lewis and the Making of the Caseg Broadsheets*. The text of the letters included is unreliable and I have quoted from the originals held by the National Library of Wales, NLW 207980. A further collection of letters was held by John Petts. These have not been published. I have kept references to the two separate.
CC Professor Christopher Cheney
FA Freda Aykroyd
GJ Professor Gwyn Jones
GL Gweno Lewis (Some of these letters appeared, in edited form, in IGT and PW.)
GT Gwladys and Tom Lewis (These letters also appeared partially in IGT but were so rewritten by Gwladys as to make quotation unreliable; references to IGT are for convenience only.)
JG Jean Gilbert
JL John Lehmann
JP John Petts (see BC *supra*.)
MF Mair Fenn (neé Lewis)
PU Phillip Unwin (and the files of George Allun and Unwin, Lewis's publisher)
RBH Lady Renee and Sir Bryan Hopkin
RM Richard Mills

Chapter I

p.9: for the history of the area I relied on *History of Cwmaman* by David Lloyd, translated from the Welsh by E.R. Morgan, Aberaman, 1913. For other information, here and in chapter two: *The Fed, A History of the South Wales Miners in the Twentieth Century* by Hywel Francis and David Smith, London, 1980, 'Sidelights on Aberdare' by R. Ivor Parry in *Glamorgan Historian*, 10, ed. by Stewart Williams, Barry, 1974, pp.65-80, and 'Leaders and Led' by David Smith in *Rhondda: Past and Future* ed. by K.S. Hopkins, Rhondda, 1975.
p.11: "enough to have": Tom Lewis to PU, 27 March, 1944.
p.12: Highland Place church: Harri Webb, 'Alun Lewis: The Lost Leader', PW, p.120
– "used to sit": letter to the author by MF.

\-   "the way from orthodoxy": *The Christian Life and Unitarian Herald*, 10 May, 1913, n.p.

p.13:   "chapel has no associations": LW, p.334.

p.14:   "an artistic and": AL, pp.4–5.

\-   "From being a happy": AL, pp. 6–7.

\-   "It was akin to": AL, pp.8–9.

Chapter II

p.17:   "The victims would be": Harri Webb, PW, p.119.

\-   "This week": Glynhafod Infants log book is in the Mid-Glamorgan archives.

p.18:   "As the lady doctor": AL, p.10.

\-   "I don't think we knew": letter to the author.

\-   "a Bible-black": PW, p.29.

p.19:   "There were no 'mod. cons'": letter to the author.

\-   "played and laughed": letter to John Lehmann, *The Open Night*, London, 1952, p.111.

Chapter III

p.21:   "[H]elping people": LW, pp.73–4.

p.22:   One master remembers: the master was Bryn Edwards, later the Deputy Headmaster.

\-   "Obey without reasoning": AL, pp.13–14.

\-   "somewhat reserved": *'A Certaine Schoole', a History of the Grammar School at Cowbridge, Glamorgan* by Iolo Davies, Cowbridge, 1967, p.292. For other information about the school see *Cowbridge and Llanblethian Past and Present* by Brian Ll. James and David J. Francis, Barry and Cowbridge, 1979, in which Bryn Edwards's memoirs are printed, p.161 ff.

p.24:   *The Bovian* is held in Mid-Glamorgan archives.

p.25:   "Youth is a time": 89, July 1923, p.2.

\-   "with minds tuned": 101, July 1927, p.2.

\-   "that noonday": *ibid.*

\-   "narrow patriotism": 114, December 1931, p.1.

\-   "though not in": 94, March 1925, p.2.

\-   "they were in deadly" *et seq.*: 96, December 1925, p.3.

\-   "We live in a": 101, July 1927, p.2.

\-   The minute book of the school Debating Society is in Mid-Glamorgan archives.

p.26:   "Who or what": letter to the author from Elonwy Kirkland.

\-   "He said that Shaw": 27 September, 1930.

\-   "worthy of the expense": 28 February, 1931.

\-   "sympathy with other men": 17 October, 1931.

\-   "the natural feelings" *et seq.*: 113, July 1931, p.1.

p.27:   "Instead of making": AL, p.14.

p.28:   Details on working at the coalface: Edward Greening, quoted in '1926 in Aberdare', *Llafur*, 2, 2, Spring 1977, p.31.

\-   "vision splendid": *The Bovian*, 97, March 1926, p.3.

\-   "Elulora", "skiff dick": see Bryn Edwards, *Cowbridge and Llanblethian*

Past and Present.

– "There was a puritan": *The Bovian*, 118, March 1933, p.3. (The number also contains a tribute from Helen Waddell.)
– 'The Tale of a Dwarf': Misc., pp.21/6.
– 'Vanité': *The Observer*, 31 October, 1937, p.20.

Chapter IV

p.29: "He was always": letter to the author.
p.30: 'It seemed to me': unpublished poem held by the National Library of Wales.
– "damned country": *Pleasant Place*, p.2.
– "Alun?": *op. cit.*, p.3.
pp. 30–31: "And when I saw": *op. cit.*, p.6.
p.31: "Why History": AL, p.16.
– "I think this was": letter to the author.
p.32: "In miles, the run": *A Welsh Eye* by Gwyn Thomas, London, 1964, pp.65–6.
Forty-nine stations: 'Alun Lewis: The Development of a Writer', Keith Evans, MA thesis, University of Lancaster, 1971.
– "The beach lacks": Gwyn Thomas, *op. cit*, p.67.
pp.32–33: "somewhat like an": *ibid.*
p.33: For the history of the college's foundation, see *The University College of Wales Aberystwyth 1872-1972* by E.L. Ellis, Cardiff, 1972.
– "Welsh students detest": *ibid*, p.162.
– "I should like": *op. cit*, p.240.
p.34: "It wasn't till": LW, p.372.
– "was a home from": letter to the author.
p.35: "the sound of the whistle": AL, p.19.
p.36: "He *never* fell": letter to the author.
– "an extremely fine" *et seq.*: Treharne's testimonial, 6 April, 1938.
p.37: "an outstanding scholarly": E.L. Ellis, *op. cit.*, p.233.
– "Why sacrifice": 31 July, 1935.
– For the Welsh: the dilemma of Welsh/English writers has been well described by Glyn Jones in *The Dragon Has Two Tongues, Essays on Anglo-Welsh Writers and Writing*, London, 1968 and *Setting Out, A Memoir of Literary Life in Wales*, Cardiff, 1982.
p.38: "The poet": Gwyn Thomas, *op. cit*, p.94.
– "messy, ugly": Gwyn Jones, *Times Like These*, London, 1936, 1979, p.53.
pp.38–9: "Let me explain": *Poetry Wales*, 7, 3, Winter 1971, pp.8–9.
p.39: "I walked my native": Idris Davies, 'Gwalia Deserta', XXIX, *The Collected Poems of Idris Davies*, Llandysul, 1972.

Chapter V

p.41: Gwladys Lewis remembers: AL, p.20.

–   "I used to think": LW, p.92.
–   "itchy dirty": IGT, p.35.
pp.41–2: "It was an evil": 'The Challenge', *The Serpent*, February 1936, p.71.
p.42: "The Norwich valuation": 'The English Activities of Cardinal Ottobuono, legate of the Holy See', May, 1937, p.127.
p.43: "I do nothing": to CC. Most of Alun's correspondence with CC is undated save for a "Tuesday" or a "Friday"; where dates are provided, they are those of CC.
p.44: "I got lost": to KL, June 24, 1941, p.413.
p.45: "adolescence's Golgotha" *et seq.*: to CC, May and June, 1937.
–   "I am still aspiring": June 1937.
p.46: "How lovely evil things": June 1937, p.154.
–   "How nearly": to CC, 12 April, 1937.
p.47: "then I'd wake": LW, pp.194–5.
–   "achieved nothing" *et seq.*: to FA, 5 August, 1943.
–   'Chestnuts': *The Serpent*, 21 (1936–7) 2, December 1936, pp.39–41.

Chapter VI

p.49: "The time hasn't": to JG, August 1937.
–   "ingrate and": to CC, 30 August, 1937.
–   "an unbalanced": LW, p.96.
p.50: Alun later came to regard: to JG, 10 January, 1938.
p.51: *Time and Tide* poems: 'The Merchant's Wife', XIX, 7, February 12, 1938; 'The Country Gentleman', XIX, 30, 23 July, 1938; 'The Poet', XIX, 33, August 13, 1938. Helen Waddell wrote to Alun praising the poems and urged him to place them in various papers at her recommendation (CC, October 4, 1937).
–   "Look, mother": to John Lehmann, *op. cit.*, p.111.
–   "each thing justified": to CC, 24 October, 1937.
–   "worst bloody": to CC, 8 November, 1937.
–   "piddling stuff": to CC, 8 November, 1937.
–   "wandering down": to CC, 9 February, 1938.
–   "I'm not much luckier": to CC, 7 February, 1938.
–   "Mother's full of": to CC, 7 March, 1938.
–   "but with definite" *et seq.*: *The Aberdare Leader*, 16 April, 1938.
p.53: "She's ever so" *et seq.*: to CC, 8 March, 1938.
–   "They would not stop": to CC, 1 April, 1938.
–   "Very cold": to CC, n.d.
–   "I apply": to CC, 12 June, 1938.

Chapter VII

p.55: "diddling about": to CC, n.d.

–   "little better": to TL, 15 September, 1938.

–   records of education: 'Education in Aberdare in the 60's', 23 July, 1938, p.3 (this was broadcast on the BBC Welsh service on 4 December, 1938, 'Overcrowding and Understaffing', 30 July, 1938, pp.7–8 and 'H.M.I.'s Reports were not Literary Models', 6 August, 1938, p.5.

–   "felt she would prefer": to CC, 6 October, 1938.

–   "she thought": letter of 20 October, 1938.

–   *The Manchester Guardian* stories: 'Picnic', 25 November, 1938, p.20; 'The Cardinelli Crisis', 7 February, 1939, p.20 and 'The Poetry Lesson', 8 June, 1939, p.20.

–   "a bit flummoxed": to RM, n.d.

p.56:   "I think I imagined": October, 1938.

–   'If War Comes—Will I Fight' and 'Munich and Peace, The Significance of Re-Armament': Misc., pp.81–5 and 85–8 resp.

–   'Anschluss': January 1939, XIV, 1, pp.4–6.

p.57:   "I wanted people": 17 December, 1938.

–   "my very pragmatic": to RM, 1 November, 1938.

p.58:   "[If you want]": LW, p. 224.

–   "To note precisely" *et seq.*: *Poems from the Forces*, ed. by Keidrych Rhys, London, 1941.

p.59:   "I'm getting more": 17 November, 1938.

–   "a mistake": to RM, 1 November, 1938.

–   "It must have been": Marjorie Walters, unpublished memoir, July 1964.

–   "Alun in the easy": to JP, May 10, 1949.

–   Geoffrey Bullough: *The Trend of Modern Poetry*, Edinburgh and London, 1943, p. 250.

p.60:   "Damn" *et seq.*: to RM, 28 November, 1938.

–   "a mort of stories" *et seq.*: to CC, n.d.

–   "Normal and sensible": to RM, March 1, 1939.

–   *The Ludovican*, III, 27, Summer 1939.

–   "a solace and": *et seq.*: to RM, 14 January, 1939.

–   "elegant sufficiency": to GJ, 16 January, 1939.

–   "quite slick": reader's report, Chatto and Windus archive, University of Reading Library.

–   "As for the poetry": to GJ, 23 January, 1939.

–   "devoutly believe": to GJ, 9 April, 1939.

–   'The Housekeeper': TLI, pp.127–38.

p.61:   "abominably lonely": LW, p.364.

–   At Whitsun: the result was published as 'English Weekend': Misc, pp.95/102.

p.62:   " . . . it wasn't like": to CC, 21 September, 1939.

–   "whether to pay": to RM, June 1939.

p.63:   "I will probably" *et seq.*: 31 August, 1939.

–   "It's making a mess": to RM, 21 September, 1939.

-     "through poverty": to RM, August, 1939.
-     "I eat it": to JG, August 1939.
-     "to synthesize": to GJ, 8 October, 1939.

Chapter VIII

p.68:   "I'm not a pacifist": to CC, September 4, 1939.
-     "Plunge in?": to CC, September 21, 1939.
-     "this might explain": to TL, n.d.
-     My description of the school draws on *The History of Lewis' School, Pengam* by Arthur Wright, Pengam, 1929. See, too, 'Between Two Summers' by C.M. Harris in *The Ludovican*, VII, 5, Summer 1966.
-     "Alun's teaching method": to RT, 8 January, 1940.

p.69:   "too much of myself": to RM, 21 September, 1939.
-     "a fine companion": to RM, August 1939.

p.70:   "This is the street": RD, p. 89.
-     "I lived on the margin": to CC, 28 December, 1939.
-     'Viking': LW, p. 97.
-     "a fountain of joy": translated from a letter to JG, 26 December, 1939.
-     "little highnecked colt": LW, p. 323.

p.71:   "I remembered how": LW, p.59.
-     "old nervous strain": LW, p.266.
-     "a horrible black" *et seq.*: LW, p.75.
-     "although we've shied": LW, p.70.
-     "real thing" *et seq.*: to RM, December, 1939.

p.72:   "sweating like a pig": to CC, 28 December, 1939.
-     "The world doesn't": to RM, December 1939.
-     Alun's reviews: 2, 1939, September (p.110), October (pp.172–4) and November (pp.231–2).
-     'The Wanderers': 2, 3, October 1939, pp.182–39.

p.73:   "[I]t is difficult": Misc, pp.102–114.
-     "I don't foresee": LW, p.104.
-     "secondary and university": to GJ, 24 April, 1940.

p.74:   "At the door" *et seq.*: 'Last Leaves of a Civilian's Journal': Misc, pp.102–114.

p.75:   "I wanted it": see Yeats's 'Sailing to Byzantium'.
-     "Last Pages of a Long Journal": Misc, pp.119–23.

Chapter IX

p.77:   "My job":LW, p.29.
-     "the adjective dominant": to CC, n.d.
p.78:   "It's ludicrous": to AD, 26 June, 1940.
-     "illiterate and" *et seq.*: to CC, n.d.
-     "snooty little": 'Lance-Jack', TLI, p.76.

–   "ideal travelling": to RM, 30 May, 1939.

p.79:   "I didn't get further": LW, p.38.

–   "a climax of disaster" *et seq.*: RD, pp.17–18.

–   'The Public Gardens': RD, pp.19–20.

–   "very quiet poems": to AD, 24 August, 1940.

–   "Poetry is becoming": to AD, 24 August, 1940.

–   "turbulence and time": 'The Soldier', RD, p.17.

–   "the problem is" *et seq.*: LW, p.101.

p.80:   "approaches to the truth": LW, p.58.

–   "glittering": RD, p.20.

–   "a poem of such feathery": *Components of the Scene, Stories, Poems, and Essays of the Second World War*, Harmondsworth, Middlesex, 1966, p.16.

–   "Blue necklace left": RD, p.15.

–   "the seed of": Misc, p.120.

–   "a sabre-toothed": RD, p.30.

–   "the ear half-catching": RD, p.31.

–   "the stench": *op. cit.*, p.32.

p.81:   "If I should go away": 'Post-script: for Gweno', RD, p.45.

–   "And has its quiet": *ibid.*

–   "One suit shall": to AD, 26 June, 1940.

–   "clerking (so-called)": to GT, n.d.

–   "a supernumerary": *ibid.*

–   "like the intelligent": to RBH, n.d.

–   "Letters are my proxies": to AD, 26 June, 1940.

p.82:   ". . . I'm fighting": LW, p.42.

–   "I'm full of": LW, p.54.

–   "my diary of": to AD, 7 October, 1940.

–   "One does things": to RBH, n.d.

–   "Conventions go" *et seq.*: 'Lance-Jack', TLI, pp.75–85.

p.83:   "horrible cul-de-sac": to CC, n.d.

–   "simpler things": RD, p.77.

p.84:   "I have left": RD, p.20.

–   "I have begun": RD, p.19.

–   "[What I fought]": a different version of 'Last Pages of a Long Journal' in 'Alun Lewis, His Short Stories and Poems' by Horst Jarka, Ph.D. dissertation, University of Vienna, 1954, p.70.

–   "fury" *et seq.*: 'The Sentry', RD, p.20.

–   'Lines on a Tudor Mansion': RD, p.25.

p.85:   "I'm not a pacifist": LW, p.41.

–   "You must see": LW, p.39.

–   "singing rib": RD, p.45.

–   "Thinking back": IGT, p.43.

–   "Climbing the steep path": 'To Edward Thomas', RD, p.21.

p.86:   "I have been garrisoned": *Horizon*, III, 13, January 1941, pp.78, 80,

reprinted in Misc, pp.118–9.
-    "He was still there": 7 October, 1940.
-    " . . . all day I watched": *ibid.*
p.88:   "really is": *Horizon, v.s..*
p.89:   "I lay awake": London, 1913, pp.230–3.
-    "as war poet": *Horizon* review, *v.s..*
p.90:   "wet, shabby": LW, p.45.
-    "Being heavy-headed": LW, p.121.
-    "when the heavy": LW, p.74.
-    "voice" *et seq.*: RD. pp.21–3.
-    "a superb moment": IH, p.24.
-    "the nearest expression": LW, p.93.
-    "In my hands": Jarka, *op. cit*, p.128.
p.91:   "hinted land" *et seq.*: RD, p.23.

Chapter X

p.92:   'Attitude': *The Dragon*, Summer 1938, pp.7–12, reprinted Misc, pp.57–68.
-    "When I was a little": Misc, p.123.
-    "I've always known": LW, p.43.
p.93:   "She's a brick": n.d.
-    " . . . it's very hard": to RM, 4 November, 1940.
-    "Mere boredom": to GT, n.d.
-    "The English, poor": to KL, p.414.
-    "the officer who is": to RM, 4 November, 1940.
p.94:   "the zero of": LW, p.84.
-    "there are heaps": to GT, n.d.
-    "I'm finicky": LW, p.88.
-    "19th-20th Century": to RM, 4 November, 1940.
-    "I *can not*" *et seq.*: to RM, n.d.
-    'New World Order': *The Sandpiper*, 6 December, 1940.
p.95:   "Let's do *something*": *ibid.*
-    "I find myself": to JL, 2 January, 1941.
-    "vague feeling": 'Farewell Binge', TLI, pp.51–7.
-    "I don't mind": Misc, p.123.
-    commendation of a visiting general: to AD, 14 June, 1941.
-    "Awful!": to GT, n.d.
p.96   "My life is the soft": to RM, n.d.
-    Graham Greene: letter of 27 March, 1941.
-    "[G]et yourself": March 14, 1941.
-    "loving self": LW, p.109.
-    "I've often": LW, p.111.
-    "distant manner": to Caton, 1 May 1, 1941.
p.97   'The Last Inspection': I, pp.9–14.

–   "a stretch of clink" *et seq.*: to JP, 28 February, 1941.

–   'Poem from Llanybri': *Poems*, London, 1944. For a fuller account of Alun's relations with Lynette, see my 'Lynette Roberts and Alun Lewis', *Poetry Wales*, XIX, 2, Winter 1983, pp.9–29.

–   "I found I was singing" *et seq.*: to KL, p.411.

–   "She's an exciting": LW, p.117.

–   "a strange uncontrollable": LW, p.153.

–   "a world of disaster": LW, p.117.

p.98   "I like your letters": n.d.

–   "*I couldn't feel*": to JP, 2 April, 1941; the journal account is unpublished.

p.99: 'They Came': TLI, pp.227/43.

–   "all that is inarticulate": to JP, 20 December, 1940.

p.100: "It's a very learned": n.d.

–   "He's made a very serious": 2 June, 1941.

–   "the old Adam": LW, p.139.

–   "strange, nervous" *et seq.*: to GT, n.d.

p.101: "a general radical": 'English Intellectuals and Politics in the 1930s', by Stuart Samuels in *On Intellectuals*, ed. by Philip Rieff, New York, 1969, p.197.

–   "Seemingly": 'Inside the Whale', *Collected Essays*, London, 1961, p.158.

–   "We must go": Misc, p.120.

–   "We are living": *The Penguin New Writing*, 6 May, 1941, pp.127–129.

p.102: "the ideology of": *Poetry Since 1939*, London, 1946, p.56.

p.115: "poems containing" *et seq.*: *The Forties*, London, 1950, n.p.

–   Connolly's advice: 'The Ivory Shelter' in *The New Statesman*, 7 October, 1939, pp.482–3.

–   "Art is not life": *New Year Letter*, London, 1941.

–   'Art for Art's sake?': *The Listener*, 11 January, 1940, pp.85–6. (Orwell, too, thought it was impossible to write books "with this nightmare going on" (*op. cit.*, p.20).

–   "Life isn't for": Misc, p.122.

–   "the quarry": 21 February, 1941.

–   "[T]here are two urgent" *et seq.*: 14 April, 1941.

p.103: "[I]t's entirely a friendly': to GJ, 19 May, 1941.

–   "continuity, almost identity": to BC, 2 June, 1941.

–   "the peasant, the soldier": to AD, 14 June, 1941.

–   "It's a lie": to GT, n.d.

–   to toe a particular party line: LW, p.120.

–   "said many sharp": to GT, n.d.

p.104: "Every true soldier": LW, p.43.

–   "You know": LW, pp.42–3.

–   a letter from Philip Unwin: 12 May, 1941.

–   "breathless with delight": to PU, 19 July, 1941.

Chapter XI

p.105: "sort of fatalism": LW, p.363.
  − "something immediately": LW, p.364.
  − "It's up to you" *et seq.*: LW, p.139.
p.106 "Dear Gweno" *et seq.*: LW, p.140.
  − "in bad moods": to KL:, p.414.
  − "atrophy": LW, p.354.
p.107: "And then you thought": LW, p.374–5.
  − "for being such a good girl": to CC, n.d.
  − "I think Gweno": n.d.
p.108: "admixture of": LW, p.348.
  − 'War Wedding': RD, pp.55–61.
  − 'The Mountain over Aberdare': RD, pp.87–8.
  − Details of Heysham Towers from a letter to RBH, n.d.
  − O.C's welcoming speech: to GT, n.d.
p.109: 'The Creation of a Class', *Horizon*, IV, 21, pp.168–171.
  − "live in blinkers": LW, p.156.
  − "drifting into": LW, p.154.
  − "quiet but definite" *et seq.*: Cadet Record Sheet, Army Records Office.
  − failed to disturb him: LW, p.156.
  − *Lilliput*: 9, 54, December 1941, pp.477–84.
  − *Horizon* plea: 'Why not War Writers? A Manifesto', IV, 22, October 1941, pp.236–9.
  − "It's all very comic": to CC, 14 September, 1941.
p.110: "You can guess": to CC, 25 August, 1941.
  − "Well, what is it": to KL, pp.418–9; the last twelve words were omitted from the printed version.
  − "with a romantic assignment": to KL, pp.416–7.
  − "symptomatic": to PU, 23 June, 1941.
  − 'The Prisoners': pp.215–225.
  − "Now why": to RM, n.d.
p.111 "a good officer": Cadet Record Sheet, *v.s.*.
  − "He was dark": IGT, p.139.
  − 'Song of Innocence': the poem appeared only as a broadsheet and has been uncollected since.
  − "fortitude with which": to PU, 2 October, 1941.
p.112: "You felt in him": Humanities Research Center, University of Texas (Austin).
  − "What will": to RM, n.d.
  − "The sort of soldier": *et seq.*: *The Listener*, 23 October, 1941, pp.566–7.
  − "given us one real": *The Listener*, 12 February, 1942, pp.216 and 219.
p.113 "to wit" *et seq.*: the correspondence has been printed in Misc, pp.134–149.

Chapter XII

p.115: "so easily upset": LW, p.185.
– "the barren": LW, p.182.
– "[T]here is always": to BC, 5 January, 1942.
– "I've had no time": to B.C., n.d.
– "like a jab" *et seq.*: to RM, n.d.
– "I shouldn't have": LW, p.181.
p.116: 'It's a Long Way to Go': TLI, pp.59-73.
– "His wife's photograph": *op cit*, pp.60–1.
p.117: "the complete village idiot": O.A. Evans in a letter to the author.
– "a rotter": LW, p.180.
– Gwynne Jones remembers: contribution to John Ormond's film 'The Fragile Universe', BBC, 1967.
p.118: "moods of black": to BC, *op cit*, p.26.
– "rather rum": Julian Maclaren-Ross, 'Second Lieutenant Lewis: A Memoir' in his *The Funny Bone*, London, 1956, p.182.
– Paul Scott: *The Mark of the Warrior*, London, 1958.
– "people who seem": LW, p.179.
p.119: "new equal endeavour": to GT, n.d.
– 'Private Jones', TLI, pp.21–43.
– "the ability of the ordinary": Alun John, *The Life and Works of Alun Lewis*, Ph.D. thesis, University of Wales, 1973, p.171.
– "I feel very out of it": n.d.
– "a pernicious": to GT, n.d.
– "My main task": n.d.
– "where selfish men": to KL, 17 January, 1942.
– "these continual petty": to GT, n.d.
– "big shots were": to KL, *ibid*.
p.120: "a queer isolated": to BC, 15 February, 1942.
– 'Dawn on the East Coast': HH, p.13.
– "strange, attractive": LW, p.193.
– "in my dreamy way": to BC, 5 January, 1942.
– "a tattered': PW, p.121.
p.121: To Alun's disappointment: to BC, n.d.
– "strong poetic thread": Misc, p.140.
– 'Mr Lewis speaks words': 16 July, 1942, pp.88 and 91.
– "dignified, epigrammatic": *Poets of the 1939-1945 War*, London, 1960, pp.19 and 21.
– "deep masculine tenderness": XVII, 2, April-June 1942, pp.54–5.
– "Mr Lewis has": March 21, 1942, p.142.
– "a young Welsh": 3 May, 1942, p.3.
– "Anyone who wishes": XXXIII, 1942, pp.169–172.
– 'War Wedding' revision: to PU.

p.122: "completed": to CC, Easter Sunday, 1942.
–   "I feel it makes": to PU, July 25, 1941.
–   "Rupert Brookeish": July 30, 1941.
p.123: "a state of benumbed": *op. cit.*
–   'Poetry of the Fifties', Carolyn Kizer and A. Alvarez in *The International Literary Annual* ed. by John Wain, London, 1958, pp.60–107.
–   "like going down": *The Journal of the South Wales Borderers*, 21 April, 1942, p.18.
–   "I find it hardest": to Llewellyn Wyn Griffith, 22 March, 1942.
–   " . . . I believe I'm": to GT, n.d.
p.124: "glittering": LW, p.200.
–   "botched": to GT, n.d.
–   "Poor Gweno": to GT, n.d.
–   " . . . I want to know": LW, p.199.
–   "I feel": LW, p.206.
p.125: "a little subaltern": LW, p.202.
–   "my inside": LW, p.197.
–   "morbidity and": LW, p.195.
–   "the attenuated": LW, p.205.
–   Maclaren-Ross: *op. cit.*, pp.181–3.
p.128: "[W]e are crawling": reprinted in Misc, pp.150–3.
–   "the dead hand": June 19, 1942, p.14.
–   "a very straight person" *et seq.*: to GT, n.d.
–   "just as if": LW, p.211.
–   "a real landslide": LW, p.212.
–   weren't objective enough: to GT, n.d.
–   Maclaren-Ross told him: Alun to GT, n.d.
p.129: 'Acting-Captain': TLI, pp.139–177.
–   'The Children': TLI, pp.179–188.
–   'Cold Spell': TLI, pp.193–206.
p.130: "the battalion moved": LW, p.218.
–   'Dusty Hermitage': TLI, pp.207–214.
–   "I'm growing": KL, p.426.
p.131: "a kind of": Ronald Blythe, *The Age of Illusion*, London, 1963, p.77.
–   "a *private* atmosphere": to KL, p.425.
–   "a happy casualness" *et seq.*: *The Listener*, 1 September, 1938, pp.426.
p.133: "The warm ones about us": In a letter to Peter Davies, TEL, pp.859–60, Lawrence expressed his sorrow at the death of Frederic Manning: "In fact I find myself wishing all the time that my own curtain would fall. It seems as if I had finished, now. Strange to think how Manning, sick, poor, fastidious, worked like a slave for year after year, not on the concrete and palpable boats or engines of my ambition, but on stringing words together to shape his ideas and reasonings. That's what being a born writer means, I suppose. And today it is all over and nobody ever heard of him. If he had

been famous in his day he would have liked it, I think, liked it deprecatingly. As for fame-after-death, it's a thing to spit at; the only minds worth winning are the warm ones about us. If we miss those, we are failures."

- "come back to": Misc, pp.119–20.
- "ate the rank's food": *Seven Pillars of Wisdom* by T.E. Lawrence, London, Harmondsworth, Middlesex, 1962, p.161.
- Andrew Rutherford: *The Literature of War*, London, 1978.
- "the best place to see": T.E.Lawrence, quoted in *The Secret Lives of Lawrence of Arabia*, London, 1969, 1971, p.194.
- "stunted version" *et seq.*: Christopher Caudwell *Illusion and Reality*, London, 1937, p.25.

p.134: "Commitment to": IH, p.39.
- "I don't know whether": to KL, p.426. Only the first sentence of the quotation appeared in the printed version.
- "the places of": LW, p.232.
- "I was fast": LW, p.311.
- "that sad afternoon" *et seq.*: LW, p.275.

p.135: told Leslie Sykes: n.d.
- "the courage to": 20 May, 1942.
- "Gweno hopes": to RM, 18 December, 1942.
- "Death in battle": LI, p.5.
- "a bit dubious": Misc, p.143.

p.136: "Mr Lewis is": May 12, 1943, p.407.
- "The stories deal": 24 March, 1943, p.376.
- "When the tide": LW, p.235.

p.137: ". . . I love you utterly": LW, p.233.
- "But darling": LW, p.239
- "No one has ever": LW, p.241.
- 'On Embarkation': HH, pp.27/31.

p.138: 'Goodbye': HH, p.24.
- "Also be *ye*": to G.T., n.d.
- "Everything is running": LW, p.251.
- "miserable interim": to G.T., n.d.

p.139: "And I remember": LW, p.264.
- "Goodbye darling": LW, pp. 280/1.

Chapter XIII

p.140: "a svelte luxury": Misc, p.160.
- "the most incredible": to GT, n.d.
- "Yet one man": IH, p.42.
- "[H]ere on this": LW, p.265.
- "a sort of incessant": LW, p.266.

p.142: "the loveliest talk": LW, p.272.
  – "none of that": LW, p.266.
  – "success fou": *The Journal of the South Wales Borderers*, 23 April, 1943, p.23.
p.143: "[A]s we went in": LW, p.267.
  – "navels like eyes": IGT, p.22.
  – "It's marvellous": LW, p.269.
p.144: "still tea at four": to JP, n.d.
  – "The moon in her": 'Chanson Triste', HH, p.33.
  – "Do you see": LW, p.279.
  – "where he'd left" *et seq.*: HH, p.34.
  – "NOT to withdraw": IH, p.41.
  – "that I'm going to be": LW, p.276.
  – "could be altered": IH, p.44.
  – "skyscraper flats": LW, p.277.
p.145: "I don't agree": LW, p.278.
  – "I don't know whether": LW, p.265.
  – "my final task": LW, p.280.
  – "I realised the significance": IH, p.44.
  – "I asked him about": Jarka, *op. cit.*, pp.139–40 and IH, p.57.
  – 'To Rilke': HH, pp.37–8.
  – 'Santa Claus': *New Year Letter*.
p.146: "Poetry is a man's": 1, 3, November 1940, pp.84–5.
  – "A few grasshoppers": LW, p.287.
p.147: "eyes like paraffin": LW, p.292.
  – "It's an amazing": to GT, 20 January, 1943.
  – "a big poem" *et seq.*: LW, p.294.
  – "a little granite": IH, pp.46–7.
p.148: "alone by a heap": HH, p.41.
p.149: "being, consciousness": *The Principal Upanishads*, ed. By S. Radhakrishnan, London, 1953, p.938.
  – "a being infinite": 1915, Harmondsworth, Middlesex, 1949, p.437.
  – "like a rubbish", LW, p.308.
  – "It is so piercingly" *et seq.*: LW, p.298.
  – "The only futile": LW, p.301.
p.150: the world spun round: see letter to GT, 20 January, 1943.
  – "My mind has" *et seq.*: LW, p.301.
  – "Thought is like": to RM, n.d.
p.151: "more morbid": LW, p.299.
  – "I'm deliberately": LW, p.303.
p.152: 'In Hospital: Poona (1) and (2)': HH, pp.52–4.
  – 'Burma Casualty': HH, pp.58–61.
  – 'The Earth is a Syllable': IGT, pp.85–90.
  – "Long cold fields": IH, p.52.

–   "breathes": *The Principal Upanishads*, *v.s.*, p.616.

p.153: "[D]on't think": LW, p.313.

–   "The sick have": 'Ward "0" 3(b)': IGT, pp.91–109.

–   "all of one breath": IGT, p.35.

p.155: "It's been an enriching": LW, p.306.

–   "brilliant and violent": LW, p.320.

–   'The River Temple: Wai': IH, p.131.

–   "wreathed in a": to RM, 23 March, 1943.

–   "Dark peasants" *et seq.*: 'The Mahratta Ghats', HH, p.43.

p.156: "guilt complex" *et seq.*: 25, 630, 20 March, 1943, pp.191–2.

–   "Well—maybe": LW, p.315.

–   'Bread for Stones': 636, 25, 1 May, 1943, p.287, reprinted Misc, pp.159–62.

–   "Life is Dangerous":IW, p. 317.

–   'Karanje Village': HH, p. 41.

–   'Motifs': HH, p. 66.

p.157: 'Bivouac', HH, p. 66.

–   For the history of the period, see *The War Against Japan*, III, *The Decisive Battles* by Major General Sir Woodburn Kirby with Captain C.T. Addis, Brigadier M.R. Roberts, Colonel G.T. Wards and Air Vice-Marshal N.L. Desoer (part of the official *History of the Second World War*, ed. by Sir James Butler).

p.158: "a fair substitute": to GT, 29 March, 1943.

–   "the arid resistancy": 28 April, 1943.

–   "There was a zareba": Misc, p.146.

p.159: "all keyed up": LW, p.317.

–   "when I've been busiest":LW, p.328.

–   "All the poems": LW, p.343.

–   "more simple poetry" *et seq.*: LW, p.326.

p.160: 'Village Funeral': HH, pp.48–9.

–   'Home Thoughts from Abroad': HH, pp.51–2.

–   'Bequest': IH, p.130.

–   'Shadows': HH, pp.50–1.

–   'Water Music': HH, pp.49–50.

–   Misc, p.122.

–   "alternation of": *Portrait of the Artist as a Young Man* by James Joyce, 1916, *The Essential James Joyce*, Harmondsworth, Middlesex, 1963, p.125.

p.161: 'Bequest—well': LW, pp.326–7.

–   "coloured more than": LI, p.5.

p.162: "in the jungle": LW, p.322.

–   "[D]eath doesn't": LW, p.354.

–   "Yesterday and the night": LW, p.335.

–   "[T]here is constantly": to JP, 28 April, 1943.

p.163: "simple restlessness": IGT, p.39.

–   'Assault Convoy': HH, p.71.

–   'The Patrol': IH, p.135.
–   'The Run-In', HH, p.132.
–   "The soldier's regiment": *Lilliput*, 13, 75, September 1943, pp.201–3.
p.164: "Perhaps it's just": to GT, n.d.
–   "He's been a missionary": LW, p.371.
–   "but only if Britain": LW, p.341.
–   "anything but a": IGT, p.48.
–   "They want Virgil's": LW, p.380.
–   "It is easy to write": Misc, pp.145–6.
–   "In many ways": 30 August, 1943.
p.165: "like floating embers": to GT, 23 June, 1943.
–   "I find": LW, p.357.
–   "the long crisis": LW, p.352.
–   "There are charcoal": LW, p.357.
p.166: "blood to follow": I. Williams, interview with the author.
–   "I tried to read": LW, pp.358–9.
–   "the freedom": to GT, June 8, 1943.
–   "natural indolence" *et seq.*: LW, p.363.
–   'A Troopship in the Tropics': HH, pp. 32–3.
p.167: "like a Youth": LW, p.364.
–   "We saw tribes": IGT, p.43.
–   "I haven't got": LW, p.364.
–   "camels, flamingoes": LW, p.366.
–   "[W]e'd come", LW, p.369.
–   "I take all": LW, p.342.
p.168: "oblivious": to GT, 17 July, 1943.
–   "colossal experience": IGT, p.43.
–   'The Orange Grove': IGT, pp.111–125.
–   "in a kind of drunkenness": to GL, 9 September, 1943.
–   "inside India": to FA, 24 August, 1943.
p.169: pneumatikos/sarkikos: see *Four Archetypes* by C.G. Jung, London, 1972.
p.170: "a mental and moral": TEL, p.244.
–   "like a soul": *The Spectator*, 18 November, 1966, p.654.
–   "Well, time" *et seq.*: LW, p.379.
p.171: "Some unstated": LW, p.381.
–   "I see life": LW, p.382.
–   Alun's meeting with Freda is derived from letters of his to her, 11 and 31
       August, 1943.
–   "more beautiful than fate": 'The House', unpublished poem.

Chapter XIV

p.172: "I'm in a mulish": 15 July, 1943.
p.174: "like all intellectual": London, 1927, p.125.

-        "marvellous feeling": to FA, 18 December, 1943.
-        "dappled moles", LW, p.387. In a letter to FA, 5 September, 1943, Alun
         recalled walking in the woods round Highfield "looking at the rose moles all
         in stipple in your little stream".
-        "I, certainly": letter to the author.
p.175:   "given purely": 'The Exquisite Moment', unpublished.
-        "There was a frailty": *Modern Reading*, Summer 1952, p.16.
-        'But today': unpublished poem.
-        'Ways', HH p.47.
p.176:   "the grey light": unpublished poem, 'The Parting'.
p.177:   'Peasant Song': HH, pp.62–3.
-        'Wood Song': HH, p.63.
p.178:   "The ruthlessness of war": Misc, p.166.
p.179:   "what no-one else" *et seq.*: to FA, 22 August, 1943.
-        "I was afraid": to FA, 15 August, 1943.
p.180:   'Yet I'm not a': 14 August, 1943.
-        "Gweno, we should": LW, pp.249–50.
-        "Why should": to FA, 15 August, 1943.
-        "a sort of hourly" *et seq.*: to FA, 2 September, 1943.
-        "[Y]ou mustn't fret": LW, pp.390–1.
p.181:   "of the anchor": letter to the author.
-        "I've growingly had": to FA, 22 August, 1943.
-        "answered 'Yes . . . '": to FA, 15 August, 1943.
p.182:   "broken rhythm": *ibid.*
-        "It matters little": unpublished poem.
-        " . . . I'd gone": n.d.
-        "ruthlessly" *et seq.*: to FA, 5 August, 1943.
p.183:   'The Way Back': HH, pp.40/2. The poem was originally called 'The
         Return' and posted to Freda in a letter (8 August, 1943) from Karachi. It
         was prefaced: "All today I've been thinking of the lake. What did it all
         mean? How did it do so much? The only answer is in your eyes, and in your
         lips". For a fuller account of the poem, see my 'Alun Lewis: The Way
         Back', *The Critical Quarterly*, Summer 1972, pp.145–66.
p.184:   "when I'm nearest": to BC, 14 April, 1941.
-        "Whenever I see": to FA, 15 August, 1943.
-        "an act of daring": to FA, 11 August, 1943.
p.185:   "Oh Frieda": to FA, 29 August, 1943.
-        "wild communion" *et seq.*: 'The Ploughman', *The Dragon*, LX, 3,
         Michaelmas 1938, p.20.
-        "there was nothing": to FA, 26 August, 1943.
-        "the clue": to FA, 5 August, 1943.
-        "Christ, don't I": *ibid.*
p.186:   "it must be *different*": 9 August, 1943.
-        "poor little *Raiders' Dawn*": 11 August, 1943.

–   "Wherever I am": 23 August, 1943.
–   "never never Land" *et seq*.: LW, p.391.
–   "I write always": 5 August, 1943.
–   "steadiness and recognition": to FA, 11 August, 1943.
–   "You say things": to FA, 24 August, 1943.
p.187: "Usually I don't know": LW, pp.399–400.
–   "I hadn't read": 19 August, 1943.
p.188: "the only place": LW, p.389.
–   'The Journey': HH, pp.45–7.
–   'By the Gateway of India, Bombay': HH, p.39.
–   "Oh such wealth": to FA, 17 August, 1943.
p.189: "You say it": to FA, 19 August, 1943.
–   "there's something wishing" *et seq*.: to FA, 22 August, 1943.
–   "One huge thing": to FA, 24 August, 1943.
p.190: "There are many sadnesses": unpublished journal.
p.191: "Fields of golden sesamum": *ibid.*
p.192: "When I lie down": LW, pp.15–16.
–   'The Attempt', *Light and Twilight*, London, 1911, p.160.
p.193: "Frieda darling": 26 August, 1943.
–   "all the time": 31 August, 1943.
p.194: "I can feel": *ibid.*
–   She wanted to believe: Alun to FA, n.d.
–   "I was *delighted*": LW, pp.391–2.
p.195: "it would be presumptuous" see letter to FA, 29 August, 1943.
–   "I want to be": to FA, 8 August, 1943.
–   "a temptation": to FA, 2 September, 1943.
–   "Welsh boys": LW, p.389.
–   "the solid realities": to FA, 2 September, 1943.
–   "You're the most selfish": LW, p.397.
p.196: "swing into a single orbit": to FA, 11 August, 1943.
–   "a kind of forest fire": to FA, 19 October, 1943.
–   "[He] wanted": VII, 40, April 1943, p.227.
–   "What twaddle": LW, p.353.
p.197: "high and unassailable": to FA, n.d.
–   "yellow-eyed beasts": to FA, 8 October, 1943.

Chapter XV

p.198: "sensations and images": to FA, 1 October, 1943.
–   "It *is* uncanny": 8 October, 1943.
–   "I know it was something": 1 October, 1943.
–   "the old childish hankering": to FA, n.d.
p.199: "I loved him always": letter to the author.
–   "an 'old' feeling": to FA, 8 October, 1943.

-     "blaze of darkness" *et seq.*: to FA, 8 October, 1943.
-     "Love had been": letter to the author.
- p.200: "Darling Gweno": LW, p.396.
-     "The problem is so": 14 October, 1943. Earlier (August 17, 1943) Alun had told Freda: "I'm not really afraid of anything except spoiling somebody else for what their good is".
- p.201: "those macabre": to FA, 14 October, 1943.
-     Cresswell's habit: Alun to FA, *ibid.*
-     "I've been reading": 17 October, 1943.
- p.202: "a shouting": LW, p.330.
- p.203: Cresswell thought him: letter to the author.
-     "I can be moderately": LW, p. 399
-     "I've got very interested": LW, p.394.
-     "There *is* such a thing": LW, p.393.
- p.204: "It's Monday afternoon": *ibid.*
-     " . . . in just a fortnight": LW, p.397–8.
- p.205: he yearned a little: to FA, end October/early November.
-     "I dread": to BC, 3 October, 1943.
-     strange poetic recession: to GL, 3 October, 1943.
-     "those cyclical expeditions": *ibid.*
-     "several deep water poems": LW, p.399.
-     "I hate this wandering": LW, p.400.
-     "I'm not busy": LW, p.405.
-     "How hard it is": LW, p.413.
-     'Pastorals': SP, p.92. I quote from the version in Misc, p.167.
- p.206: "NO NO NO": n.d.
-     "There's a maniac": to BC, 3 October, 1943.
-     "where I can at least": to FA, n.d.
- p.207: 'Renewal': SP, p.94.
-     'Lady in Black': Misc, p.164.
- p.208: "I had a swift" *et seq.*: n.d.
-     "nearness and": LW, p.373.
-     "the big cloudy": LW, p.379.
-     "up in that": LW, p.387.
-     "[Gweno] says": 29 November, 1943.
-     "If he was sometimes": letter to the author.
- p.209: "I've been indifferent": to FA, n.d.
- p.210: "depressing thoughts" *et seq.*: to GL, 2 November, 1943.
-     "I feel sometimes": LW, p.403.
-     "I knew I needed": LW, pp.403–4.
-     "negative, null": to RM, 14 August, 1943, describing his "black periods".
-     "the horrible slump": to GL 2 November, 1943.
-     "It was simply" *et seq.*: to FA, 8 November, 1943.
-     "I'm trying to simplify": to KL:, p.340. Similarly, he told Freda (26

-   "I'm trying to simplify": to KL:, p.340. Similarly, he told Freda (26 November, 1943) that he had "lost any belief in [my poems] I may have had. I feel all the time that I'm either washed out or waiting to start. It may be either. I'm waiting to see."

p.211: When he next wrote: 8 November, 1943.
-   "I know that": letter to the author.
-   "I'm very far away": 14 November, 1943.

p.212: "Sunday gone": LW, p.405.
-   "the coarse": LW, p.409.
-   "I was very conscious" *et seq.*: to FA, 18 December, 1943.

p.213: "a universal pining": LW, p.409.
-   "like water in a sump": LW, p.410.
-   "quietly and persistently": LW, p.409.
-   "death in life": LW, p.410.
-   "At other times": to FA, 14 November, 1943.
-   "a faith-keeping": *Modern Reading, v.s.*, p.20.
-   "You were afraid": to FA, 14 November, 1943.

p.214: 'A Fragment': HH, p.73.
-   "But I am still": 17 August, 1943.
-   "I regret": IGT, p.51.
-   "Daddy is the rock": to FA, 26 November, 1943.
-   "a sort of symphonic": LW, p.408.

p.215: "I shall be glad": to FA, 26 November, 1943.
-   "still waiting": to GT, 6 December, 1943.
-   "I had everything": n.d.
-   'The Reunion': IGT, pp.127–136.

p.216: 'Grenadier': *Bugle Blast*, Second Series, ed. by Reginald Moore and Jack Aistrop, London, 1944, pp.161–180.
-   "A sort of nervousness": *The Life and Letters of Edward Thomas*, London, 1939, pp.79–80.
-   "I wish I hadn't": to FA, 18 December, 1943.
-   "I must let go": to FA, 7 December, 1943.
-   "The jungle really": to GT, 22(?) December, 1943.

p.217: isolated from: to FA, 18 December, 1943.
-   "I'm simple again": *ibid.*
-   "a separate world": LW, p.412.
-   "impatient to have": n.d.
-   "You chide me": LW, p.414.
-   "My main reason": LW, p.415.
-   " . . . Gweno, Frieda": Christmas Eve, 1943.

p.218: "I'm afraid": to FA, 1 January, 1944.

p.219: "content with the green": to RM, 14 January, 1944.
-   "absurdly unreal": LW, p.418.
-   "all the coldness": *ibid.*

- "the climacteric": LW, p.419.
- 'The Jungle': HH, pp.67–71.

p.220: "All you and your sort": *Rhondda Roundabout*, London, 1934, p.67.

p.222: "mort": see Misc, pp.30–33.

p.223: "I remember": *I am my Brother*, London, 1960, pp.234, 237.
- "a world I wouldn't" *et seq.*: 3 October, 1943.
- "England is easy'": Misc, p.149.

p.224: "more objective": to FA, 24 January, 1944.

p.255: "He mocketh": Job, ch. 39.
- "an expression of sorrow": to MF, 22 January, 1944.
- "The transit was": *Satis*, 1960, p.19.
- "periods of spiritual death": Misc, p.148.
- "into origins": Misc, p.149.

p.266: Keith Evans: *op. cit.*, n.p.
- 'Midnight in India': HH, pp.74–5.
- "I couldn't decide": Misc, p.147. Alun felt he hadn't digested the experience of Coonoor sufficiently to write about it. He told Freda (29 August, 1943): "And yet it is true that I cannot write you the poetry that is yours. Until long after this is over and it is part of me and I have made myself see the world again with my new eyes that you said were blind, as of course they are, as a newborn animal's are . . . . But of course I can't write the real real real poems yet. A very big thing happens and after it, under its impact, one is for a long time apparently smaller. Like concussion."
- "I can't look": to FA, 24 January, 1944.

p.227: "*If undelivered*": n.d.
- "from a strange wilderness": letter to the author.
- "phlegmatic humour" *et seq.*: 15 January, 1944.
- "I'm not going": IGT, p.59.
- "crazy machinery": to GL, 11 February, 1944.
- "I don't know why": IGT, p.62.
- "You know the cloud": 9 February, 1944.
- "I've put a huge":LW, p.421.
- "God knows where": 7 February, 1944.

p.228: "I don't mind" *et seq.*: 10 February, 1944.

p.230: "to rest and build": AL, p.44.
- "trying so hard" *et seq.*: LW, p.422.
- "black mood": LW, p.423.
- "alive with sunlight": LW, p.424.

p.232: "Waking up": LW, p.244.
- "when Tudor": LW, p.398.

Chapter XVI

p.234: The court of enquiry record is at the Army Records Office. The battalion

p.235: "Obviously the whole point": letter to the author.
–   "Alun I considered": letter to GL.
–   "One felt that character": letter to the author.
–   "Kamerad": LW, p.105.
p.236: "well-being and well-doing": HH, p.7.
–   "Like the Welsh poet": to Gwladys Lewis, AL, p.48.
p.238: "Another death": unpublished poem.
–   "Speak in me": unpublished poem.
–   "Alun must have suffered": letter to the author.
p.239: "A thing there was": *Mrs Dalloway*, London, 1925; Harmondsworth, Middlesex, p.204.
–   "a healer and an illuminator": *Quite Early One Morning*, London, 1954, p.151. The broadcast was on 5 January, 1946. Alun held the highest opinion of Thomas's poetry but the two never met or corresponded.
–   "a very noble spirit": *The Listener*, 4 May, 1944, p.497.
–   "some sort of guide": Humanities Research Centre, *v.s.*
–   "The personality which": *The Listener*, *v.s.*.
p.240: "A hospital ward": 22 July, 1945, p.3.
–   "His term in India": IGT, pp.139–141. In a letter to Professor Jones (3 October, 1944) Gwladys Lewis wrote: "Even now I can scarcely bear to write of it but I needn't tell you that Alun was a most splendid son and brother and we all adored him. Huw, writing from the Chin Hills, says, 'Alun was more than a brother to me. He was a way of life' and to me it is in very truth a limb torn from the living."

Gwladys Lewis had earlier written a poem and sent it to Alun while he was at Heysham in 1941. After his death, she sent it to Professor Jones, who was just then starting up *The Welsh Review* again. "I can't bear to think of your first issue coming out without a contribution from Alun. So just to keep the family flag flying I am offering this if it comes anywhere near your standard."

To My Sons (Overseas)

> Freed by the joyous pain of birth
> From your soft vigil in my womb,
> You, to whom I owe so much,
> Have taught me all I know of worth.
>
> And by the love that you owe me,
> I beg you, come to me again,
> Here, on this living breathing Earth,
> I dare not say "Thy Will be done."

–   "not born of" *et seq.*: *An Acre of Land*, Newtown, 1952, p.25.
–   "a poetry steeped": *New York Herald Tribune* Weekly Book Review, 19,

45, 7 April, 1943, p.13.

p.241: "decent sententiousness": Kingsley Amis in *The Observer*, May 2, 1976, p.30.

–   "rigorous economy in": 18 March, 1944, p.7.

–   "The letters read": London, 1948, pp.328–9.

p.242: "an imaginative understanding" *et seq.*: 11 June, 1949, pp.619–20.

–   "We feel it about": 24 June, 1949, p.408.

APPENDIX A

p.244: "a matter of policy": n.d.

–   the following programme: n.d.

p.245: Vernon Watkins's donation: to BC, 9 December, 1941.

–   "the idea I have": to BC, 15 February, 1942.

APPENDIX B

p.247: "I don't think I'll": n.d.

p.248: "Very recently": 17 November, 1953.

p.251: "I try to take care": 22 November, 1953.

–   "is all a complicated": 1 November, 1953.

Index

A

* 'A Fragment', 214, 226
* 'A Pattern', 46
A Passage to India, 130
A Portrait of the Artist as a Young Man, 160
* 'A Soldier's Journal', 84
* 'A Troopship in the Tropics', 166
Aberdare Leader, The, 54, 55, 56
* 'Acting Captain', 129
* *Adam* (unpublished novel), 72-73
* 'Administration of the Forests, The', 36-37
Aeschylus, 123
* 'After Dunkirk', 80
Aistrop, Jack, 94, 103, 247
'Aldershot', 112
* 'All day it has rained . . . ', 86-89, 91, 96, 97, 98, 108, 122, 150, 166, 216
Allen, Walter, 242
Allen & Unwin (see also Philip Unwin), 104
Alvarez, A., 123
An Indian Day, 174
* 'Anschluss', 56
* 'Assault Convoy', 163
* 'Atropos to Ophelia', 49, 50
* 'Attitude', 92
Auden, W.H., 58, 101, 102, 145, 220, 222
Aykroyd Freda 171, 173-75, 176, 180-81, 182, 183, 184, 185, 186, 187, 188, 189, 193, 194, 195, 196, 197, 198, 199, 200, 203, 204, 205, 206, 208, 209, 210, 211,213, 214, 215, 216, 217, 218, 224, 226, 228, 229, 236, 238, 243, 249, 252
Aykroyd, Gilly, 171, 173, 212, 229
Aykroyd, Juliet, 250
Aykroyd, Peter, 173
Aykroyd, Wallace, 171, 173, 175, 196, 198, 211, 249

B

Bayliss, John, 128
Bell, H. Idris, 246
* 'Beloved, beware', 179, 183, 184
* 'Bequest', 160, 161
Berridge, Elizabeth (Lisa), 247, 252, 253-59
Bevan, Aneurin, 128
* 'Birthday', 51
* 'Bivouac', 157
Blythe, Ronald, 80
Bovian, The, 25, 26, 28, 35
Bowen, Elizabeth, 136
'Boychick, The', 250, 251, 255-57
B.B.C., 55, 94
Brooke, Rupert, 81, 96, 122
Browning, Robert, 25
Bugle, The, 94
Bugle Blast, 247
Bullough, Geoffrey, 59
* 'Burma Casualty', 152, 157, 184
* 'By the Gateway to India, Bombay', 188

C

Calcutta Statesman, 173

Call Wind to Witness (ed. Derek
  Stanford), 128, 213
★ 'Captivity, The', 122
Carlyle, Thomas, 25
Caseg Broadsheets, The, 102-103,
  244-46
Caton, Reginald, 25, 96
ap Cedifor, Peryf, 246
Chalfont, Lord, see Jones, Alun
  Gwynne
Chamberlain Brenda 99, 100, 102,
  103, 111, 115, 118, 119, 158, 205,
  206, 223, 227, 244, 245, 246
Chekhov, Anton, 55
Cheney, Christopher, 42, 43, 45, 52,
  59, 60, 61, 62, 68, 110, 122, 236,
  243
★ 'Chestnuts', 47
★ 'Children, The', 129
Clouds Hill, 130-136
★ 'Cold Spell', 129-30
Coles, A.T.E., 117
Collected Poems of Edward Thomas, 78
Collected Poems of W.B. Yeats, 78
Connolly, Cyril, 88, 96, 100, 101, 102,
  109, 121
Connors, Bill (Cassandra), 94
Conrad, Joseph, 164, 215
Constant, Benjamin, 45
Coonoor, July-August 1943, 172-186
Cowbridge Grammar School, 1926-
  32, 21-28, 30, 68
Cox, C.B., 170
★'Creation of a Class', 109
Cresswell, R.S., 165, 166, 201, 202,
  203, 204, 205, 231, 232, 234, 235
Crewe-Read, R.O., 231, 232, 234
Crozier, W.P., 55
Curry, R.N., 121
Cwmaman, 9-20

D

Daily Herald, The, 37
Daily Mirror, The, 94, 116
Daily Telegraph, The, 54
Dante, 90
Davies, Andrew, 79, 86, 135, 264
Davies, Barry, 61

Davies, Becky, 92
Davies, David, 33
Davies, Howell, 92, 97, 103
Davies, Idris, 38, 39, 60
★ 'Dawn on the East Coast', 120
★ 'Defeated, The', 245
'Dejection', 69
Desjardines, Paul, 44-45
★ 'Desperate, The', 44
★ 'Destruction', 69-70
Dickens, Charles, 69, 101, 214
Dobree, Bonamy, 109
Dragon, The, 35, 39, 50, 92
Drew, Elizabeth, 240
Drummond, D.M., 117, 235
Dublin Magazine, The, 56, 121, 123
Durrell, Lawrence, 146
★ 'Dusty Hermitage', 130-134

E

★ 'Earth is a Syllable, The', 152, 153
Edwards, Bryn, 24
Eliot, T.S., 35, 60, 222
Ellis, Eiluned, 128
Ellis, Gweno, (see also Lewis Gweno)
  62, 69, 70, 74, 75, 76, 77, 79, 81, 83,
  85, 92, 93, 94, 97, 100, 101, 104,
  105-07
Ellis, William, 76
Empson, Sir William, 102, 109
England is My Village, 110
English Historical Review, The, 52
Eumenides, The, 123
Evans, Bridget, 12
Evans, Caradoc, 37
Evans, Keith, 226
Evans, Melchezedic, 11-12, 13, 15
Evans, O.A., 117
Evans, Sarah Jane, 15
Evans, Selwyn, 117
★ 'Everlasting Ultimatum, The', 206

F

★ 'Farewell Binge', 95
★ 'Fever', 44
★ 'Field, The', 177
FitzGerald, Edward, 114, 123, 131

Fletcher, Joseph, 131
Forster, E.M., 102, 130, 131
Forsyte Saga, The, 196
Fortune Anthology, The, 128
Fortune Press, The, 96
Foyle, Christina, 55
★ 'From a Play', 123
Fry, Roger, 185-86

G

Galsworthy, John, 196
Gandhi, Mahatma, 149
du Gard, Roger Martin, 45
Germanacos, Chris, 34, 51, 70
Gibbon, Edward, 47
Gide, Andre, 45
Giffard, Sir George, 219
Gilbert, Jean, 45, 49, 57, 243
Gilford, Maurice, 107
Goch, Iolo, 244
Goddess, The, see also Muse, The,
    144, 152, 226
Goff, Lt. Col., 111
★ 'Goodbye', 138
Grafton, Evelyn, 19
Graves, Robert, 112, 113, 114, 121,
    134, 135, 158, 164, 215, 223, 225,
    226, 236
Greene, Graham, 96
★ 'Grenadier', 216, 249
Griffin, Ruby, 32
★ 'Grinder, The', 122
Gunn, David, 107
Gush, Jack, 117, 147, 219
Gwalchmai, 246

H

★ *Ha! Ha! Among the Trumpets*, 224-
    26, 235-36, 239
Habbakuk, John, 42
Hall, George, 37
Hall, John, 251
Hamblett, Charles, 128
Hamilton, Ian, 90, 134, 144
Harden, Albert, 78, 95
Hardie, Keir, 14
Hardy, Thomas, 130
Hemingway, Ernest, 195

Hillary, Richard, 196, 197, 202
★ 'Home Thoughts from Abroad', 160
Hopkin, Sir Bryan, 42, 119
Hopkin, Lady René, 119
Horizon, 86, 88, 89, 96, 97, 100, 101,
    104, 109, 196, 211
★ 'House, The', 172
★ 'Housekeeper, The', 60, 61, 69, 70
Howard, Queenie, 129
Humphreys, Emyr, 60

I

★ 'If War Comes – Will I Fight?', 56-
    57
★ 'In Hospital, Poona (1)', 152, 160,
    204, 208, 221
★ 'In Hospital, Poona (2)', 152, 153,
    208
★ 'In the days when I could choose',
    178
★ *In The Green Tree*, 153, 241
★ 'Interuption', 43
★ 'It seemed to me the truth lay at
    rest', 30
★ 'It's a Long Way to Go', 116, 136

J

Jacob, E.F., 42, 54
James, Ethel, 62
Jefferies, Richard, 90
Jones, Alun Glynne, 117, 149, 201,
    238
Jones, Glyn, 38, 60, 245, 246
Jones, Gwyn, 38, 60, 103, 111, 240,
    241
Jones, Iris, 29, 31
Jones, Jack, 38, 220
Jones, Lewis, 38
Jones, Mairwen, 32
Jones, Thomas, 31
★ 'Journey, The', 188, 190
Joyce, James, 160
★ 'Jungle, The', 219-224

K

Karachi, August-September 1943,
    188-195

* 'Karanje Village', 148-49, 156, 170
Keats, John, 72, 181
Khayyam, Omar, 114
Khulla, Lt., 182
Kipling, Rudyard, 25
Knight, Bernard, 235
Knight, Stanley, 68
Koestler, Arthur, 109, 196

L

* 'Ladybird Awakes, The', 39
* 'Lady in Black, The', 207
* 'Lance-Jack', 82, 83, 85, 90, 96, 131, 156, 170, 205, 222
Larkin, Philip, 70
* 'Last Inspection, The', 97, 104
* *Last Inspection, The*, 43, 100, 116, 130, 135-36, 156, 241
* 'Last Leaves of a Civilian Journal', 74
* 'Last Pages of a Long Journal', 75, 92, 101, 133, 150
Lawrence, 48, 99, 101, 110, 149, 162, 195, 199, 209
Lawrence, T.E., 60, 130, 131-33, 170, 196, 202
Lee, Laurie, 109
Left Book Club, 39, 55
Lehmann, John, 95, 165, 223
* 'Letter from a Long Way', 226
* 'Letter from the Cape', 226
* *Letters from India*, 241
Lewis Alun see Contents page and entries under (i) *Aberdare Leader*, (ii) Bombay September 1943, (iii) Caseg Broadsheets, (iv) Clouds Hill, (v) Coonor, July-August 1943, (vi) Cowbridge Grammar School, (vii) Cwmaman, (viii) Karachi, August-September 1943, (ix) Lewis School, Pengam 1938-40, (x) Manchester 1935-37, (xi) Muse The, (xii) On the Welsh Mountains (Aberdare 1935-37), (xiii) Pontigny May-June 1937, (xiv) Poon Hospital January-March 1943
Lewis, C. Day, 109
Lewis, Dewi, 34

Lewis, Edward, 11, 18, 32
Lewis, Glyn, 14, 18, 215, 216
Lewis, Gweno (see Ellis, Gweno) 108, 109, 110, 111, 112, 114, 115, 118, 120, 121, 124, 125, 128, 129, 130, 134, 135, 136, 137, 138, 139, 142, 145, 149, 150, 151, 152, 153, 155, 156, 159, 162, 165, 166, 167, 170, 179, 180, 181, 187, 194, 195, 196, 200, 201, 203, 204, 205, 206, 208, 210, 211, 214, 216, 217, 224, 226, 227, 228, 229, 230, 232, 235, 236, 241, 242, 243, 248, 250
Lewis, Gwladys, 9, 11, 12-13, 14, 15, 19, 21, 27, 30, 31, 36, 41, 47, 51, 52, 60, 108, 138, 214, 216, 227, 229, 230, 236, 240, 264
Lewis, Huw, 18, 31, 63, 93, 239
Lewis, Jane, 18, 61
Lewis, Job, 11, 18
Lewis, Mair (a.k.a. Fenn, Mair), 11, 18, 31, 43, 75, 229, 250
Lewis, Tim, 33, 39, 70, 78
Lewis, Tom, 9, 11, 13, 14, 15, 18, 19, 21, 31, 33, 49, 51, 52, 60, 68, 214, 216, 227, 230, 264
Lewis, Tony, 136, 147
Lewis School, Pengam, 60, 68-75, 78
* 'Leyborn, Roger, and the Pacification of England 1265-67', 52, 55
Life and Letters Today, 82, 246
Lilliput, 109
* 'Lines on a Tudor Mansion', 84
* 'Lines to Edward Thomas' (see also
* 'To Edward Thomas'), 89
Listener, The, 112, 121
Llewelyn-Williams, Alun, 241-42
Llyn, William, 246
* 'Lost Man, The', 250, 252-55
* 'Love', 188
* 'Love Letter', 211
Ludovican, The, 60

M

Maclaren-Ross, Julian, 125-27, 128
MacNeice, Louis, 109

Maddox, Elonwy (a.k.a. Kirkland, Elonwy), 29
* 'Madman, The', 247
* 'Mahratta Ghats, The', 155, 166
Makin, Clifford, 104
Manchester, 1935-37, 41-46
Manchester Guardian, The, 55
* 'Manuel', 163
* 'Map', 178
Marx, Karl, 69
Menai, Huw, 37, 245
Miall, Bernard, 104
* 'Midnight in India', 226
Mill, John Stuart, 25, 45
Mills, Richard (Dick), 54, 56, 60, 62, 63, 68, 69, 71, 78-79, 83, 93, 98, 112, 135, 148, 150, 151, 171, 172, 179, 195, 201, 208, 227, 228
* 'Miner's Son, The', 49
Modern Reading, 247
Moon, I.O., 117, 201, 234
Moore, Reginald (Graham), 247, 252, 259
Morgan, D.M., 117, 234
* *Morlais*, 63-67, 71
Morris, G.T., 152
* 'Mortuus', 55
* 'Motifs', 156, 157
'Mountain over Aberdare, The (see also 'On the Welsh Mountains'), 108, 119, 123, 245
* 'Munich and Peace, The Significance of Re-Armament', 56, 57
Muse, The (see also Goddess, The), 28, 64, 168, 188, 190

N

Nehru, Jawarhalai, 130
New Statesman, The, 128, 156, 165, 242
New Writing, 95
News Chronicle, The , 55
* 'Night Journey', 247
* 'Nothing About the Dead', 178
* 'Novice, The', 46, 72

O

Observer, The, 104, 121
* 'Odyssey, The', 83, 123
Oldfield, Maurice, 42
* 'On Embarkation', 137, 222
'On the Welsh Mountains (see also 'Mountain over Aberdare, The') 60, 65, 108,
On the Welsh Mountains (Aberdare 1938-39), 51-67
* 'Orange Grove, The', 168-69, 172, 191, 195, 205, 212, 227, 242
Orwell, George, 101, 109
Owen, M., 139
Owen, Wilfred, 76, 89, 96

P

* 'Parable', 80
* 'Pastorals', 207
* 'Patrol, The', 163, 191
* 'Peace', 97, 98, 148
* 'Peasant Song', 177, 185
* 'Peasants, The', 203
Perry, Bill, 93
Petts, John, 99, 100, 102, 103, 111, 119, 122, 153, 158, 206, 245, 246
Phelps, Laurie, 19
Pile, Bernard, 26
Plath, Sylvia, 207
Pleasant Place, 30
Plomer, William, 109
* 'Ploughman, The', 185
* 'Poems from the Chinese', 51, 122
Poems from the Forces, 112
* 'Poet, The', 51
Poetry (London), 96, 146
Poetry Review, 121
Pontigny, May-June 1937, 44-46, 50, 53, 115
Poona Hospital, January-March, 1943, 149-55
Popham, V.J.F., 116, 117, 142, 165, 202, 229, 235
* 'Post-script: for Gweno', 85, 96, 166, 177
Powell, Barbara, 26
Price, Nansi, 51

Prince, F.T., 123
* 'Prisoners, The', 110
Pritchard, John, 245
* 'Private Jones', 119, 136, 249
Prosser, Glyn, 55, 57
Prys-Jones, A.G., 37, 245
* 'Public Gardens, The', 79, 80
Punch, 136

Q

Qureihoi, Lt., 232, 234

R

* 'Raid, The', 163
* 'Raiders' Dawn', 99, 111-12, 166, 246
Raiders Dawn, 44, 49, 56, 59, 80, 111, 121-23, 136, 148, 175, 186, 222, 226, 254
Reed, Henry, 123
Reid, Eric, 24-26, 28, 31
* 'Renewal', 208
* 'Reunion, The', 215-16, 223
Rhys, John Ll., 110
Rhys, Keidrych, 60, 97, 102, 112, 212, 239, 244, 245, 251
Ridler, Anne, 109
Rilke, Rainer Maria, 50, 74, 79, 120, 145, 148, 151, 154, 170, 179, 241
* 'River Temple: Wai, The', 155, 160
Riviere, Jacques, 45
Roberts, Lynette, 60, 97-98, 112, 130, 134, 205, 211, 244, 245, 246, 251
Robeson, Paul, 56
Rook, Alan, 121
Ross, Alan, 102
Rowse, A.L., 241
* 'Run-In, The', 163
Ruskin, John, 25
Rutherford, Andrew, 133

S

Sandpiper, The, 95
Sassoon, Siegfried, 89, 96
Scott, Paul, 118
Selected Writing, 247

* 'Sentry, The', 84, 102, 166
Serpent, The, 43
* 'Shadows', 160, 184
Shaw, G.B., 26
Shelley, Percy Bysshe, 45, 160, 239
* 'Soldier, The', 79, 112
* 'Song' (Oh Journeyman), 242
* 'Song' (On seeing dead bodies), 144
* 'Song of Innocence', 246
* 'Songs of Innocence', 111
Spectator, The, 96
Spender, Stephen, 100, 101, 109, 195
* 'Squibs for the Guy', 50
Stevenson, W.H., 37
* 'Stones for Bread', 165
Straus, George, 128
'Such Aching', 238
Sunday Times, 239
Sykes, Bill, 86, 93
Sykes, Lesley, 86, 92, 93, 135, 237

T

* 'Taliesin', 53
Taliesin, 246
* 'Tale of a Dwarf, The', 28, 30
Tambimuttu, 96, 247
Tatler and Bystander, The, 136
Tennyson, Alfred, 25
* 'They Came', 99, 136
Thomas, Dylan, 28, 38, 60, 69, 109, 239, 245, 246
Thomas, Edward, 61, 63, 78, 83, 85, 86, 87, 88, 89, 90, 91, 96, 99, 100, 122, 130, 131, 150, 152, 170, 192, 206, 209, 216, 220
Thomas, Gwyn, 32, 38
Thomas, Huw, 73
Thomas, R.S., 240
Thomas, Stan, 238
Thomas, W.D., 239
Thompson, Edward, 174
* 'Threnody for a Starry Night', 59, 74, 108
Time and Tide, 51, 55
Times, The, 164, 241
Times Literary Supplement, 242
'To Edward Thomas' (see also 'Lines

to Edward Thomas') 85, 90, 91, 96,
   98, 220
★ 'To Rilke', 145
Tolstoi, Leo, 133
Toynbee, Philip, 156
*Transactions of the Honourable Society
   of Cymmrodorion*, 241-42
★ 'Transmigration of Love, The', 197
Treharne, R.F., 33, 36, 37
Tribune, 128
Tudor, Harry, 232
★ 'Tunnel, The', 47, 50, 72

U

Uhland, Ludwig, 236
Unwin, Philip (see also Allen &
   Unwin), 104, 110, 121, 122, 123,
   128, 135, 235
Upanishads, The, 193

V

★ 'Vanite', 28
★ 'Village Funeral', 156, 160, 166
Virgil, 90
★ 'Visit, The', 50
Vivian, 117
★ *Voyager, The* (see also *Ha! Ha!
   Among the Trumpets*), 186

W

Waddell, Helen, 28, 51

Wales, 60, 97
Waller, John, 112
Walters, Marjorie, 50, 53, 55, 61, 128
★ 'Wanderers, The', 72, 99
★ 'War Wedding', 108, 121, 122, 191
★ 'Ward "O" 3(b)', 153-55, 165, 191,
   242
★ 'Water Music', 160, 161-62, 166,
   184, 220
Watkins, Vernon, 241, 245
'Way Back, The', (see also 'Return,
   The') 183, 184, 185, 186, 187, 188,
   191, 195, 210, 219-220
★ 'Ways', 175-76
Webb, Harri, 17, 120
★ 'Wedding, The', 50
Welsh Outlook, The, 38
Welsh Review, The, 60, 72, 99, 241
Western, Dilys, 52, 53, 227
Western Mail, 39, 54
Williams, Bronwen, 35-36, 43, 44, 50,
   110
Williams, Greta, 118
Williams, Kemble, 118
Williams, Richard, 22, 24, 28
Williams Parry, Robert, 245
Wodehouse, P.G., 101
★ 'Wood Song', 177, 229
Woolf, Virginia, 185, 239

Y

Yeats, W.B., 78, 113, 149, 160, 169,
   182, 184